DEVELOPING
the
GLOBAL
ORGANIZATION

Strategies for Human Resource Professionals

THE MCD SERIES
MANAGING CULTURAL DIFFERENCES

Series Editors: Philip R. Harris, Ph.D., and Robert T. Moran, Ph.D.

Managing Cultural Differences, Third Edition
Philip R. Harris and Robert T. Moran

Developing the Global Organization: Strategies for Human Resource Professionals
Robert T. Moran, Philip R. Harris, and William G. Stripp

Dynamics of Successful International Business Negotiations
William G. Stripp and Robert T. Moran

Transcultural Leadership: Empowering the Diverse Workforce
George F. Simons, Carmen Vazquez, and Philip R. Harris

Multicultural Management: New Skills for Global Success
Farid Elashmawi and Philip R. Harris

Forthcoming

Case Studies in Managing Cultural Differences
Robert T. Moran, David O. Braaten, and John E. Walsh

International Directory of Multicultural Resources

DEVELOPING the GLOBAL ORGANIZATION

Strategies for Human Resource Professionals

Robert T. Moran
Philip R. Harris
William G. Stripp

Gulf Publishing Company
Houston, London, Paris, Zurich, Tokyo

THE **M🌐🌎SERIES**
MANAGING CULTURAL DIFFERENCES

Developing the Global Organization
Strategies for Human Resource Professionals

Gulf Publishing Company
Book Division
P.O. Box 2608, Houston, Texas 77252-2608

10 9 8 7 6 5 4 3 2 1

Library of Congress Cataloging-in-Publication Data

Moran, Robert T., 1938–
    Developing the global organization : strategies for human resource
professionals / Robert T. Moran, Philip R. Harris, William G. Stripp.
        p.   cm.—(Managing cultural differences series)
    Includes bibliographical references and index.
    ISBN 0-88415-071-2
    1. International business enterprises—Management.
2. Communication in personnel management. 3. Intercultural
communication. 4. Cross-cultural orientation. I. Harris, Philip R.
(Philip Robert), 1926–   . II. Stripp, William G.   III. Title.
IV. Series.
HD62.4.M658   1993
658.3—dc20   92-21197
                                                                CIP

Printed in the United States of America.

This book is dedicated to the human resource professionals in business, government, academia, and elsewhere who, during the past decade, have worked to make their organizations more global.

We invite human resource professionals to share with us their effective strategies on the themes of the book for inclusion in subsequent editions.

CONTENTS

ACKNOWLEDGMENTS

The authors have learned much from the organizations they were privileged to work with over the past few years. We thank each. Specific citations and references have also been made in the text to the many colleagues whose thinking influenced our own. We also want to acknowledge the special assistance rendered to this project by Timothy Calk, senior editor at Gulf Publishing Company, and Judith Soccorsy, our incomparable editorial assistant.

The original idea for this book evolved from discussions during a seminar with a few graduate students of human resource management. Sanjeev Chowdhury, Kevin Lilly, and Terri Lloyd had many ideas and influenced the original discussions. They subsequently made important contributions to several sections of the book. We also acknowledge the assistance of Douglas Henson, Kathleen Boemer, Paul Damiani, and Sonja Mussler.

Finally, we are grateful to the international executive, consultant, author, scholar, and former ambassador, Dr. Stephen H. Rhinesmith of Stamford, Connecticut who wrote the Foreword.

SERIES PREFACE

To thrive and, in many cases, to survive in the 1990s, it is necessary for organizations to globalize in strategy, structure, and people. Companies have realized that developing strategies or managing people as if the internal and external environments of the organization had not changed is a major mistake. "Bashing" others rather than taking the inward journey and becoming a revolutionary learning organization is dysfunctional and counterproductive to corporate survival. As expected, many organizations in various countries have taken the inward journey and are effectively managing this challenge. Some are not.

The *Managing Cultural Differences Series* is intended to stimulate and support the effort of globalization in all of its dimensions. The books have been widely accepted in academic circles and by practicing internationalists.

As series editors, we are pleased that Gulf Publishing Company has risen to the challenge of addressing questions of people, cultures, organizations, and strategy in a rapidly changing, highly interdependent community.

Philip R. Harris, Ph.D.
Robert T. Moran, Ph.D.

FOREWORD

The 1990s mark a turning point in the role of the human resource professional in today's corporation. With the increasing speed of change and globalization in the world's marketplace, corporations are under new pressure to recruit, train, and develop a work force with managers and leaders able to meet the demands of a fast-paced global world.

The CEOs of the world's major corporations, realizing the need to globalize their companies to remain viable in a world of cross-border joint ventures, strategic alliances, and global sourcing of capital, technology, and people to take advantage of new market opportunities, are turning to their chief human resource officers for help. Sadly they are too often discovering that their human resource executives have grown up in a different era and are unprepared to meet the challenges of developing people for a global marketplace.

The duties of today's human resource professional have evolved over the last twenty years from the traditional personnel functions of recruitment, training, compensation, and union negotiations to those that demand HR professionals become part and parcel of the corporate strategic management team. For these people, and for the CEOs seeking to find HR people with broader perspectives, this book is a splendid resource.

Bob Moran and Phil Harris have contributed mightily over the last decade to the exploration of the human side of global management. They are pioneers in their ground-breaking approaches to managing cultural differences and cultural synergy, and they have now combined their talents with Will Stripp to write a lively guide for HR professionals who are seeking to redefine and broaden their role in global organizations.

In this book, Moran, Harris, and Stripp have made a major contribution to reshaping the human resource professional's arena of action. Reaching far beyond traditional assumptions of HR responsibilities, the authors examine the strategic linkage of the HR professional to the total management of today's modern global corporation. They outline new areas for growth and development, new arenas for thought and inquiry, and new approaches to developing human resources as a strategic competitive advantage.

Because real global management begins with the determination of strategy, the authors correctly believe that HR professionals need to be "in at the beginning," developing the strategic intent of a corporation, rather than called in "after the fact" to determine the HR implications of a new strategic direction. As a result, they begin by reviewing the role of the HR professional in developing the total organization strategy. They provide an overview of the elements of business strategy and provide a vocabulary within which an HR professional can work with line management as an integral part of the strategic planning process.

This new strategic role, however, is only the starting point for their redefinition of the HR manager's role in a global corporation. After strategy and structure have been outlined for new global directions, the HR professional will be held accountable for delivering the workforce knowledge, skills, and attitudes necessary for the company to compete effectively in new global arenas. This requires the identification of new global management competencies, the development of selection, compensation, and promotion criteria that reflect these competencies, and the promotion of a global corporate culture and organizational values within which globally-oriented people can contribute, thrive, and be recognized.

This new HR challenge is a large order for many of today's HR professionals and will demand that they rethink and reframe their role as strategic thinkers, systemic managers, and cross-cultural experts who can meet the needs of a global work force for a global marketplace.

To assist in this process, the authors conduct a thorough examination of the emerging role of the HR professional as a global manager, including traditional HR functions such as developing cross-cultural employees, cross-cultural teams, and managing cross-cultural conflict and meetings. These chapters provide rich new insights to well-known areas and have helpful suggestions and references that can be consulted for further thought and development.

Not content with adding new perspectives to traditional areas, the authors also launch into some uncharted waters, exploring the role of the HR professional in marketing, negotiating, and technology transfer. In these chapters they chart the way through legal, tax, consumer, and technological issues that are often overlooked when examining the HR role in organization management.

The authors not only provide new perspectives on global HR management, but also outline the context within which today's HR professional must operate, the skills they must develop, and the resources available for a new and creative approach to HR management.

This is a timely book that should challenge and help today's professional HR manager who is seeking to make a meaningful contribution to the future success of his or her company's global operations. It is an invaluable addition to the world's library on managing the human side of global enterprise.

Stephen H. Rhinesmith, Ph.D.
Rhinesmith and Associates, Inc.
Stamford, Connecticut

DEVELOPING the GLOBAL ORGANIZATION

Strategies for Human Resource Professionals

INTRODUCTION

The idea for this book, written for human resource professionals interested in or responsible for the globalization of an organization, had its origin in two events. The first occurred during a consulting activity of one of the authors.

Senior managers from a large multinational company who seemed to be well advanced in their globalization efforts were asked to write on a blank sheet of paper answers to two questions: "What is your definition of globalization for your company?" and "What strategies is your organization using to globalize?" These managers then analyzed the responses and concluded unanimously that surprisingly they didn't agree on what globalization is, and they didn't have a common plan to globalize.

Shortly after this experience an interview with Percy Barnevik, president and CEO of ABB (Asea Brown Boveri), was published in the *Harvard Business Review* (March–April 1991). He was asked, "Is there such a thing as a global manager?" His response, "Yes, but we don't have many. One of ABB's biggest priorities is to create more of them; it is a crucial bottleneck for us." The interviewer continued, "Where do these new managers come from?" Barnevik responded, "Global managers are made not born."

In this book we examine the idea of "making" global managers by providing a theoretical foundation, practical information, and suggestions for "globalizing" an organization. The aim is to help those responsible for globalization efforts by focusing on the specific themes of:

- Training Leaders for a New Work Culture
- The Cross-Cultural Strategist
- Cross-Cultural Team Building
- Solving Conflicts in a Multicultural Environment
- Cross-Cultural Technology Transfer
- The Cross-Cultural Employee
- The Cross-Cultural Marketeer
- The Cross-Cultural Negotiator

- Effective Cross-Cultural Meetings
- The HRD Role in Globalizing an Organization and Transforming Theory into Action

Steven H. Rhinesmith [4] tries our understanding of globalization with the following:

> Ask Andy Grove, the scion of Silicon Valley and founder of INTEL, whether INTEL is a global corporation. He will answer emphatically, "yes." Ask Dov Frohman, director of INTEL's Research Center in Israel, the same question and he will just as emphatically answer "no." Ask Sharon Richards, cross-cultural coordinator for INTEL and she will answer "yes" in strategy, but "no" in the skills and attitudes of the people and the corporate culture of the company.
>
> Who's right? All three are—and that's the first problem with globalization. Nobody—even in the same company—seems to have the total picture of how to make globalization work. . . .

Effective globalization involves three levels of corporate activity: strategy/structure, culture, and people.

A similar perspective is reflected in the following [1]:

> The 1990s will test the capacities of multi-national corporations (MNCs) to react rapidly to global changes in human resources as in all other areas of the company. . . . Traditional human resource methods must be refined, expanded, and applied to address new challenges that range from a changing work force profile to the importance of corporate restructuring on existing international business relationships.
>
> Already prized at the highest levels of global companies, international experience on the part of executives will become increasingly critical to business success in coming years. At the same time, however, an increasingly tight labor market will put added pressure on companies to properly manage and develop their international work force. Convinced that executives must learn to think globally and act locally, MNCs are directing their most promising executives towards international development assignments designed to foster a corps of seasoned global managers. As international business success has become synonymous with corporate success, international experience on the part of executives has become identified with upward mobility within the company.

This book can also be used by persons involved in organizational change. However, Andre Laurent [2] pointedly states,

> The management of organizational change can hardly exceed our capacity to conceive it. This capacity is often constrained by our premises, assumptions, and conceptions about the nature of organizations and the nature of change. Major or strategic organizational change requires a transformation of the actors' view of the organization.

Joint ventures and strategic alliances are now a routine aspect of international business. With the increases in strategic alliances, the way in which businesses see themselves and their competition are being drastically altered. Corporations must change the way they think about their organizational and financial structures, as well as their style of management. Obviously, the people who must address the most difficult issues will be the corporate managers. Because reluctance to change is common in almost any corporate culture, herein lies the paradox. Although most managers heartily dislike joint ventures, they predict that they will be involved in more and more of them. The success of the joint venture can be critical to the companies involved. A successful venture can bring in enormous profits, while a failed one can drain the organizations of both financial and human resources. Hamel, Doz, and Prahalad [2] even suggested that "organizations must learn to collaborate with competitors—and win."

When managers around the world are asked whether a joint venture or a wholly-owned subsidiary is more difficult to manage, it is likely the joint venture will be named. Further questioning is apt to reveal that this is not because joint ventures have more difficult tasks to perform, but because they are a much more difficult form of organization and in the organization the human resource dimension adds increasing diversity.

Throughout this book the reader will be expected to question premises, assumptions, change, and values. In some ways this means there will be an unlearning and then relearning. This is difficult for many of us who have learned certain ways to think and behave, and it may be necessary to de-mystify our beliefs about what globalization really is.

There have been many books that describe and explain aspects of globalization and the resulting necessary organizational, structural, cultural, and people changes. What makes this book unique is that where many have fallen short in providing useful approaches to facilitate change, ours provides the reader with action strategies to be used in the organizations. It is these activities, we believe, that will facilitate the paradigm shifts required in globalization. We have included and cited a variety of features and activities relating to different training techniques such as case studies, demonstrations, discussion groups, role playing, films, lectures, workshops, and resource lists.

Problem areas also arise within joint ventures among multiple parents. One is at the board of directors level, and the other is at the joint venture general manager level. The board of directors of a joint venture contains representatives from each parent and it is here that differences in practices, directions, and perhaps values emerge. Typically, when management teams form, different cultures mean the speed and amount of information necessary to make decisions can vary greatly. The results usually are confusion, frustration, and, quite possibly, bitterness. Peter Killing gives a good example [4]:

> The board of directors of one company in my study, consisting of American and British managers, continually disagreed vehemently about the amount of data required before a decision could be made. The British could not understand why the Americans wanted "all those numbers." The Americans, on the other hand, believed the British were totally "flying blind." This problem was serious, as it meant that either the Americans had to agree to proceed with what they considered to be insufficient information, or the British had to incur a delay and spend extra money collecting information which they did not feel was necessary.

It is obvious from these statements that American managers do not really trust the information given to them by the British, prompting the British managers to say, "Why have a joint venture if you don't trust our judgment?"

A successful joint venture general manager must have a high tolerance for ambiguity, excellent negotiating skills, and a good feel for what matters to each parent, because this may not be communicated explicitly. Problems do not surface while the venture is running smoothly. When the organization is faced with adversity and put under stress "true colors" begin to show. Killing gives another excellent example [3]:

My primary allegiance is to the joint venture, not to either of the parents. Of course, most joint venture general managers would probably say that, but in my case it is true. The reason is that I did not have a permanent job in either parent company before coming to work here, and I do not particularly expect to be promoted into either of them if I leave this job. The fact that I spent six months training in Germany offsets the fact that I am in more frequent contact with the Americans in my day-to-day job. . . . So I consider myself neutral; and more importantly, I think both parents see me in the same way.

In the case of this general manager, it seems that he has attained a high level of trust.

In an early 1980 survey Royal Dutch Shell found that one third of the corporations on the *Fortune 500* list in 1970 had disappeared. Comparisons between 1990 and 1980 yield similar statistics. Peter Senge [6] argues that organizations "learn poorly" because of "the way they are designed and managed, the way people's jobs are defined, and, most importantly, the way we have all been taught to think and interact."

This book has been written by three persons having different styles, backgrounds, and different work experiences—consulting, training, and academic credentials—to name but a few. We hope our differences contribute to the usefulness of the theoretical perspectives and practical applications that we have presented.

Generally, each chapter has been organized to assist the reader by beginning with an introduction to the subject matter, including a theoretical overview on a central theme, citing practical cases or illustrations of the theory, presenting some strategies useful in human resource development, and sometimes including an instrument that can be used for data-gathering or self-analysis. Some of the proposed HRD strategies are quite unique and innovative. Various critical incidents, tables, and figures have been grouped together under the heading of exhibits.

References

1. *Business International Research Report.* New York: Business International Corp. 1991.

2. Evans, P., Doz Y., and Laurent A. (eds) *Human Resource Management in International Firms.* New York: St. Martin's Press, 1990.
3. Hamel, G., Doz, Y., and Prahalad, C. "Collaborate with Your Competitors and Win." *Harvard Business Review,* January–February 1989, pp. 133–139.
4. Killing, J. P., *Strategies for Joint Venture Success.* New York: Praeger, 1983.
5. Rhinesmith, S. H. "An Agenda for Globalization," *Training and Development Journal.* February 1991.
6. Senge, P. *The Fifth Discipline.* New York: Doubleday/Currency, 1990.

CHAPTER 1

TRAINING LEADERS FOR THE NEW WORK CULTURE

Introduction

On the threshold of the 21st century, all systems and institutions are in the process of transition—from the old ways of operating for the past decades to a new way of functioning. A profound cultural transformation is underway not only in societies as a whole but also within the cultures of individual corporations, associations, or agencies. To survive, no less develop, our organizations must move beyond the Industrial Age way of doing things to operate effectively within a post-industrial mode, an Information Society. Those with human resource responsibilities in such enterprises are challenged to exercise transformational leadership. With personnel at all levels, they become agents of change in creating awareness and skills for the emerging work environment. With institutions and systems, they must "reframe" organizational culture [15].

In that regard, our message here is aimed particularly at the human resource (HR) professionals in organizations. Sometimes their functions are divided into human resource development (HRD), which recruits, selects, trains, evaluates, and consults employees; and human resource management (HRM), which is more concerned with standard personnel activities such as hiring, promotion, compensation, benefits, assignments or deployment, and firing or retiring, as well as contracting with consultants and negotiating with unions, if they exist. Whether such human resource functions are separated or combined, performed by specialists or line managers, the practitioners deal with human assets whose undertakings are increasingly cross-cultural and global in scope. We prefer the explanation of Leonard Nadler [21], professor emeritus of George Washington University: "Those with human resource responsibilities engage in a series of organized activities, conducted within a specified time, and designed to produce behavioral change in personnel." For those in HRD, Nadler points out that the most common manifestations are *training* (learning for the present job) and *education* (learning about the future job).

It is on the latter arena that this book is focused, indicating the ongoing and forthcoming changes in the work culture. Thus, the chapters to follow underscore the directions to go, the priorities to set, and the strategies to try, whether as trainers or HR specialists, managers or consultants responsible for career development of one's self or others.

In the context of setting priorities, "tearing down the walls," the Berlin metaphor, is not just about dismantling national or geographical walls, but the psychological or ideological barriers that separate diverse peoples, disciplines, and industries. The need is for more integrated, synergistic, multicultural leadership that is able to globally focus our economies, markets, and businesses as well as our entertainment and health services.

For more than a dozen years, we (Harris and Moran) have been advocating the *managing of cultural differences* [13], especially by global managers who must become more cosmopolitan and synergistic in their thinking and actions. Originally, we maintained that a cross-cultural component should be a part of all management development; now we contend that cross-cultural training or learning should be incorporated into *all* human resource development (HRD).

Therefore, our attention here is on preparing *cross-cultural leaders* for the global work culture. The process involves the altering of adult perceptions and learning how to overcome one's cultural conditioning [19]. Such endeavors at re-orientation must extend beyond management to encompass all employees, whether hourly workers, technical, or professional personnel. For it is in the transformation of human assets or resources that the organization will be renewed.

There are seemingly four major forces that are awakening management and trainers to the importance of including cross-cultural training in their HRD programs:

1. The pressure of international competition and the globalization of the marketplace.
2. The imbalance in the export/import trade, as in the USA and increasingly in the European Community.
3. The explosion of articles, books, and media features on the influence of culture upon trade, management, organization, business, and the professions.

4. The impact of the transition from an industrial to a post-industrial economy and way of life.

It is the latter that may prove to be the biggest cross-cultural challenge and where we will begin examining the type of leadership necessary to meet that challenge.

New Work Culture Leaders

Leaders are more than excellent executives or managers; they are people who may be found anywhere in a system, who make things happen to achieve organizational goals. We hope they will be found, especially, among those who call themselves human resource professionals, for leaders influence planned change and organizational transformation. But what is leadership, particularly the type that can be described as cross-cultural? Volumes have been written on that subject, and how to enable people to exercise it [6, 14]. Here in this chapter, we can offer only an overview on the topic within the framework of global business wherein a leader is not only attuned to cross-cultural sensitivities at home and abroad, but also able to negotiate and communicate effectively throughout the world with diverse peoples [20]. Next, we examine how HRD leaders may contribute to a creative work environment, one which turns its personnel "on" and stretches employees' capacities through an organizational climate and culture, as well as management style, that stimulates high performing workers.

Leadership is defined differently by various cultures and schools of management thought. The dictionary indicates that "to lead" is to go before, to show the way, to guide or influence in a direction, to take the initiative, and to demonstrate how something can be accomplished. These various meanings of the word extend from to precede and persuade, to excel or to be in the vanguard.

If one conceives of an organization as an energy exchange system, then leadership is the generation and direction of people's energies toward the achievement of personal and organizational goals. To position an organization within a rapidly changing competitive environment, Bennis [3] proposes five leadership qualities to cultivate (Exhibit 1-1). However, Bennis does not identify cross-cultural competencies, which are essential for successful leadership both today and tomorrow.

Exhibit 1-1
Leadership Qualities To Cultivate*

Warren Bennis cites five qualities considered essential for successful leadership. Notice that under "people skills," he fails to include cross-cultural competence:

- Technical Competence—the combination of knowledge, broad experience, and the ability to do whatever one does as well as possible; usually pragmatists who have risen through the ranks as smart, insatiably curious and tireless workers.
- People Skills—the possession of self understanding of one's talents and flaws, plus the ability to eliminate the latter or to compensate for them; also the capacity to understand and work with others in terms of common needs.
- Conceptual Skills—a viewpoint and a vision that permits one to capitalize on existing opportunities and anticipate future ones.
- Judgment—the artful mix of brains and heart that translates into understanding and steadiness; with it, leaders see and understand what's happening, responding immediately, decisively, and intelligently.
- Character—the perfect balance of ambition, ability, and conscience; capable of doing the right thing and taking full responsibility for ones's actions and those of his/her organization.

*Source: "Presidents as CEOs," by Warren Bennis, *Los Angeles Times,* March 6, 1988, Part IV/p. 3. Also see Reference 3.

Leaders for Cultural Renewal

Remember that culture expresses the customs, traditions, viewpoints, practices, and lifestyles of a particular people at a specific point in time. As this 20th century closes, the human family and global business in particular are increasingly intercultural and interdependent. We are in passage from a work culture that conditioned most of us when the Industrial Revolution recast our physical world and reality through mechanization, quantification, and consolidation. We are in transit to a Knowledge Society, dominated by high technology and information processing, a culture marked by mediation (describing and interpreting our world), by simulation and virtual reality (VR), and by circularity (events whipping around us, interacting and shaping experiences). In these circumstances, between epochs, everything we do is cross-cultural and dynamic. Advances in communication, transportation, and other technologies have reduced the actual obstacles that separate humans—the big barriers left that hamper progress and pluralism are in our own minds and imaginations. How else can we explain the persistence of ethnocentrism and provincialism that spawn prejudice, bigotry, and sexism?

Our concern here, generally, is about leading in the creation of this emerging culture; more specifically, toward designing a high-performance environment within globalized organizations. John Sherwood [27] confirms these observations by arguing for high-performance, high-commitment *work cultures* (see Exhibit 1-2). But unfortunately, he fails to mention how those cultures should deal with increasingly multicultural work forces to achieve such productivity and loyalty. We suggest that when leaders value pluralism, and are cross-culturally sensitive, performance improves.

Exhibit 1-2
Succeeding Through High Performance Cultures [27]

Sherwood makes a compelling case for such a strategy, citing many progressive companies such as General Electric, Procter and Gamble, Digital Equipment, and Ford, who are innovating in the redesign of work and organizational structure. As a result, he maintains that personnel expend energy because work is then challenging and significant; in such firms, continuous "learning" is emphasized and rewarded for quality performance. As a tool for this purpose, he recommends design teams to redesign socio-technical systems.

Sherwood believes that management will only succeed in gaining a competitive advantage when leaders change their views about people and the design of work, linking human and technical resources in a collaborative work system. He advocates many of the same approaches suggested in this text, underscoring that leaders inspire and articulate the organization's vision—that is, its mission and a set of values for achieving its goals. For Sherwood, this is the foundation of an organization's work culture, which anticipates the future and encourages high performance.

The principal ingredients of the metaindustrial work culture include those who lead by being attuned to the *changing nature* of society and organizations, of the economy and market, of work and the worker, of leadership and management [9,10,12]. To transform an industrial mindset and environment into a high performing, superindustrial work environment calls for innovative managers who again lead by example and by continuous learning in what has been summarized in Exhibit 1-3.

Exhibit 1-3
New Work Culture Leadership [17, 29]

- Provides improved, more open communication and information to personnel, customers, and suppliers. This is accomplished both personally and electronically, such as through effective use of communication and computer technology. Because work is increasingly information oriented, data must be distributed and differentiated more rapidly, then shaped and paired into information that when refined becomes knowledge.
- Creates more autonomy and participation, so that workers have increasing control over their own work space and opportunities for involvement in the enterprise. This is achieved in various ways that offer employees psychological or actual ownership in the business. The democratization in the workplace ranges from sharing in planning, problem-solving, and decision-making to team management, and profit-sharing.
- Promotes an entrepreneurial spirit in innovative ventures, especially of a technological or service nature. This can be done through encouragement and funding of new start-up, fast-growth enterprises, or by fostering entrepreneurial activities within existing organizations.
- Enhances the quality of work life, so that it is more meaningful, fulfilling, and psychologically rewarding. This incorporates the above strategies, but builds into human systems, wellness programs, sabbatical leaves, incentives, and other entitlements that strengthen loyalty and morale, as well as peak performance.
- Generates innovative, high performing norms and standards that foster competence and excellence, a means to productivity and profitability. This is attained by cultivating work attitudes, agreements, and policies which develop a new work ethic of professionalism in which personnel strive to give their best, to offer quality service at all costs.

- Uses more informal, synergistic organizational relations, so that cooperation and trust are reinforced among the work force. This can be furthered by resisting hierarchial and status relations in preference to adaptive, temporary, cross-functional or interdisciplinary, collaborative activities, and networking.
- Advances technology transfer and venturing, as well as research and development. Because work is becoming more technically oriented, this trend involves more than the introduction of office automation and robotics. It means investing more in R & D by the private sector, emphasizing more technical training and the use of technology for education of people, seeking more applications of new technologies to improve productivity and performance.

These are some of the new directions toward which HR leaders should be pointing their organizations. But there is a missing element without which the work culture will not be transformed. The workplace must value the *diversity of its personnel and their varied talents.* The new culture is not only accepting of women, minorities, and foreign workers, but also capitalizes upon their resources and differences and offers opportunities for career advancement. Such a culture espouses a global perspective that positively reinforces effective intercultural communication and synergistic performance.

Thinking managers no longer view business in domestic and international categories, but have a more cosmopolitan view. The parts to their products, as well as their customers, owners, and personnel, literally come from around the world, as well as their customers, owners, and personnel. No wonder that Louis Korn, an executive search expert, argues that organizations should seek, train, and reward leaders who are forward-looking and effective across cultures, as well as capable of managing technological change. Korn observed (*Los Angeles Times,* January 20, 1982, J2):

> Tomorrow's executives must possess a broad understanding of history, of culture, of technology, of human relations. They must be as comfortable with history, anthropology, sociology, mathematics, and with the physical and natural sciences, as they are with cash management.

Examples of the New Work Culture

Although one may believe that what has been described is tomorrow's organizational culture, there are examples of these characteristics at work today, particularly among some of the high-tech, take-off companies around the globe. Just as there is a similarity in the subculture of management worldwide, so too is there a similarity in the organizational cultures of high-tech enterprises, whether in San Diego, Taiwan, India, Hungary, or reforming Russia. Consider the implications of these seven mini-cases of the changes underway in the work culture.

1. Tandem Corporation

James Treybig, president and principal founder of Tandem Computers, Inc., described the principal features of his company's environment as follows:

- *Fast-growth by high performers*—only 19 years old, Tandem is already listed in the *Fortune 500* for going from zero to half a billion dollars in business, and from 4 to 5,000 employees.
- *High productivity and creativity*—attributed to its competent people who continue to learn, especially about customer satisfaction (*Datamation* magazine rates them number 1 on the latter criteria because of outstanding, motivated, dedicated personnel).
- *Open-door policy with workers, visitors, customers*—managers are responsive and egalitarian with their people, as demonstrated in a weekly "Friday Popcorn" social mixer of two hours for unstructured communication.
- *Emphasis on self and peer management by workers*—Tandem people are expected to take on responsibility and to be held more accountable because they are so involved in its computer business, feel part of the corporation, and enjoy working.
- *Information and technology oriented*—Tandem prides itself on being a "paperless factory" because personnel not only build computers, they use them totally to conduct their business. It is every worker's tool —all have a terminal for setting his or her own quality standards and reviewing personal quality production; everyone controls quality, which is not a separate department. Electronic mail connects personnel from California to Switzerland. Tandem encourages personnel to

use it to help one another, especially in global problem-solving. The company also has used its electronic network to produce a daily, real-time, internal newspaper that combines words/media/voice in a package, and employees from all over the world submit news. Other innovations include a journal that discusses corporate strategy; a TV network in forty-three locations to promote organizational communications, trust, and marketing; training through computer business simulations.

- *Everyone is part of the management process*—each person shares supervisory responsibility through membership in various manufacturing committees that are concerned about everything from quality to asset management. Worker democracy extends to voting on corporate policy. As they contribute to the success of the enterprise, rewards may be bonuses, stock, sabbaticals, and other forms of recognition. Everyone, including worker families, knows where the company is going, so the five-year corporate plan is shared, even with spouses of employees.

- *The Outstanding People Seminar*—called TOPS. This is an annual conference of an organization's highest achievers and their spouses or loved ones. Held during seasons of business downturn as a means of maintaining high morale and productivity, 7% of employees who are truly outstanding performers are rewarded for their extra effort and sacrifice for the past year. Groups of seventy include guest managers, thus mixing every level and function of the company. Because they all are top workers, special relationships are formed that engender professional respect, regardless of status or education, and strengthen a family atmosphere. Executives are convinced that this group socializing builds mutual respect and creativity, as well as an effective and unstructured communication network which contributes to further business success. As Treybig describes it [29, Chapter 1],

> The key to productivity in our business, and in fact in 90% of the jobs in our company, comes from its emphasis on people. We develop people concepts; we involve people in what we do. . . . The bottom line for business is that the major change facing companies in the United States today is the shifting roles of managers and individuals. Managers must integrate several functions—caring about people, working on strategy, expanding communication, generating creativity and innovation, raising productivity, improving quality, and strengthening the organization.

In essence, these types of leaders are the agents of planned change in the work culture.

2. Intel Corporation

The president of this high-tech firm in northern California, Andrew Grove, even wrote a book that details its approach [8]. It involves adapting management style to personnel; structuring decision-making to enlist people support; forecasting and resolving potential problems; enhancing meeting performance and productivity; systematizing performance indicators and reviews; leveraging high performance through raises, bonuses, and promotions; and improving employee career interviewing.

These are successful strategies for leveraging maximum performance at work; imaginative leaders translate them into concrete programs within their company or agency, and then devise even better ones.

As more corporations become transnational in operations, their HR executives must acquire global perspectives and skills to deal with their culturally diverse work force. The next five mini-cases deal with the HR perspective of these forward-looking companies.

3. Ferro Corporation

This Cleveland-based company has been in international business for almost three-quarters of a century. It operates in twenty-two countries on six continents with 60% of its revenues from foreign operations; two-thirds of its employees are foreign nationals. Only since restructuring has Ferro become a global company according to David R. Woodbury, vice president of human resources:

> There was quite a bit of sharing of information and technology among our operations in various countries, but each foreign division or subsidiary operated highly independently, formulating much of its own strategy for manufacturing, marketing, finance, and human resources. . . . Now each business thinks of the world as a marketplace. We're developing broad-based global strategies, with increased communications and a greater sharing of assets throughout the world.

Woodbury was involved in the transformation of Ferro's human resource program, which placed emphasis on recruiting and training people with an international outlook, skills, and experience who could be developed into real global managers in practice.

4. Fluor Corporation

This $7.4 billion engineering firm has 22,000 employees in more than eighty countries, of which there are 500 international HR professionals and about the same number that takes care of domestic personnel. HR management is involved globally not only in the traditional HR functions of administering payroll, benefits, training, and internal consulting, but also in project bidding and management when contracts are awarded. The diverse and worldwide staff of HR professionals do project team training and personnel trouble-shooting. In the Flour-Daniel subsidiary many employees are truly international business people, spending six months to six years, sometimes even decades, away from their homelands as they travel from one construction project to another.

5. General Electric's Medical Systems Group (GEMS)

This $3 billion Milwaukee-based division derives over 40% of its income from outside the USA. Therefore, the company was compelled to integrate internationally, including its human resource policies and programs. The centerpiece of this effort is its Global Leadership Program, a multi-year process in which selected managers from the Americas, Europe, and Asia devise an organized framework to solve problems on important global projects such as improving worldwide engineering productivity, sharing technical expertise, and a common strategy for a network of suppliers. One G.L.P. team is working on a worldwide employee integration plan to increase commitment and a sense of belonging.

Transforming Human Resources

Bernard Bass [1, 2] observes that too much of current management development is on transitional rather than transformational leadership, which most institutions need today. Exhibit 1-4 compares the two leadership styles. Based upon a concept first described by James McGregor Burns, and Bass [1, 5] rightly maintains that leadership research has been focused upon autocratic and democratic or participative issues of leadership for too long, whereas a new paradigm is required that transforms individuals and systems. He concludes that quantum leaps in performance may result with a leader who has innovative or revolutionary ideas, offering a vision of future possibilities, such as when John Fitzgerald Kennedy set a national goal to land a man on the moon in a decade. Perhaps the "Soviet" leaders Mikhail Gorbachev and Boris Yeltsin would fit in this category?

Exhibit 1-4
Transitional Versus Transformational Leadership [2]

Definitions: *Transition* is the movement or passage from one position, place, condition, state, stage, concept, or paradigm to another. . . . To *transform* is to change or alter in form, appearance, structure, or character. Therefore, transformational leadership literally implies a "metamorphosis," for example from one expression of culture to an entirely new manifestation.

Transitional:

- Recognizes what actions sub ordinates must take to achieve outcomes; then clarifies these role requirements for them, so as to instill confidence.
- Identifies subordinates' needs and wants, so as these are satisfied, employees make the effort to achieve the desired outcome.
- Employs leadership training and other positive reinforcements ments to sustain performance, such as raises, promotions, or desirable assignments.

Transformational:

- Raises consciousness level about importance and value of designated outcomes and ways of reaching these, thus contributing to confidence building by members.
- Raises the need level of members from survival and security to higher levels of recognition and self-actualization, thus heightening motivation for extra effort.
- Inspires individuals to transcendence over self-interests for sake of the team, organization, or larger cause leading to higher expectations and performance.

Human resource transformational leadership is necessary to enable employees to "tear down" their psychological walls and transform their mindsets about the new work culture, the globalization underway, and the realities of the new multicultural work force. Transformational leadership is somewhat charismatic, capable of provoking extraordinary effort because leaders have a personal approach to people and instill a sense of larger mission in them, thus creating a high performing atmosphere. It is a leadership style in which the manager becomes a coach, cheerleader, facilitator, and consultant. Bass' research with senior executives and military officers confirmed that they had known such transformational leaders whose vision and expectations inspired them to work long hours, produce an outstanding performance, and express total commitment. The subjects described these high performing leaders as persons they wished to emulate because such leaders:

- Gave followers a sense of autonomy and fostered their self-development.
- Treated them in a friendly, informal, and equal way, like a benevolent parent who was always accessible.
- Provided a model of integrity, fairness, and high standards, while being capable of formality and firmness, reprimanding or correcting as appropriate.
- Encouraged them with advice, help, support, recognition, and openness, while sharing knowledge and expertise.
- Prompted reactions in them of trust, enthusiasm, admiration, respect, pride, and loyalty.

Thus, the transformational leaders are role models who offer followers individualized attention and consideration—the opportunities for inputs of information and inspiration. In an era of knowledge workers, such leaders transmit intellectual excitement by getting people to think and mind-stretch, to visualize the future and what might be done, to arouse awareness in combatting stereotyping of people, gender-bias, and other practices that inhibit the development of human potential. They cause their group to restructure their constructs or perceptions for more timely and relevant responses. As Burns [5] reminds us, these are moral leaders who express people's fundamental and enduring needs, mobilizing followers toward more meaningful and comprehensive values. John Watson of IBM, John Welch of General Electric, John Scully of Apple, and Akio Morita of Sony are corporate examples of transformational leadership. As Harvard's Richard Reich rightly noted, this type of manager transforms an economy, an industry, or a corporation by seeking to innovate with new products and processes, by focusing on human capital and trust. Certainly, this kind of leader is in stark contrast to those executives who wish only to assemble or rearrange portfolios of assets, "number crunchers" who forget their companies are human systems to be developed.

In the transitional period underway, there are numerous mergers and acquisitions among organizations, which in the '80s were to acquire new sources of capital, and now in the '90s are more often for economic survival. The HR leader can accomplish much to ease the human pain involved, while assisting in the synergistic merger of two distinct organizational cultures [18].

Transformational leadership may very well involve confronting archaic structures and procedures, suitable for the industrial age, but inappropriate in a metaindustrial culture. A case in point may be found in the political arena worldwide. Globally, citizens are getting frustrated with politicians who conduct "business as usual" and fail to exercise leadership in the fundamental restructuring of governmental institutions and processes. In North America, for instance, this discontent manifests itself in voter revolt against candidates from traditional parties and the search for an "outside" leader. The typical American is aware of the gridlock between the legislative and executive branches and demands leadership that will change the system. The election of Bill Clinton and the campaign of Ross Perot illustrate this attitude. In Canada, as in the United Kingdom, there is movement toward "devolution" or separatism (e.g., the French in Quebec and the Scots in Great Britain). The whole of Eastern Europe has fragmented as totalitarian regimes are being ousted and people seek democratic leaders to transform their societies toward free-market enterprise. More slowly the same trends manifest themselves in Latin American, the People's Republic of China, and even the two Koreas. Whether in the public or private sectors, the new knowledge workers follow those capable of bringing excessive ambition into a healthier balance by effective leadership, personal growth, and organizational progress [16].

The concept of transformational leadership, as described by Tichy and DeVanna [30], implies the leading edge of change, innovation, and entrepreneurship, especially by empowering personnel. Bennis and

Nanus [4] suggest that the leader's role is to energize learning behavior toward changing realities, whether in knowledge-base, its people, the environment, or technology. This may imply some "unlearning" of obsolete information and attitudes, reinterpreting organizational history, experimenting with change, and analyzing trends and emerging issues. If an enterprise is a dynamic energy exchange system, then it is a learning organization.

Many businesses are striving to adapt to the new work climate by strategic self-analysis, restructuring, and other mechanisms for survival and renewal. But how many turn to their top-performing employees to share their leadership in these processes? How many managers really channel the energy or power within their people?

James O'Toole [23] surveyed 200 top-performing managers in successful companies to ascertain key characteristics in their work environment that accounted for their success. In summary, his findings reveal that a vanguard corporate environment is distinguished by

- A careful balance of and attention to the interests of the varied stakeholders in the business.
- A dedication to high purpose—more visionary and concerned with long-term performance and future orientation.
- A commitment to continual learning, including the fullest development and use of human resources.
- An orientation toward technology to improve both product and service.
- A passion for free-enterprise, market dictates, and openness to new ideas.

HRD Strategies

There are many opportunities within organizations to exercise leadership by sharing this chapter's insights with colleagues, especially by computer networking [26]. For example, some of the issues and strategies reviewed here could be reviewed at staff meetings or used in training sessions. The following are career development possibilities for individual analysis or group process to improve work performance or cross-cultural effectiveness.

High Performance Workshop (HPW)

Bruce Qualset of Professional Development Services and author Harris developed the following process for expanding the leadership abilities of top-performing employees. The model developed has been successfully tested with Navy jet pilots, savings and loan personnel, public utilities supervisors, and even moving company managers. The process follows:

Preliminary Data Gathering. Identification by key management of five critical management concerns, such as matters of performance, productivity, organizational communications, or even globalization and other issues discussed in this chapter. Then, one must determine what constitutes a top-performing employee, the criteria and means for selecting such personnel. Next follows the nomination and selection of high-achieving employees capable of problem-solving the targeted issues.

Designing and Conducting a Workshop. A two-day session is planned and scheduled to deal with the identified problems. Twelve to fifteen high-achieving personnel are invited to participate with a facilitator. The total program is videotaped. To perform group tasks, suitable handouts and instruments are prepared to facilitate data gathering and analysis. The focus is on the major subjects that planners have chosen previously, and the discussions are duly recorded. The sessions begin with key questions about how these participants become top performers—their personal success stories, how they react to the problems presented to them by management, and the solutions they have to offer. At the end of the meetings, participants are asked to summarize what they learned from the experience, as well as make recommendations for organizational changes on the issues under consideration.

Analysis and Reporting. The consultants present during the learning sessions then replay and analyze the videotapes for feasible solutions and organizational insights. They later give an oral briefing to key management and report their findings, as well as offer guidelines for tape review. The videotapes are powerful feedback for management to consider either in summary or full format. A digest of the principal recommendations or insights on the issues may be prepared and distributed as a report of the High Performance Workshop.

The value of this strategy is that it is participative management and can involve employees at any level in the organization who deal with relevant and timely issues. For example, suppose HR leaders wanted to know more about top performance in overseas operations. They could bring together expatriate employees from foreign assignments who have a track record of effective acculturation and performance in international operations. The HPW media sessions focus on what these employees did abroad to facilitate their performance, what problems other employees had in such development, how to interact effectively with the locals, how the organization was supportive of them during their international assignment, and what improvements they recommend. Such videotapes then are used in the orientation process for new organizational representatives going abroad.

This strategy recognizes the high achievers within the enterprise and uses them as behavior models with ordinary workers. The videotapes can be edited for other training sessions. Top performers are today's innovators who help to establish tomorrow's organizational standards. In two such workshops with field and customer service supervisors at Michigan Consolidated Gas and Electric Company, it became apparent that many of the participants had not been told previously that they were outstanding workers; selection for the workshop was the first recognition of this type.

The Bag Lunch Seminar

There are informal opportunities that HR leaders use for career development. A simple approach is a weekly luncheon discussion among six to eight like-minded employees. A site is chosen where one can bring "lunch in a bag" for the learning experience. The participants decide a yearly theme about which they wish to learn more, and the weekly topics as the "umbrella" issue. For example, suppose the theme was "toward globalization-cross-cultural learning," then every chapter heading in this book might become a discussion topic. The subject matter and dates for the meetings are typed and distributed in advance. The first ground rule is that each week a member serves as chairperson, preparing an analysis, leading the discussion, and making any necessary arrangements. The role rotates among the group. To prime the intellectual pump, the second rule is that each person will read ahead on the agreed topic before the meeting (e.g., an article, newspaper story, book chapter). That pre-reading provides the input for discussion and mind-stretching. The final ground rule is that the last half hour of the session is devoted to developing personal *action plans* based on the learning.

As an illustration, suppose the topic for next week is "international management culture." To stimulate discussion, the chairperson might choose an appropriate quotation to reproduce and circulate among the group, such as this one [28]:

> International management culture is an integrative force. As the speed of communication and travel shrink the globe, organizations in different parts of the world are coming to resemble each other in their practices and standards. English has become the almost universal second language of choice in this management culture. The structure of computer hardware and software has added its own rules and norms. Much American management technique has been adopted and adapted to serve this culture, including some things that Americans themselves practice badly or not at all. For better or worse, we are all becoming global managers—all of us can benefit by being more aware that the "right way of doing things" is much more likely to be the result of each culture's contribution than "doing it my way." Our best choice is to learn from each other. Otherwise, we are likely to behave like the frog under the coconut shell who thinks that it sees everything, but in fact its vision is severely limited. Together, we are strong; divided, we collapse.

The chairperson might use this as a discussion opener, asking questions such as:

1. What do you agree or disagree with in this statement?

2. Are international managers from various cultures more comfortable with one another than with hourly workers from their own culture?

3. How do international managers network across cultures?

There are some companies using this method that have renamed it "The Bag University" and actually offer academic or extension credit toward a graduate degree for participation in such seminars. It is not unlike an independent study group on campus.

Data Gathering Instruments

Inventories or questionnaires can be developed or purchased to gather information on how employees think/feel about certain organizational issues and management practices. The HR leader can use such instruments to diagnose an organization's culture or a specific problem. The data collected can be used for self or group analysis, team discussion, individual or work unit evaluation. The ground rule is to collect and analyze the data, then let the findings speak for themselves and form the basis for self or organizational improvements. Here are a few companies that produce them commercially (request a catalog (by writing to):

- National Computer Services Assessments, P.O. Box 1416, Minneapolis, MN 55440
- Talico Inc., 2320 South Third St., Ste. #5, Jacksonville Beach, FL 32250, USA (904-241-1721)
- University Associates, Inc., 8517 Production Ave., San Diego, CA. 92121, USA (619-578-5900)

References

1. Bass, B., *Leadership and Performance Beyond Expectations,* New York: The Free Press, 1985.
2. Bass, B., "Leadership: Good, Better, Best," *Organization Dynamics,* Winter 1985, Vol. 13, #2, pp. 26–40.
3. Bennis W., *Why Leaders Can't Lead,* San Francisco, CA: Jossey-Bass, 1990.
4. Bennis, W. and Nanus, B., *Leaders: The Strategy of Taking Charge,* New York: Harper & Row, 1985.
5. Burns, J. M., *Leadership,* New York: Harper & Row, 1978.
6. Clark, K. E. and Clark, M. B., *Measures of Leadership,* West Orange, NJ: Leadership Library of America, Inc., 1990.
7. Giffi, C., Olson, T., Roth, A.V., and Seal, G. M., *Competing in World-Class Manufacturing—America's 21st Century Challenge,* Homewood, IL: Business One Irwin, 1990.
8. Grove, A., *High Output Management,* New York: Random House, 1983.
9. Harris, P. R., *New Worlds, New Ways, New Managements,* Ann Arbor, MI: Masterco Press/AMACOM, 1983.
10. Harris, P. R., *Management in Transition—Transforming Managerial Practices and Organizational Strategies for a New Work Culture,* San Francisco: Jossey-Bass, 1985.

11. Harris, P. R, *Living and Working in Space: Behaviour, Culture and Organization,* Chichester, UK: Ellis Horwood (USA-Prentice Hall, Englewood Cliffs, NJ), 1992.
12. Harris, P. R., *High Performance Leadership—Strategies for Maximum Productivity,* Glenview, IL: Scott, Foresman/Harper/Collins, 1989.
13. Harris, P. and Moran R., R. T., *Managing Cultural Differences,* Third Edition, Houston: Gulf Publishing Company, 1991.
14. Freeman, F. and King, S. (eds.), *Leadership Education,* Greensboro, NC: Center for Creative Leadership (5000 Laurinda Dr., 27438), 1992.
15. Frost, P. F. and Moore, L.F., *Reframing Organizational Culture,* Newbury Park, CA: Sage Publications, 1991.
16. Kaplan, R. E., et al, *Beyond Ambition: How Driven Managers Can Lead Better and Lead Better,* San Francisco, CA: Jossey-Bass, 1991.
17. Kuhn, R. L. (ed.), *Handbook for Creative and Innovative Managers,* New York: McGraw-Hill, 1988. [NOTE: Ch. 61, "The New World of Creative Work" by P. R. Harris.]
18. McManus, M. L. and Hergert, M. L., *Surviving Merger and Acquisition,* Glenview, IL: Scott Foresman/Harper/Collins, 1988.
19. Mezirow, J., *Transformative Dimensions of Adult Learning,* San Francisco, CA: Jossey-Bass. 1991.
20. Moran, R. T.(ed.), *Global Business Management in the 1990s,* Washington, DC: Beachman Publishing, 1990.
21. Nadler, L. and Nadler, Z., *Every Manager's Guide to Human Resource Development,* San Francisco, CA: Jossey-Bass Publishers, 1992.
22. Nanus, B., *The Leader's Edge: Seven Keys to Leadership in a Turbulent World,* Chicago, IL: Contemporary Books Inc. (180 N. Michigan Ave., 60601), 1990.
23. O'Toole, J., *Vanguard Management,* New York: Doubleday & Co., 1985; (paperback ed.), New York: Berkley Publishing Group, 1987.
24. Reich, R. B., *The Next American Frontier,* New York, NY: New York Times Books, 1983.
25. Reich, R. B., *The Work of Nations—Preparing Ourselves for 21st Century Capitalism,* New York: Vintage Books, 1992.
26. Rossman, R., *The Emerging Worldwide Electronic University,* New York: Greenwood/Praeger, 1992.
27. Sherwood, J., "Creating Work Cultures with Competitive Advantages," *Organizational Dynamics,* Winter 1988, pp. 5–26.
28. Simon, G. M., Vazques-Colin, C., and Harris, P. R., *Transcultural Leadership—Strategies for Empowering the Multicultural Workforce and Capitalizing on People Diversity,* Houston, TX: Gulf Publishing Co., 1993.

29. Smilor, R. W. and Kuhn, R. L. (eds.), *Managing Trade-off in Fast Growth Companies,* New York: Praeger, 1986 (see Ch. 7 "Corporate Culture" by P. R. Harris).
30. Tichy, N. M. and DeVanna, M. A., *The Transformational Leader,* New York: John Wiley & Sons, 1986.

CHAPTER 2

THE CROSS-CULTURAL STRATEGIST

Introduction

Culture and Strategy

Culture is a group problem-solving tool that enables individuals to survive in a particular environment [11]. All cultures use some form of strategy to help in the survival effort. Strategy, which is derived from a Greek word meaning "the art of the general," was originally limited to military applications. Today, the concept of strategy encompasses a wide variety of planning systems for promoting the vital interests of various organizations.

The interlacing of culture and strategy in modern organizations can be either an asset or a liability. All cultures have various strengths and weaknesses. An organization's strategy must be designed to maximize cultural strengths, while minimizing cultural weaknesses. Unfortunately, the lack of effective cross-cultural interaction in many organizations often results in either a debilitating polarization or a cultural stagnation that allows negative traits to grow. This can offset or diminish cultural strengths and reduce the global opportunities available to the organization.

For example, homogeneous cultural groups, such as those found in Japanese corporations, are able to act with such uniformity and dedication that they can often out pace more heterogeneous competitors. However, this homogeneity can also result in a cautious rigidity that reduces the flexibility needed to survive during periods of rapid change. Globalization requires the inclusion of all cultural groups within the organizational framework. Japanese organizations have been faced with increasing resistance to their products and been subjected to cultural "bashing" by groups that feel excluded and preyed upon.

Some educators and consultants feel that the Japanese are allowing their cultural homogeneity to become a liability. U.S. Labor Secretary Robert Reich observes [14]:

> In fact, even the most cosmopolitan Japanese companies are finding that the general reputation of Japanese business for putting Japan's interests first is creating a competitive disadvantage, making it increasingly difficult for these companies to export their products or undertake foreign investment around the world without encountering political opposition.
>
> Furthermore, the well-known predilection of Japanese companies to do business with each other and in a way that uniquely benefits Japan has created a backlash among corporate competitors. In recent years, U.S. and European global managers have grown wary of depending too heavily on Japanese companies for critical high-tech components. Specifically, they worry that Japanese suppliers will allocate the parts they make to other Japanese corporations first and withhold them from foreign partners or that Japanese companies will use the parts to gain a predatory foothold, gradually displacing their foreign partner as the relationship becomes more and more lopsided.

The cultural rigidity displayed by Japanese organizations has opened up new opportunities for organizations from culturally diverse nations, such as the United States and the new European Community. Multiculturalism has become a source of competitive advantage. Combinations of different cultural traits can result in innovations, flexibility, and speed necessary for success in the modern world. If directed properly, multiculturalism is the most valuable asset that a global organization owns.

It is the job of the cross-cultural strategist to direct the organization's multiculturalism in such a way that minds are opened, innovation is spurred, flexibility is increased, and speed is maximized. This chapter presents a broad overview of the concept of strategy, followed by ideas and suggestions for HR professionals to use in developing cross-cultural strategies for their organizations.

The Military Paradigm

The concept of strategy has military roots. Many executives look to military authors in developing strategies for their corporations. For example, Richard Holder, president and chief operating officer of Reynolds Metals Company, emphasizes the Prussian General Erich Ludendorff's concept of "total war" [3]:

> Ludendorff's "total war" meant the complete commitment of the nation state's entire portfolio of resources—all its population, its economy, its financial structure, its agriculture, its raw materials and its production facilities, and its total will—to the task at hand.
>
> A global corporation that is able to martial its entire worldwide resources to focus on a single market, or a single product category, or a single country would have no problem fitting into Ludendorff's thought process.
>
> The emergence of global and multinational corporations all lean, mean, and combat-ready, willing to compete for markets anywhere, has added new dimensions to transnational trade issues and has made the notion of competition very different from what it was in the past.

Military analogies are also used by consultants. Preston Townley, president and chief executive officer of the Conference Board, agrees with the advice of Prussian Field Marshall Von Moltke. Townley observes [21]:

> At GE, Jack Welch regularly asks the top managers in the company's 14 major businesses to answer a series of questions about the global competition. We should all constantly ask ourselves these questions:

> - What are your global market dynamics today, and where will they be over the next several years?
>
> - What actions have your competitors taken in the last three years to upset those global dynamics?
>
> - What have you done in the last three years to affect those dynamics?
>
> - What are the most dangerous things your competitor could do in the next three years to upset those dynamics?
>
> - What are the most effective things you could do to bring your desired impact on those dynamics?

> I like this strategy because it acknowledges the power of other people to upset our apple carts today. Without knowing it, Prussian Field Marshall

> Von Moltke, who originated the modern method of directing armies in the field, may have created the best global business strategy. Long ago he warned, "A plan is valid only until your opponent makes the first move."

Human resource professionals can pick and choose from the writings of a wide array of military strategists in making important points about the realities of global business. The most cited strategic works include those of Carl von Clausewitz [24], Baron de Jomini [4], B.H. Lidell Hart [2], Sun-tzu's [18], Miyamato Musashi [11], and Alfred Thayer Mahan [6].

Despite the widespread use of military concepts in the development of business strategy, many consultants are worried about the implications of the military paradigm and refuse to "pick up the sword."

We will begin our discussion with the presentation of a sample training program that uses the martial art of kendo to expose business persons to cross-cultural aspects of strategy. This will be followed by the presentation of a universal strategic model and an in-depth discussion of the model's components.

A Cross-Cultural Strategy Training Program

Kendo and the Way of the Sword

There are many ways to learn about cross-cultural aspects of strategy. One way is to involve clients in physical activities, including martial arts exercises. In observing a variety of martial arts training exercises, business persons are often able to develop new cross-cultural strategic perspectives. For example, the observation of Chinese kung-fu, Japanese karate, and Korean tae-kwon-do can be of assistance in developing an Asia-Pacific strategic perspective.

One of the most impressive martial arts to use in a cross-cultural strategy training program is Japanese kendo. Kendo is "the way of the sword." Very few knowledgeable business persons would question the proposition that the Japanese have become the premier strategists of the global marketplace. An understanding of kendo is of great assistance in understanding why the Japanese are so good at what they do, and why they are in danger of losing their current position.

With the founding of the samurai class in 8th century Japan, military arts became the highest form of study. Samurai children were schooled in the Chinese classics and fencing exercises. Rather than the pen being mightier than the sword, it was "pen and sword in accord." Schools of kendo were created as early as the Muromachi period (1390–1600), and are still attended by Japanese business persons and politicians today.

Rather than simply being a sport, kendo is a code of personal honor and discipline. Training in kendo requires an individual to overcome self-indulgence, build up a tolerance of pain through grueling exercise, and conquer the fear of death. To become a master of the sword, the kendo novice must resolutely accept that death can occur at any moment.

The kendo ideal is perhaps best expressed by the 17th and 18th century samurai, Yamamoto Tsunetomo. After his master died, Tsunetomo was prohibited from committing *seppuku,* ritual self-disembowelment. Instead, he was granted permission to retire and become a Buddhist priest. During the last years of his life in a hermitage in Kurotsuchibaru, Tsunetomo was visited by a young samurai named Tashiro Tsuramoto. Their conversations lasted for seven years and were recorded by Tsuramoto in a widely-read book entitled *Hagakure* [23]. One passage from the book is especially revealing:

> The way of the samurai is found in death. When it comes to either/or, there is only the choice of death. It is not particularly difficult. Be determined and advance. To say that dying without reaching one's aim is to die a dog's death is the frivolous way of sophisticates. When pressed with the choice of life or death, it is not necessary to gain one's aim.
>
> We all want to live. And in a large part we make our logic according to what we like. But not having attained our aim and continuing to live is cowardice. This is a thin dangerous line. To die without gaining one's aim is a dog's death and fanaticism. But there is no shame in this. This is the substance of the way of the samurai. If by setting one's heart right every morning and evening, one is able to live as though his body were already dead, he gains freedom in the way. His whole life will be without blame, and he will succeed in his calling.

Just think about what this quote says about the Japanese approach to strategy! Japanese strategy is not merely a planning system, it is an honorable way of life. There is no dishonor in dying like a dog without meeting one's goals. Just set your heart straight and march forward regardless of the personal consequences. Is it any wonder that Japanese manufacturers have such disciplined, dedicated work forces? Will this cultural rigidity result in the demise of Japanese global organizations?

Although kendo schools of the 18th century continued to emphasize the resolute acceptance of death, they began to use less lethal equipment to reduce the chances of mortal wounds. Today, the sword is represented by a *shinai,* or bamboo sword. The shinai is made of four lengths of split bamboo bound with leather thongs. It is about 43 to 46 inches long with a leather covered hilt.

Protective clothing prevents contestants from receiving serious injuries. In preparing for a match, the traditional *uwagi* (jacket) and *hakama* (floor-length, pleated skirt) are put on first. Then the contestant kneels with his buttocks resting on his heels, and puts on the *tare* (hip and waist protector) and the *do* (chest protector). A cotton towel is then wrapped around his head, and the *men* (mask) and *kote* (padded gloves) are put on.

Kendo matches take place on a wooden floor in an area about twenty-nine to thirty-six square feet. After the contestants rise and bow, they stand with the right foot slightly advanced and the left foot slightly raised. The shinai is held in both hands, with the tip pointed at the opponent's throat.

During the match, contestants must try to hit their opponent with the shinai. Points are awarded for hits delivered upon the left side, right side, or top of the head; the right or left wrist; the right or left side of the body; and for a thrust to the throat. These are the only scoring areas. The attacker must call out the name of the point struck at the moment that he hits it. For example, as you hit your opponent with a downward strike to the middle of the head, you must call out, *men* (mask). A contest is won by the first combatant who scores two points. Points are verified by judges.

Several years ago, Stripp brought his son, Sage, to a kendo class in Niigata, Japan. Although Sage had absolutely no experience with kendo, the students were gracious enough to include him in their training program. Every student in the class fought a match with their American visitor. Unfortunately for the Japanese students, the wild young American had absolutely no conception of proper kendo form. He continually gave the Japanese students low blows, hit them in their arms and legs, and caused quite a few bruises. Through it all, the Japanese students displayed the utmost courtesy to their guest and gave him a rousing cheer when the session ended.

What did the Japanese and American students learn from the kendo matches? The American learned of Japanese discipline, respect for ceremony, and courtesy to guests. The Japanese learned of American courage, informality, and willingness to try new things. All in all, it was a valuable lesson for both sides.

Business persons can learn a great deal about the Eastern mindset from kendo and its background, and this knowledge can be incorporated into training sessions.

Universal Principles of Strategy

Strategy comprises general principles that have remained fairly constant throughout history and are universally applicable. Strategy always involves long-term planning; defining objectives; analyzing one's own and the competitor's strength; understanding the geography of the land or environmental conditions; planning moves accordingly; assessing options and preparing contingency plans; organizing transport, supplies, and communication; anticipating the competitor's actions; and determining when and where to act.

The general principles of strategy always include a central purpose, a set of objectives, an intelligence function with emphasis on analysis of internal and external strengths and weaknesses, a consideration of alternative actions, a strategic choice, and a means of coordination and control. Strategy considers the whole picture, determining when and where to act. Logistics organizes the internal resources and develops the lines of communication, supply, reinforcement, and retreat. Tactics occur at contact and determine the manner of execution and employment of resources. All of this is driven by policy, which is an outgrowth of individual and group philosophy.

The basic framework for developing corporate strategy is the same for domestic, international, multinational, transnational, and global operations (see Exhibit 2-1). However, as a corporation increases its global involvement, the corporate planning model must be expanded to include a complex panorama of environmental variables.

Exhibit 2-1
Basic Framework for
Developing a Global Strategy

1. General Philosophy: What is the firm's basic reason for existence?

2. Analysis and Diagnosis:
   - External: Are there opportunities outside of the domestic environment that can benefit the organization?
   - Internal: Can the organization meet global opportunities if they are present?

3. Mission Statement: Given the results of the analysis and diagnosis, what is the organization's vision for its future existence as a global enterprise?

4. Objectives: Within a specified time period, what outcomes does the organization desire to achieve?

5. Strategic Alternatives: How can the organization take advantage of the available global opportunities while avoiding global threats?

6. Strategic Choice: Which alternative is most appropriate to the organization's situation?

7. Contingency Plan: Given the possibility of failing, which alternative should the organization fall back upon?

8. Implementation:
   - Leadership: Who will be selected to implement the global strategy?
   - Personnel: How will personnel be chosen?
   - Logistics: How will the lines of global communication and supply be organized?
   - Tactics: How will global resources be deployed?

9. Evaluation: How does the organization know if its plan is working? What provisions are made to alter or realign strategy based on feedback or new input?

General Philosophy

The single most important task of business leaders is to give their employees a sense of direction. Strategy cannot be formulated until the leader's philosophy is properly articulated. Therefore, the human resource professional's first job in helping a corporation develop a cross-cultural strategy is to discover what the corporate philosophy is. The corporate philosophy includes the fundamental beliefs, concepts, and attitudes that caused the corporation to be created. It represents both the personal values of top management and the values imposed upon the corporation by stockholders and society. It is the broad direction that the corporation is supposed to pursue.

The personal values of top management are extremely important to the direction of the corporation. Top management's values influence the way middle and lower level managers perceive situations, solve problems, make decisions, look at individuals and groups, evaluate the business, determine what is and is not ethical, and decide where the business should go.

Management's value system may lead the corporation to seek rapid growth over profits, to produce only technically sophisticated products rather than mass-produced items, to sell only in U.S. markets and not go abroad, to seek profits over all other considerations, to stabilize employment at the expense of stock dividends, and so on. Values have an obvious relevance to the basic objectives of the corporation.

For example, the basic duty of a business is to generate a profit. Most corporations are purely profit-oriented. They were created with only one purpose in mind—to make money. They will add and subtract product lines, change locations, and hire and fire employees as long as the fundamental purpose of maximum profitability is reached.

However, to succeed within some cultural contexts, it may be strategically wise to redefine or realign corporate purpose with phrases such as "to provide profitable service." In other words, within some cultures, "to make money" would be rejected as crass materialism, while providing profitable service would be an acceptable philosophy.

In talking to executives from these firms about corporate philosophy, the human resource professional may receive a response such as, "I'm in this for the money, pure and simple." This response is helpful, and may be sufficient to form the foundation of the corporation. Profit-driven businesses often have a maximum of flexibility and can concentrate on providing customers with what they want.

On the other hand, legal and social limitations prevent corporations from entering certain areas of business. For example, drug dealing is illegal in most countries of the world, with penalties ranging from monetary fines to the death sentence. Business persons who are "in it for the money" may not be willing to go so far as engaging in illegal activities to make money. Therefore, their philosophy might be more properly articulated as, "I'll do anything for money, as long as it's legal."

If you take it a step further, managers might want to make money, but may have great personal pride in their work. Maximum profitability is not as important as attaining the highest quality in their products or services. They want to stimulate quality in management and employees and are devoted to principles such as top quality management or zero defects management. Such executives might express a desire to "seek the highest quality in all of our products."

Other managers are concerned with the atmosphere of the work place. They want the corporation to provide opportunities for personal growth and fulfillment. Values such as equal opportunity and the education of all employees are promoted. Co-workers are like a family. These executives might say, "We want to be a good place for people to work."

The best way for a human resource professional to discover the corporate philosophy is to spend time with top management. The HR professional can do this in various ways: go to dinner with managers, play golf with them, take a camping trip together, or go sailing. Any activity where you can spend time together is helpful in developing a profile of top management.

With the profile in hand the HR professional can help top management create a simple written statement of corporate philosophy. The statement will be used as the cornerstone of the corporation's direction and method of operation. It should also be designed with public image in mind. Stockholders and the general public take great interest in statements of corporate philosophy.

The statement of philosophy should express the basic purposes of the company and the values of top management. This includes ethical values as well as philosophies and chosen practices in achieving or adhering to them. The ethical values refer to personal conduct, moral duty, or an expression of what is considered right or wrong within the organizational culture.

It is best to keep the statement of philosophy short. A direct and simple statement, which clearly and concisely states top management values, will minimize confusion and increase the chances of success. For example, "The purpose of the Los Alamos Car Corporation is to make nuclear powered automobiles at a profit while being a conscientious community citizen." This statement includes three major purposes, (1) line of business, (2) profits, and (3) corporate social responsibility.

Classic examples of short philosophy statements include Du Pont's "Better things for better living through chemistry," RCA's "The most trusted name in electronics," Union Carbide's "The discovery company," and Celanese's "To retain our global business leadership through new products and research, supported by aggressive marketing."

The CEO may want to use a slogan to express the corporate philosophy. Slogans were originally battle cries or gathering calls of the Scottish clans. In many instances, a good battle cry can be half the battle. A classic example of a corporate battle cry is Stephen Davison Bechtel's, "We'll build anything, anywhere, any time." This battle cry has helped turn Bechtel into one of the world's greatest engineering and construction firms.

Developing a Global Philosophy

Kenichi Ohmae, a Japanese management consultant with McKinsey, feels that the path to becoming a global company begins with the development of the proper attitude. Prahalad believes the proper attitude is an obsession with winning [12, 13]. The obsession takes the form of a "strategic intent" that permeates the total organization and is nurtured and sustained for a long period of time.

Prahalad believes that the obsession with winning must go all the way down from the chairman of the board to the lowest level employee. Each member of the organization must believe in and share the same fundamental competitive agenda. To gain this obsession for winning corporate members must recognize that "the enemy is outside." Without a shared competitive agenda and a clear view of the enemy, a corporation ends up in a collective paralysis and an inability to globalize.

In trying to build a global philosophy, HR professionals can constructively follow Prahalad's lead by thinking in terms of a worldwide athletic competition. A world-class athlete is one who has proven worthy to compete with the best the planet has to offer. World-class competitiveness requires that all employees be involved in the pursuit of continual and rapid improvement. The key is training. Everyone must develop a passion for satisfying the customers.

The use of the idea of a worldwide athletic competition in developing a global philosophy has particular appeal in multicultural situations. For example, Hiromi Gunji, chairman, president, and CEO of Brother International recognizes that we live in a multicultural world, but believes that global executives should never lose sight of their roots. His philosophical objective is to cultivate a spirit of cultural understanding with host nations and create an atmosphere of global harmony akin to the Olympic Games. This approach allows business persons to retain their cultural heritage and be respectful of other cultures, while engaging in fierce competition at the same time.

Analysis and Diagnosis of Global Opportunities

The HR professional's second task in developing a corporation's cross-cultural strategy is to assist in determining whether or not there are international opportunities that can benefit the corporation. The international environment changes so fast that managers need to systematically analyze and diagnose it. Environmental analysis is the process by which strategists monitor the international environment to determine opportunities and threats to the corporation.

In keeping track of the world environment, strategists must pay particular attention to international economic indicators, national governments, legal structures, competitors, suppliers, technology, geography, and local markets. HR professionals can assist in monitoring these areas by pointing out information sources, providing information, and facilitating discussion.

Although there is an abundance of written and documentary information available, top executives normally search for international opportunities by talking to other people. The higher up the executive is in the corporation, the more likely verbal information is relied upon. If written and documentary information is used at all, it is used by middle and lower level managers, who will provide a brief oral summary of relevant information to top management.

The network of human sources used by top executives for scanning the international environment is primarily inside the corporation. Company salespersons can be particularly good sources. Outside the organization, the primary information sources are personal and professional contacts, including customers, suppliers, government officials, bankers, insurance agents, and advertising agencies. Some corporations obtain additional information by either spying or hiring competitor's employees.

There are severe problems with relying upon these verbal information sources. The effectiveness of corporate strategy largely relies upon the accuracy and validity of the environmental assessment. However, most of the information provided to top management is either anecdotal or highly subjective. Information about international opportunities is often distorted by both geographic distance and cultural differences.

HR professionals, both internal and external, can help prevent distortion by bringing the various information sources together and holding global environmental assessment workshops. During the workshops, participants can compare written and documentary information with verbal reports of international opportunities. HR professionals can act as facilitators.

Prior to the workshop, HR professionals can obtain economic information through various government agencies, international organizations, and large banks. The U.S. Commerce Department (14th Street between Constitution Avenue and E Street, NW, Washington, D.C. 20230) publishes *Global Market Surveys, Country Market Sectorial Surveys, Overseas Business Reports, Foreign Business Trend Reports,* and *Market Share Reports.* The Commerce Department's "country desk officers" are extremely good sources of information on global trade opportunities. HR professionals might also want to contact their state international trade office for information on global trade opportunities.

Other good sources of information on doing business with foreign countries include:

- The U.S. International Trade Commission (500 E Street, SW, Room 112, Washington, D.C. 20436; Telephone: 202-205-2000).
- The Bureau of Economic and Business Affairs, U.S. Department of State (2201 C Street, NW, Room 6822, Washington, D.C. 20520; Telephone: 202-647-1942).

- The Office of International Trade, U.S. Small Business Administration (409 3rd St. SW, Room 501A, Washington, D.C. 20416; Telephone: 202-205-6720 or 800-827-9722).
- United Nations (46th & 1st, New York, N.Y. 10017). The U.N. publishes *The Statistical Yearbook, The Demographic Yearbook,* and *Yearbooks of Industrial Statistics, Labor Statistics,* etc.
- The World Bank (1818 H Street, NW, Washington, D.C. 20433) publishes *The World Development Report* and *The World Bank Tables.*
- Japan Information Access Project, IEEE 1730 Massachusetts Ave. NW, Washington, DC 20036, USA (202/833-4545;FAX: 728-9614).
- The Global Forecasting Service, *The Economist* Intelligence Unit, 40 Duke St., London W1A 1DW, UK (44 71/493-6711;FAX: 499-9767).

There are also various private commercial organizations that provide excellent economic information:

- Business International Corporation (Dag Hammarskjold Plaza, New York, N.Y. 10017).
- *The Economist* Intelligence Unit (75 Rockefeller Plaza, New York, N.Y. 10017).
- Euromonitor (18 Doughty Street, London, WC IN2 PN, England) which publishes a wide variety of regional economic reports.

Legal information can be obtained through insurance companies, accounting firms, and law firms. Good written sources of legal information include the Price Waterhouse guides, Dun and Bradstreet's Exporter's Encyclopedia, and Business International's Licensing, Trading, and Investment series.

Some international accounting firms offer a free volume containing taxation information on eighteen countries. *Taxation of Cross-Border Mergers and Acquisitions* can be obtained from KPMG Gebouw's International Tax Centre (Burg, Rijndersl 20, 1185 MC Amstelveen, The Netherlands).

All HRD programs and training must be aligned with the organization's strategic plan and contribute to achieving its goals. To help in this process, the *BNAC Communicator* is a free newsletter on topics and resources for training, including many video programs. Available from

BNA Communications, Inc. (9439 Key West Ave., Rockville, MD 20850, USA; Tel. 1-800/233-6047).

In conjunction with the *Managing Cultural Differences* Series, the strategist will find useful Gulf Publishing Company's *Multicultural Resources Databank and Directory* (3301 Allen Parkway, Houston, TX 77019; Tel. 1-800-231-6275). This source offers a comprehensive listing of organizations, publications, and learning materials that will enhance people's intercultural and international skills.

Global Business Analysis from the Experts

HR professionals can consider the advice of the following six consultants and scholars on the environment for global business in the 1990s:

1. George Stalk [17], vice-president of the Boston Consulting Group, says that strategy has become extremely dynamic. Competition now involves a "war of movement" in which success depends on anticipation of market trends and quick response to changing customer needs. Successful competitors move quickly in and out of products, markets, and sometimes entire businesses in a process more akin to interactive video than to chess. In this environment, the essence of strategy is not the structure of the company's products and markets, but the dynamics of its behavior. Size doesn't count as much anymore. Many corporations are successful because they are niche players and fast movers.

2. Harvard business Professor Michael Porter, author of *The Competitive Advantage of Nations* argues: "The successful industries in virtually every nation are ones where companies, through aggression and emotion and sometimes sheer hatred, are really propelling each other to advance." Successful nations are those where industries constantly upgrade themselves by investing in research, technology, or people to innovate faster than their foreign rivals.

3. Lester Thurow, dean of MIT's Sloan School of Business, believes that America should create a business environment that is both cooperative and competitive at the same time. In terms of cooperation, businesses should pool resources for activities such as industry-wide training programs or research. When it comes to manufacturing and marketing, antitrust laws aimed at fostering competition should be

vigorously enforced to ensure innovation and dynamism in the market place.

4. C.K. Prahalad [12, 13], professor of corporate strategy and international business at the University of Michigan believes that:

- The nature of competition is shifting toward new product development.
- The idea that emphasis on cost reduction and improvement of quality would lead to market share is no longer true. Customers now expect good quality and good prices.
- Businesses must realize that their competitors may have shifted from end products and services to "core" products that provide function. Share in core products leads to manufacturing share as distinct from market share for end products.
- The next round of competition is going to be about competence. People are going to be a lot more concerned with the capacity to create new businesses rather than being efficient in existing businesses. Competence is going to provide companies with the differential advantage. Competition is not going to be over technology, resources, size, regulations, subsidies, or investor pressures. Competition is going to be over ideas.

5. Peter Drucker predicts that Europe will gradually become the world's leading economic power, replacing the U.S. and Japan. Drucker feels that both Japan and the U.S. have peaked and Europe will move ahead because of its size, affluence, and new political power and market dynamics.

6. On the other hand, Alain Gomez [8], CEO of Thomson S.A., feels that the future is in Asia. Gomez stated: "There is no question that the center of the world is moving toward Southeast Asia. Not only are the costs much lower but the workers are very good, as are the engineers and the professionals. It is a function of social coherence and education and valuing hard work and family."

Internal Analysis and Diagnosis

The HR professional's third job in helping a corporation develop a cross-cultural strategy is to assist in determining whether or not the corporation has the internal resources to take advantage of present and future international opportunities. To do this, the corporation must perform an internal audit. Factors to look at include financial strength, marketing and distribution systems, production and operations, personnel, and corporate resources.

One of the key areas to look at is the "core competence" of the corporation. C.K. Prahalad and Gary Hamel, lecturer in business policy and management at London Business School, believe that long-run competitiveness derives from an ability to build, at lower cost and faster than competitors, the core competencies that spawn unanticipated products. The real sources of competitive advantage are to be found in management's ability to consolidate corporate-wide technologies and production skills into competencies that empower individual businesses to adapt quickly to changing opportunities.

Core competencies revolve around the collective learning of the organization, especially how to coordinate diverse production skills and integrate multiple streams of technologies. The development of core competencies requires communication, involvement, and a deep commitment to working across organizational boundaries. The entire organization, from the chairman on down, must become involved.

Three tests can be applied to identify core competencies in a company. First, a core competence provides potential access to a wide variety of markets. Second, a core competence should make a significant contribution to the perceived customer benefits of the end product. Third, a core competence should be difficult for competitors to imitate. A rival might acquire some of the technologies that comprise the core competence, but it will find it more difficult to duplicate the more or less comprehensive pattern of internal coordination and learning.

At the level of core competence, the goal is to build world leadership in the design and development of a particular class of product function. To sustain leadership in their core competence areas, companies seek to maximize their world manufacturing share in core products. The manufacture of core products for a wide variety of external and internal customers yields the revenue and market feedback that, at least partly, determines the pace at which the core competencies can be enhanced and extended.

Mission Statement

The HR professionals fourth task in developing a corporation's cross-cultural strategy is to assist in creating a mission statement.

The starting point for global success must begin with a relentless focus on satisfying customer needs. HR professionals need to learn how to energize both management and workers. Minds must be focused on the customer.

The best way to focus the corporate mind on the customer is through the use of a "mission statement." Drawing upon their personal and corporate philosophy, top management evaluates global opportunities in light of existing corporate resources. They choose a course of action which is labeled a "mission." The most powerful missions are expressed in simple terms. The mission statement should present a message that is so simple and compelling that employees are driven to follow it. Top management must articulate the mission in a written statement, which will be used by middle and lower level managers as a guide for action.

Human resource professionals can assist in formulating a mission statement by asking top management to answer ten basic questions designed to focus top management on the needs and wants of customers, and to determine: "What is our business?"

1. Who are our customers?
2. What products and services do our customers buy?
3. Why do our customers buy these products and services?
4. Where do our customers buy these products and services?
5. Which of our customers' wants are not being satisfied by the products or services we offer today?
6. Which of our customer's unsatisfied wants can we satisfy?
7. How will we satisfy those wants?
8. Who should our customers be?
9. What should our business be?
10. What will our business become?

It is vital that HR professionals emphasize the importance of identifying customer needs before products are manufactured. Many American corporations manufacture products before they know if customers want them. This is "old-style marketing." Corporations produce something and then rely upon their salesmen to sell it, whether anybody wants it or not. In the aftermath of World War II, when no other products were available, American corporations could get away with this approach. Today, it won't work. There are too many alternatives available in the global marketplace.

To be successful today, corporations must use "new-style marketing." A corporation must identify who the customer is and what the customer wants before it manufactures anything. Then the corporation must determine if it can produce the product at a lower cost and/or a higher quality than competitors. This involves a global search for the best opportunities available.

Developing a Global Mission Statement

The key to the success of a global corporation is developing and implementing a common strategic mission as expressed by their mission statement.

NEC has a fairly simple statement of their long-term destiny— "C&C"—computers and communications. NEC believes that computers and communications will converge, and they want to be a part of the convergence. They make sure that all of their publics, including employees, customers, suppliers, and investors, know that they are focused on C&C, covering a wide product range, from laptops to satellite dishes. NEC's mission is very clearly understood both inside and outside the organization.

HR professionals might want to consider following Dow Chemical's formula for developing a simple global mission statement. Dow Chemical asks five key strategic questions:

1. What is the thrust or focus for future business development?
2. What is the scope of products and markets that will, and will not, be considered?
3. What is the future emphasis or priority and mix for products and markets that fall within the scope?
4. What key capabilities are required to make the strategic vision happen?
5. What does this vision imply for growth and return expectations?

HR professionals can also use Exhibit 2-2 as a guideline.

Objectives

The human resource professional's fifth task in helping a corporation develop a cross-cultural strategy is to assist in the formulation of

---

Exhibit 2-2
Mission Statement for Globalization

- We will search the globe for the best opportunities available.
- We will place our investments around the world to achieve the highest return at the least risk.
- We will purchase raw materials, partially processed items or manufactured items wherever in the world we can do so most economically.
- We will produce either the components or the finished product wherever we can do so most productively.
- We will market our manufactured products wherever we can do so most profitably.
- We will conduct a worldwide search in recruiting our personnel.
- We will conduct our research and development wherever we can capitalize at optimum cost on the technical capabilities that exist in the world.

---

objectives. The mission statement comprises abstract guidelines meant to provide general direction for the corporation. From the mission statement comes "action commitments," which are termed objectives. An objective is a desired outcome to be achieved by the corporation within a specified time-period.

Objectives are the heart of the strategic plan. They indicate what the corporation is trying to achieve and become. Without objectives, organizations waste energy and flounder aimlessly without direction. With objectives, a corporation is provided with specific direction and knows what it is trying to accomplish.

Objectives determine the desired future state of the business or one of the business units. They should lay out what performance each managerial unit is supposed to achieve, what contribution different managerial units are expected to make in helping other units meet their objectives, and what contributions managers can expect from others.

Objectives should provide clear, unambiguous, measurable results, a deadline, and a specific assignment of accountability. To be useful for business managers, objectives should be close-ended. Open-ended objectives are described in very general terms and are of limited value, because they cannot be measured and it is not known when or if they can be achieved. Close-ended objectives are precise descriptions of intended results that management has the ability to achieve.

Building a "network" of related objectives is a rigorous process, which should be performed by middle and lower level managers. Managers determine what the objectives should be. They also determine goals for each area of objectives. HR professionals can recommend the following approach to building corporate objectives:

1. Use top management's philosophy as a starting point.
2. Express preliminary business objectives, including:
   - What specifically is to be accomplished.
   - A time limit for achieving each goal.
3. Rate the relative priorities of the objectives.
4. Develop an overall time frame for the firm's efforts.
5. Structure goals and sub-goals in a hierarchy, including:
   - What specific goals will lead to achieving broader goals?
   - Which organizational units do what?
6. Refine an overall objectives system, including:
   - Final statements of specific measures and dates.
   - Delegation of authority and responsibility.

Human resource professionals can use Exhibit 2-3 to create model objectives for every functional area.

Exhibit 2-3
Example of a Corporate Global Objective

General Objective: Minimization of Operating Costs
Performance Objective: Globalize Management
Measures of Performance Objective:
    Performance sub-objective #1: Latin American Managers
       Increase Latin American managers by 10% in 1995.
    Performance sub-objective #2: Latin American Absenteeism
       Reduce Latin American absenteeism by 25% in 1995.
    Performance sub-objective #3: Latin American Productivity
       Increase Latin American productivity by 5% in 1995.

Developing Global Objectives

Senior management should spend a significant amount of time developing a corporate-wide strategic architecture that establishes global objectives. Key objectives in the quest to become a world-class company include extremely high quality levels, reduced manufacturing cycle time, and dedication to serving the customer.

The president of the Reynolds Metals Company suggests the following eight objectives for world competitiveness [4]:

1. We must reduce debt and increase financial strength.
2. We must have the courage to get out of businesses where we have no chance of being competitive.
3. We must allocate resources to those areas that have the most promise.
4. We must concentrate on increasing the value-added of our products and services.
5. We must build "partnership alliances" with our suppliers, built upon trust, quality, service, and low costs.
6. We must invest in the technology and create the operating processes to allow us higher quality products at lower costs.
7. We must be uncompromisingly aggressive in our quest for quality improvements.
8. We must be more entrepreneurial—get close to the customer, find out what he needs and deliver on time, on spec, and at a price that provides him with good value.

Motoman Inc., a joint venture created by Hobart Brothers Co. and Japan's Yaskawa Electric, follows a good approach for setting global objectives. The company starts with a five-year plan and the "president's objectives," i.e. a set of goals for the coming year. These goals are then broken down and built back up, department by department. This participation helps to build commitment to the goals, as well as a strategy for achieving them. After goals are set, departments are asked to evaluate their performance every month. To do so, they answer the following four simple questions: (1) What did you say you were going to do? (2) What did you actually do? (3) Why is there a difference? (4) What are you going to do about it?

Strategic Approaches

The HR professional's sixth task is to assist in evaluating strategic alternatives. In general, corporations can follow one of four different strategic approaches: international, multinational, regional, or global.

International strategy is a composite of several individual foreign market entry plans. An entry strategy is needed for each product in each foreign market. The firm must choose (1) a target market, (2) the objectives in the market, (3) an entry mode to penetrate the market, (4) the marketing plan to enter the target market, and (5) the control system to monitor performance.

Multinational strategy is based upon portfolio planning theory. Individual markets are evaluated on a stand-alone basis. The multinational corporation (MNC) continuously assesses the strengths and weaknesses of existing and potential subsidiaries through managerial audits. They also evaluate threats and opportunities in existing and potential markets through environmental profiles. Each market is then ranked in terms of potential profitability and growth. The MNC will aggressively pursue entry into high-profit or high-growth markets, while avoiding or abandoning weak markets.

Regional strategy is centered around regional strongholds that concentrate on markets within the region's sphere of influence. The corporation is highly interdependent on a regional basis. Regional headquarters control local subsidiaries and collaborate with other regions to attain broad objectives.

Global strategy is an integrated system for dealing with corporate opportunities and threats on a worldwide basis. The global strategist coordinates a worldwide system of market positions, facilities, and investments, focusing on leveraging positions in one country market against those in other markets. For example, the global enterprise may establish "blocking positions" in nations where rivals are attempting to set up base for global competition. By undercutting the competitor's price, the global enterprise can prevent the competitor from getting the cash flow necessary to go global.

In light of its philosophy, mission, and objectives, a corporation must decide what strategy to follow in taking advantage of global opportunities. The HR professional can assist in this process by reviewing a list of strategic alternatives with corporate executives (see Exhibit 2-4). HR pro-

---

Exhibit 2-4
Strategic Alternatives in World Trade & Investment

- Strategic alliances
- Transnational ownership of equity securities
- Transnational management organization
- Wholly-owned manufacturing branch plant or subsidiaries
- Consortium
- Joint ventures
- Cross-production agreements
- Turnkey operations
- Manufacturer's contracts
- Research consortium
- Outsourcing agreements
- Franchising
- Licensing with partial ownership
- Cross-licensing agreements
- Licensing
- Management or technical assistance contracts
- Cross-distribution agreements
- International barter and countertrade
- Foreign branch sales office
- Foreign warehouse
- Export directly to the "end user"
- Export directly to a "foreign distributor"
- Export directly through a "foreign sales agent"
- Export indirectly through an "export management company"
- Export indirectly by hiring an "export agent"
- Export indirectly by "piggybacking" on an international company
- Export indirectly by selling to an "export merchant"
- Export indirectly by selling to a "commission buying agent"

---

fessionals should develop checklists for evaluating the pros and cons of each alternative.

Alternatives should be reviewed in global problem-solving conferences that include managers from all functional areas. At the conferences, middle and lower level management must review top management philosophy, the corporate audit, the list of environmental opportunities, the corporate mission statement, and the corporate objectives. Based upon this information, managers must make suggestions on how the corporation should take advantage of the opportunities to meet corporate objectives. Top management will choose the alternative that is most appropriate for the corporation.

In reviewing possible strategic alternatives, HR professionals should consider that a global corporation must:

1. Be prepared to enter all three of the world's most important markets—North America, Europe, and Asia.
2. Develop new products for the whole world.
3. Replace profit centers based on countries or regions with centers based on product lines.
4. Make decisions on strategic questions about products, capital, and research, but let local units decide tactical questions about packaging, marketing, and advertising.
5. Overcome parochial attitudes by sending employees off on frequent trips and conducting frequent teleconferences between national offices.
6. Open senior ranks to foreign employees.
7. Do whatever seems best wherever it seems best, even if people at home lose jobs or responsibilities.
8. Find allies in markets that cannot be penetrated on their own.

Implementing a Strategic Plan

It is much more difficult to implement a strategic plan than it is to create one. HR professionals should spend the bulk of their efforts in seeing that the strategy comes to fruition. Important areas for HR professionals to be involved in include helping to select and train global leaders, choosing global personnel, helping with the organization of lines of global communication, and becoming involved in the deployment of global resources.

The CEO must be heavily involved in the globalization effort. Effective and profitable global thinking does not result from a flood of memos or directives from the CEO. It is a product of personal communication throughout the company. Global management must be practiced as a "contact sport." The CEO must develop direct contacts with employees around the world.

The CEO must visit as many markets and subsidiaries as possible, and the visits should not be whirlwind tours. The CEO must conduct detailed meetings with middle managers, customers, and government officials. One of the CEO's primary tasks on the road is to encourage management teams to meet the challenges of globalization and assure them that they will be rewarded for doing so.

The CEO's globetrotting often involves brutal travel schedules. It is not unusual for global trips to span 30,000 miles and three continents. This can take a heavy toll on the CEO's family life and personal health. HR professionals can help by developing exercise programs for the CEO and offering counseling sessions for the CEO's family. The family must understand that the success of the global strategy may require the CEO to be away from home for extended periods.

The CEO must ensure that top managers are involved in the nitty gritty of operations. Many corporations have been severely hurt due to management separation brought on by acquisitions, divestures, and portfolio management. Management cannot allow walls to be built around corporate divisions. Departments must be required to share technology, sales forces, and wisdom.

Yoshinori Taura, president of Mazda Motor of America, fought management separation by dividing the company's entire senior management into teams. The teams were sent around the U.S. to visit personally with local dealers and get grassroots input. Taura believes that it is important for the president to keep track of the pulse of the company and for employees to see the boss and senior managers face-to-face.

HR professionals can assist the CEO by seeing to it that the global managers have stamina and dedication. HR professionals must prepare potential global managers for the rigors of the road. Global managers have to be willing to work extremely hard to get results. The life of a global manager is very tough. They cannot afford to be lazy.

Percy Barnevik, president and CEO of Asea Brown Boveri (ABB), says that only about 3% of ABB's managers are truly "global." Beyond having stamina, global managers must have exceptionally open minds. They must respect how different countries do things, and have the imagination to appreciate why they do them that way.

Global managers also must be incisive, pushing the limits of various cultures. Global managers don't passively accept it when someone says, "You can't do that in Italy or Spain because of the unions," or "You can't do that in Japan because of the ministry of finance." They sort through the debris of cultural excuses and find opportunities to innovate.

To build a culture of trust and technological exchange, ABB created three forums: (1) A management board for each business area that meets four to six times a year to shape global strategy, monitor performance, and solve big problems; (2) A rotating staff of veteran managers who each have worldwide responsibility for activities in critical areas, such as purchasing and R & D. They travel constantly, meet with the presidents and top managers of local companies, and drive the coordination agenda forward, (3) Functional coordination teams that meet once or twice a year to exchange information on details of implementation in production, quality, marketing, and other areas. The teams include managers with functional responsibilities in all the local companies, so they come from all over the world.

The real value of these programs comes from the informal exchange that occurs throughout the year. People spend time together, and get to know and understand each other. This builds trust, and promotes the sharing of expertise that the company needs to build new products and to be a global competitor.

HR professionals also must be actively involved in personnel decisions. Recruitment and promotion play a significant role in growing and sustaining the global mindset. When HR professionals are involved in the recruitment process, they should stress the global nature of their organization and make it clear that promotions, transfers, and opportunities are made on a global basis.

HR professionals should spend a great deal of time trying to close the cultural gaps between headquarters and foreign subsidiaries. HR professionals can promote the following ideas to help create a global mindset among the employees:

1. All employees should be encouraged to learn at least one additional language.
2. Employees should be given opportunities to work overseas. Short-term business exchange programs should be aimed at all employee levels, not just managers.
3. Employees should be encouraged to read a book or two about the other countries.

4. Employees should be encouraged to vacation abroad and consider sending their children on summer exchange visits with children of their business counterparts.

The Human Resource Strategist

Specialists in the fields of human resource management and development usually have not been prime movers in developing the organization's strategic plan and management system. However, in the new work culture, HR professionals must get involved directly in these processes. HR professionals need to become corporate strategists not only in terms of personnel administration and development, but for overall organizational development [7, 16]. However, to be effective, the HR leader must study and learn from strategic management and research literature [22]. There are skills to be acquired in environmental scanning, forecasting, and strategy methods [5, 9, 15]. There are organizations to join so as to enhance one's competence in this regard, such as the World Future Society (7910 Woodmont, Suite 450, Bethesda, MD 20814, USA).

Whether as external or internal consultants, such professionals can make a significant contribution to organizational diagnosis, health, and maintenance. Once the HR experts have mastered this body of knowledge, they can formulate training programs to share such information with line managers and other employees. This is an opportunity for the HR professional to implement strategic goals through in-service education, whether by means of workshops, team meetings, or computer-assisted instruction. Given the trend toward globalization, training programs in strategic business planning must now include a cross-cultural component, both in terms of macro- and micro-cultures.

The changing economic conditions worldwide, as well as globalization, have accelerated the process of organizational acquisitions and mergers. For many corporations, this means downsizing [20]. For others, it has meant trying to integrate two or more different organizational cultures. Thus, the challenge for HR leaders is continuous strategic development in the light of altered conditions and realities. These transitional times toward a new world order and economy present great, sometimes somber, challenges to any cross-cultural strategist, as the mini-case in Exhibit 2-5 illustrates.

Exhibit 2-5
Bank Merger Realities

With the Bank of America and Security Pacific Corporation merging into their nation's second largest bank, the director of human resources for the combined banks has a tough assignment. The current strategic plan requires cultural synergy and calls for a melding of a 91,000 person work force, including the elimination of 12,000 positions. The HR professional implementing that goal is Kathleen Burke, 40, who sees her role as "keeping the dialogue going with employees, and helping to curb uncertainty." This has meant improving management communications and helping personnel to prepare for contingencies. Thus Burke and other executives devised a broad severance package with generous pay, retraining grants, business loans, and subsidies for non-profit work. With the downsizing, each employee will be walked through the opportunities offered by this program.

As a result-oriented person, Burke, the new Executive Vice President and Director of Human Resources for Bank of America, draws upon a background that includes studies in political science, law, and foreign languages, along with broad business experience.

The essence of global business is the ability to tap into the talents of good people. Everyone in the organization must become personally involved. Communication and bridging cultural gaps must be the top priorities. People should be learning something new everyday and applying it throughout the corporation. Multiculturalism should become the global corporation's greatest competitive advantage.

Finally, the human resource leader must be alert to socio-political changes within the countries where the organization operates or has future market expectations. He or she must seek expert counsel in analyzing issues, trends, and events that impact business. For example, the break-up of the former Soviet empire and the shift to a market economy, the reemergence of tribal warfare in Central Europe (as in the Serbian "ethnic cleansing" within the former Yugoslavia), the intervention of the United Nations into a region and its effect on economic activities (e.g., Cambodia and Somalia). It is the responsibility of HR professionals to prepare a digest of ongoing global happenings for key management, and to indicate their implications for revisions in strategy.

References

1. Dentzer, S., "The Coming Global Boom," *U.S. News & World Report,* July 16, 1990. pp. 22–28.
2. Hart, B. H. Liddell, *Strategy,* New York: Frederick A. Praeger, 1956.
3. Holder, R. G., *"The Global Corporation: A Strategy for the '90s,"* Vital Speeches of the Day, South Carolina: City News Publishing, December 1, 1989. pp. 98–100.
4. Jomini, A. H., *The Art of War* (translated by Capt. G. H. Mendell and Lieut. W. P. Craighill), Westport, Connecticut: Greenwood Press, n.d.
5. Makridakis, S. G. and Associates, *Single Market Europe: Opportunities and Challenges for Business,* San Francisco, CA: Jossey-Bass, 1991.
6. Mahan, A. T., *The Influence of Sea Power Upon History,* 1660–1783. Boston: Little, Brown & Co., 1945.
7. Manzini, A. and Gridley, J., *Integrating Human Resource and Strategic Business Planning,* New York: AMACOM, 1987.
8. McCormick J. and Stone, N., "From National Champion to Global Competitor: An Interview with Thomson's Alain Gomez," *Harvard Business Review,* May/June 1990. pp. 127–135.
9. Millet, S. and Honton, E., *Managers Guide to Technology Forecasting and Strategy Analysis Methods,* Ohio: Battell Press, 1991.
10. Moran R. T. and Stripp, W. G., *Dynamics of Successful International Business Negotiations,* Houston: Gulf Publishing, 1991.
11. Musashi, M., *A Book of Five Rings* (translated by Victor Harris), Woodstock, New York: The Overlook Press, 1974.
12. Prahalad, C. K. and Hamel, G., "The Core Competence of the Corporation," *Harvard Business Review,* May–June 1990. pp. 79-91.
13. Prahalad, C. K., *"The Changing Nature of Worldwide Competition: Reversing the United States' Decline,"* Vital Speeches of the Day. April 1, 1990. pp. 354–357.
14. Reich, R. B., "Who Is Them?" *Harvard Business Review,* March/April 1991. pp. 77–88.
15. Schwartz, P., *The Art of the Long View,* New York: Doubleday/Currency, 1991.
16. Sibson, R., *Strategic Planning for Human Resources Management,* New York: AMACOM, 1992.
17. Stalk, G., Evans, P., and Shulman, L. E., "Competing on Capabilities: The New Rules of Corporate Strategy," *Harvard Business Review,* March/April, 1992. pp. 57–69.
18. Sun Tzu, *The Art of War* (translated by Samuel B. Griffith), Oxford: Oxford University Press, 1971.
19. Taylor, W., "The Logic of Global Business: An Interview with ABB's Percy

Barnevik," *Harvard Business Review,* March/April 1991. pp. 90–105
20. Tomasko, R., *Downsizing and Reshaping Organizations for the Future,* New York: AMACOM, 1990.
21. Townley P., "Going Global in the 1990s: The Case for Trading Blocks," Vital Speeches of the Day, July 15, 1990. pp. 589–593.
22. Tracey,W., *Leadership Skills,* New York: AMACOM, 1990.
23. Tsunetomo, Y., *Hagakure.* (translated by William Scott Wilson), Tokyo: Kodansha International Ltd., 1983.
24. Clausewitz, Carl Von, *On War* (translated by Col. J. J. Graham), New York: Penguin Books, 1832, 1984.

CHAPTER 3

CROSS-CULTURAL TEAM DEVELOPMENT

Introduction

On July 22, 1990, just south of Scotland's Grampian Mountains, Dr. David L. Dotlich and twenty-five other Groupe Bull executives slid rubber rafts into the swirling waters of the River Spey. But theirs wasn't to be an afternoon of fun in the sun. These men from nine nations had just reviewed Bull's business prospects in countries ranging from Albania and Algeria to Germany and Yeman. The white-water rafting trip upon which they were embarking was to be a metaphor for how they'd have to pull together to successfully navigate some tough months ahead. Bull believes that team building is essential to global success into the twenty-first century. Challenges such as this year's outing in Scotland or the ascent of Mont Blanc that Bull chairman and CEO Francis Lorentz led last year, are part of a considered strategy.

"I think it builds trust quickly. It demonstrates international cooperation. It helps people learn what each other's styles of management behavior are. It provides a common base of experience," states Dr. Dotlich, executive vice-president for Corporate Resources at Bull HN Information Systems Incorporated. "The biggest problem with globalization is that all human beings are blinded by their cultural assumption, whether they know it or not. So when you provide a common experience like an outdoor rafting trip, people have a way of getting at what those assumptions are." The demands of the moment force them to confront their differences of perspective and look towards achievement of common goals.

Significantly, Bull does not limit team-building exercises to senior executives who are presumably in their positions because they have already bought into the approach. In a variety of two- to five-week education and development sessions, lower level executives and managers on severalt continents come together to solve problems that go beyond national boundaries. Some recent examples include; design and development of a new UNIX product, the formulation of a worldwide advertising and branding strategy, and the worldwide consolidation of engineering designs. "We try to explain that what is happening at the senior management level is a coming together of common interests to build a global team and that they have to do the same," says Dr. Dotlich.

Are people frustrated by having to develop new relationships and tap new resources of information and expertise? "Yes," says Dr. Dotlich. Is it very difficult? "Very," he responds. Do people believe that things are out of control? "Often," he states. But the bottom line is that, "We'll do anything to build a global team" [7].

One of the principal reasons for this team emphasis is the shift in the new work culture to network organizations. Raymond E. Miles et al.[9] describe why and how large-scale organizations, like IBM, are transitioning from hierarchial command structures to smaller, more focused corporations guided by market forces. Miles et al. [9] point to such causes as global competition, rapid technological change, deregulation, and demographic shifts. To survive and be competitive, the multilevel, vertically organized bureaucracies are forced to transform to clusters of downsized, focused, enterprising business units attuned to the customer. Thus, Professor Miles and his colleagues at the Haas School of Business in Berkley developed conferences within the university extension program that enabled managers to reshape their strategic roles and redeploy resources. In the emerging network organizations, boundaries, and memberships are flexible, work units are fluid and easily re-assembled, and resources—both human and material—are deployed readily across organizational and national boundaries to meet product or service life-cycle demands.

These new ad-hoc networks require team management and development.

Teams and Team Development

A dictionary would describe a team simply as a number of persons assembled in some joint action, as the selected group of senior executives discussed. But team management implies much more. To appreciate the concept the human resource (HR) leader should view the term within the context of the organization and the relationships of its people.

Human relations take on a new dimension within an organization or team, thus impacting the performance of the people therein. Such relations may be viewed from three perspectives—interpersonal (between individuals), intragroup (within and among members of a group), and intergroup (between and among groups that make up the organization or with external groups). Those in leadership roles should be aware of how these relationships affect their own behavior, and how they may be used to enhance or undermine productivity. Organizational relations impact clients or customers, suppliers and contractors, as well as government and community officials with whom the organization interacts—good will and profitability may be increased, or decreased, by such. Within the global marketplace, the insights provided in this chapter have cross-cultural applications to improve the organization's international relations.

Throughout the organization, people enter into a "psychological contract" in which they contribute their energy and information in return for role definition and compensation, which may take the form of money, benefits, or other types of rewards for their productivity. In the modern corporation, for example, management is permitted to exercise some power and authority over workers, but the employees enforce their expectations by giving or withholding work effort and energy. It is the quality of management relationships with personnel that influences performance and determines the success of organizational outcomes, such as products and services.

So relationships are the key to successful individual and institutional performance. Career development, increased sales or profitability, organizational effectiveness—all are dependent, to a great degree, upon positive "human" relationships. Again, if we resort to the dictionary, it would describe "relationships" as merely involvement or establishing a connection with another individual or group. Apart from kinship through birth or marriage, it refers to developing a special affinity, alliance, or association with one's fellows, such as with co-workers or professional colleagues. However, in a deeper sense, a person confirms and expresses self in terms of one's relationships with other human beings and living creatures. In its profoundest expressions, relationships may be seen in the love between parent and child, husband and wife, friends, and even business partners. Our focus here will be upon *team relations* as part of one's vocational activities.

To better comprehend the significance of organizational relations, think of these in the form of:

- Dyad—two persons interacting as when two peers work together, or relations between a supervisor and a subordinate who reports to that individual. This is the basis of interpersonal relations.
- Triad—three persons, the beginning of group or intragroup relations. Team relations begin here.

These relations affect morale and job satisfaction, performance and productivity.

When HR leaders understand the importance of organizational relations as a lever for high performance and team management, they devote time and energy to group characteristics, space, and change; group goals, norms, and values; group style, leadership, and influence; group roles, relationships, and responsibilities; group image, communication patterns, and feedback; and group decision-making and problem-solving.

Furthermore, such leaders apply these insights to improve the management of work units in general, and teams in particular. They also learn to become more skilled in team formation and building. We will not only examine what makes for productive teams, but how to energize its members and promote a helping relationship.

The composition of work teams is becoming increasingly multicultural. People may come from different disciplines, work units, or levels within the organization. Members may come from diverse parts of a country or from several nationalities. Women are more often a part of what used to be all-male teams. The racial or ethnic mix may be complex. Team leaders must be able to practice intercultural competence.

The team is a sub-system of a larger system, the corporation, association, or agency. As such, the organization is an energy exchange system with varied inputs, throughputs, and outputs. Miller [8] explains a *group* as a set of single organisms, commonly called members, which, over a period of time or multiple interrupted periods, relate to one another face-to-face, processing matter, energy, and information.

Thus, when we use a systems approach to envision people in either an organization or a group, we can analyze functional interrelationships. Human beings enjoined by common goals and needs in a social system can then be studied from their complex interlocking relationships within the total institution, or national or regional arrangement. In the disappearing Industrial Age organization, relationships were rather stable within a department or division. In our present postindustrial period, relationships are more dynamic and temporary because of membership in more project teams or task forces, or because of mergers and acquisitions.

Organizational culture contributes powerfully to the quality of relationships that people develop in a work unit or team. In acculturating the individual to the institution or group, there are forces at work within both the personal and organizational spaces that influence behavior—image, needs, values, ideas, principles, standards, expectations. Sometimes these may conflict and cause "binds" or frustrations for members. Sometimes the HR leader can act as a facilitator and resolve such conflicts, while promoting synergy between and among the enterprise and its people.

The more people have in common, the easier it is to develop a team. It is difficult enough to develop teams among one's own nationals. When one crosses cultures and tries to assimilate "foreigners" onto the team, team development becomes very complicated—even when all the team members are employed by the same global organization. By understanding something about organizational and group dynamics, leaders are enabled to synthesize differences and create consensus among divergent persons. One military analogy is the "esprit de corps" and training system of the U. S. Marines, which has made it possible for countless drill sergeants to weld together raw recruits from diverse backgrounds into successful fighting units. A sports analogy would be baseball's ability to integrate players from varied races, nationalities, and education into an effective team, based largely on competence— if you can *play well,* the industry does not care if you come from the middle of Mexico, or Santo Domingo. Similarly, in the new work culture, high technology firms are more concerned about your ability to perform, rather than your gender, race, or place of origin.

The mix of organizational relations influences attitudes and behavior of members. Leaders not only must learn how to cope with these human factors or forces and within the institution, but how to control and manage them, so as to actualize the person and the organization's potential. The challenges to HR leaders today are to

1. Provide for role enlargement, so that individual participation in the group and organization becomes more meaningful and effective.
2. Create temporary and supportive networks, groupings, and arrangements that cut across traditional structures and divisions, promoting cross fertilization of ideas, knowledge, and specializations.

3. Increase the span of control over work space so as to enhance individual initiative and responsibility.
4. Decrease distance between people at various levels within the organization by limiting pseudo distinctions that act as barriers to organizational communications.
5. Cut across boundaries that separate people and prevent them from working together cooperatively and effectively.

Team Productivity

The scope of problems facing global managers today are simply too big for local solutions. Only by integrating overlapping jurisdictions and efforts can there be results. This will force multicultural teams to play a big part in solving problems.

There are large differences between the productivity of homogeneous and heterogeneous teams. Cultural diversity within teams increases potential productivity. It also increases the complexity of the process. Thus, culturally diverse teams have potential for higher productivity than culturally homogeneous groups, but greater risk of loss due to a faulty process.

Nancy Adler [1] states that a team's productivity can best be described by the following formula:

Actual Productivity = Potential Productivity – Faulty Process Loss

A team's productivity depends on its task, resources, and process. The actual type of task is the first important determinant of productivity. *Diverse groups are better suited for specialized tasks, whereas homogeneous groups are better suited for routine repetitive tasks.* This is important to remember when choosing team members. Team management is being employed when an organization's activities are less repetitive and predictable. Such an approach increases the need for liaison, management by exception, and sharing of authority and information. All this is contrary to traditional organizational culture.

A team's resources include everything at their disposal for performing an assignment: people, information, materials, time, money.

The process includes all productive and non-productive actions taken by each member and the team as a whole while working to achieve the team's goal. The group process can be seen by examining all interpersonal and intrapersonal actions by which people transform their resources into a product, which would include all non-productive actions prompted by frustration and lack of understanding.

Culturally diverse teams are more or less effective than homogeneous teams, but rarely equal. An obvious goal of team building is to make your team fit into the highly effective category. To meet this end, let's look at some of the differences and similarities between highly effective and ineffective teams.

Effective vs. Ineffective Teams

High and low effective teams differ in how they manage diversity. Highly effective teams look at problems as opportunities and are proactive in finding a solution to the problems they are presented. Highly effective teams make a productive resource of diversity. Low effective teams make problems out of diversity. This can be any kind of diversity including the make-up of the team.

Some team members may view other members' actions as inappropriate. The communication of these perceptions in a positive way will enhance the effectiveness of the team and increase dialogue among members.

Cultural diversity makes interaction between team members more difficult because teams see situations, understand them, and act upon them differently based on their cultural assumptions. Cultural diversity makes compromise and agreement more difficult because group members have more difficulty in communicating. There may be slower speech patterns as members who speak different languages try to communicate. There also may be problems in translation and less accurate communication of meanings. As Nancy Adler suggests, poor communication can be broken down into misperception, misinterpretation, misevaluation, and miscommunication.

There is also implicit and explicit disagreement on expectations, appropriateness of information, and the nature of the decision to be made. Diverse cultural teams are subject to increases in ambiguity, complexity, and inherent confusion in the group's process. There may be stereotyping, and more conversations between people within one culture. Initially, there is a lack of cohesion between culturally diverse teams.

ty Gains from Cultural Diversity

Increases in productivity may more than compensate for the difficulties that are experienced by culturally diverse teams. Culturally diverse teams often have more, creative, and better ideas. The creativity used in finding solutions is greatly enhanced by these groups because members don't see the situation from the same standpoint. Often the most innovative solutions are rendered by these diverse teams.

Groupthink can be described as "a mode of thinking that people engage in when they are deeply involved in a cohesive group," and is usually a subconscious act. This can be detrimental to group creativity and entice groups to not consider all options, thus rendering poor decisions. The inherent inability for a culturally diverse group to fall prey to groupthink is a major benefit.

The team will strive to be cohesive as this will enable it to act as one and to perceive, interpret, and act on its goals in similar and mutually agreed upon ways.

Team diversity is beneficial in that it makes team members concentrate on other members' ideas, messages, and arguments, because team members must really listen to comprehend the messages given by others.

Nancy Adler [1] recommends the following guidelines for managing diversity within teams:

1. When selecting team members for a specific task, choose members for the abilities that they provide for the project at hand. Keep in mind that members should be homogeneous in ability levels, while heterogeneous in attitudes. The criterion for team selection should be competence. The individual should have some knowledge, information, or expertise that can help the group.

2. Team members should recognize the cultural differences of group members, not ignore them. This will minimize misperceptions, and alleviate problems due to ignorance rather than a rejection of the differences between members. It is important that members don't minimize cultural differences. Communication is facilitated by better understanding of cross-cultural differences. Each member should strive to be aware of their own stereotypes without limiting their expectations, understanding, and actions. Try to understand why the people in different cultures think, feel, and act the way they do.

3. Teams should superordinate the team's goals. Multicultural groups have more difficulty with agreeing on the purpose of their task. Thus, to maximize effectiveness, the group leader must help the group to agree on a superordinate goal, one that transcends individual differences. The team's goals should give direction and focus to the team's activities. Make these goals include cooperation. This will decrease prejudice and increase mutual respect.

4. Give equal power to all group members. Each team member must be given the opportunity to contribute to the group and thus enhance the group's output.

5. Mutual respect between group members is a must. There is no room for ethnocentrism whereby one member views their culture as the center and all other cultures as scaled and rated with reference to it. There can likewise be no prejudice whereby a person or group is judged as inferior to one's own. To reduce prejudice, use equal status, close contact, and cooperative efforts. To build mutual respect between members, select members of equal ability, make prior accomplishments and skills known to the group, and minimize early judgments of group members.

6. Managers should give positive feedback to individuals and the group as a whole early in the group's life together. This helps the group see itself as a team, teaches the team to value its diversity, helps the group recognize contributions made by other members, and helps the group trust its collective judgment.

Characteristics of Effective Groups

As social beings, humans take readily to group affiliation and formation. Some groups form naturally out of common interest, cause, or concern. Others come into being because of a common task or assignment, such as a product or project team. Consider what we are about to report on groups in terms of a work unit or team. A leader who becomes astute in group dynamics understands his or her own behavior in relation to the team, as well as being able to observe the process and activities of that group.

For collections of people to become a *team,* in the full sense of that term, they develop the following ten characteristics. A manager may analyze and assess the team's performance and development of these characteristics by using the suggested questions after each attribute.

1. Group Background. Every group develops a history in relation to its immediate environment or setting. Individually members contribute to the group's uniqueness by reason of their own attitudes, interests, feelings, and competencies. At the moment of assembly, each member has preconceived notions, prejudices, and orientations that bear directly upon the life and work of the group until that individual leaves it. The activities, responses, and feelings that the group generated in the past, impact its present and future. For example, technicians who work on a project team eventually develop some unwritten agreements as to who does what and when; newcomers must discover these arrangements.

What is this team history like? What traditions has it developed? How does all this affect relationships within the team and with other groups or the total organization?

2. Group Participation Patterns. Teams develop involvement patterns, and the forms of group participation may frequently change. Participation in group activities and accomplishment is one way in which power is exercised—influence upon the behavior, direction, and work of the team. Some of these patterns place great emphasis upon status, politics, forcefulness, or even competence. Participation patterns affect what members may do in a group, so that an overly dominant member who talks eighty-five percent of the time reduces the participation possibilities for the others. On the other hand, when there is free and democratic exchange within the group, the opinions and input of all are sought.

Is there sufficient opportunity for participation in this team, so as to bring out all that the various members can contribute? How do leaders and members share participation and involvement?

3. Group Communication Patterns. The system of communication within a group can be objectively analyzed, both verbally and non-verbally. Who talks to whom? What do they say? What are the effects? Verbally, leaders should examine one's clarity of expression, commonality of vocabulary, and the results of verbalization. Equally, the postures, facial expressions, and gestures of the members' body language can be studied. The streamlining of bureaucracy should enable top management to communicate more quickly and easily with employee groups.

How clearly are the group's leader and members expressing their ideas, especially those who may speak English as a second language? Does everyone understand the group's mission and what is going on? Is both the verbal and non-verbal interaction getting the job done well?

4. Group Cohesion. When the group is working well together, it is attractive to members. Usually, cohesion is evident when morale is high, and members like one another, but are interdependent. People demonstrate teamwork when they feel free to invest themselves in the group and contribute fully to the accomplishment of its tasks. Cohesion means that members work as one, or a unit, for the common cause, and are concerned about the welfare of each member as well as the whole team.

How well does this collection of people work together as a team? Do individuals exercise a helping relationship toward other members? How willing are members to accept and act readily upon group decisions?

5. Group Atmosphere. To what degree does the group permit informality, freedom of expression, and acceptance of individual differences? In an unfriendly, formal, and rigid situation, members are unwilling to be open and to express themselves, especially when feelings and ideas may seemingly be in conflict with the group's direction. Instead, members tend to say what authority figures want to hear and group energies may be wasted. When the group climate encourages frankness and participation, it facilitates sharing, leveling, and creative exchange.

How free do members really feel to express themselves in this group? How willing are members to listen and to share personal feelings or beliefs? How would you rate the group on its friendliness and informality?

6. Group Standards. As a group, members adopt, formally or informally, norms of behavior, a code of operations. This results from the need to coordinate group effort and activities toward a common goal. Such standards or expectations provide a framework or guide for adjusting individual needs and resources toward the group's requirements. These norms stabilize group energies and contribute to cohesiveness and improved performance.

Has this group developed standards for member responsibilities or team discipline? Are group expectations clear on matters such as ethics, operational behavior, protocol, dress, or whatever distinguishes this team's culture?

7. Group Procedures. Every group needs to define ways for getting its work done, its mission accomplished. Again whether these are formally set down or just commonly understood, such policies and practices facilitate a united team effort when they are adequate and appropriate, rather than burdensome. Task accomplishment is hastened when these procedures allow for flexibility and innovation. For example, procedures regarding group decision-making are critical for high performance.

What kind of procedures does this group use to get its principal work done? How appropriate are these in relation to the type of group task and its accomplishment?

8. Group Goals. Members must agree and accept what are considered the group's primary purposes. Top management may have set forth this mission and tasks to be accomplished, or the group may have established its own objectives and priorities. These goals may be long range or immediate. When the group is clear on its goals and all members endorse them, members tend to be more supportive and committed. When such goals are realistic in terms of resources, then group energies can be better mobilized toward their achievement. Group goals motivate the membership when they are found to be compelling, offer mutual advancement, include interim objectives that are attainable, and are subject to alteration when the situation requires.

Do members have a clear understanding of the group's goals? Are the goals attainable given the group's resources? Are members supportive of these goals?

9. Group Leadership. The group may have an appointed or elected leader, or may simply share the leadership function. Sometimes designated leaders, such as project managers, may not be the real leaders; more "natural" leaders may emerge. Rather than authoritarian leadership, the trend today is democratic and participatory. Within groups, leadership style must be flexible and respond to the situation and people, using both formal and informal structures and communication. With knowledge workers, for instance, those in leadership roles must exercise skills at facilitating and experimenting, resolving conflict, and attaining consensus.

How is leadership influence exercised in this group? How are leaders chosen and held accountable?

10. Group Alignments. Group life usually involves development of sub-groups of one kind or another, and affiliation with other groups of like concerns. Within the group, the formation of such relationships depends somewhat on its total size, and may result from the member's mutual needs, interests, shared friendships, antipathy toward another or the group's direction, or simply because the persons live in the same neighborhood or work together in a functional unit. The make-up of these sub-groups change in relation to new tasks, forces, or issues. While a normal occurrence, in the interest of healthy group relations, leaders should be able to diagnose the phenomenon and respond creatively. For example, the formation of "cliques" based solely on race or gender, on hetero- or homosexual preference, on harmful habits or substance abuse, on some perceived exploitation, may undermine group effort unless confronted. Similarly, groups interface with other groups, and may form coalitions or working relations, so as to be mutually helpful.

What sub-groups exist, and do they tend to work together as a whole, or do they dissipate group energies? What are the needs, issues, or forces that arise to which these sub-groups relate? How does this group align itself with other similar or nearby groups, and for what purpose?

For HR leaders engaged in cross-cultural team development, these ten categories provide a way to assess group performance, particularly by asking the questions at the end of each section. At the end of this chapter is an instrument that facilitates this process.

Improving Team Performance

In the disappearing Industrial Age, organizational relations tended to be long term. Today, the new work culture often features intense temporary relationships with colleagues. The high performing business environment, for example, emphasizes team management that involves ad hoc relations through task forces, project or product teams, and time-limited work arrangements. Such groups come rapidly into being, function for a period, and then are phased out. Personnel must, therefore, learn to jump quickly into such task-oriented situations, establish connections and communications with co-workers from different disciplines or work units, and then disengage when the mission is accomplished. All this may happen while one maintains a dual relationship with another group that serves as one's base in manufacturing, marketing, finance, information systems, or whatever. The organizational situation may be formalized through some type of matrix management system that involves reporting to two supervisors—one from a functional group, and another who coordinates a special project. Once the latter finishes its task or achieves its goals, then the worker may be assigned to another temporary group and the cycle repeats itself.

Organizational realities such as these make new demands upon leaders and knowledge workers to develop team skills. [For more detailed information about team management see References 5 (Chapter 8) and 10 (Chapter 7)]. But what should we be aiming for in team development?

Our research indicates that there are certain behaviors practiced by team members that facilitate their relations with others in the group, as well as with other groups in the organization. In addition to the ten characteristics previously listed, here is a summary of other approaches to improving team relations and performance:

- Take an interest in both individual and team accomplishment.
- Tolerate ambiguity and seeming lack of structure at times.
- Give and receive feedback sensitively and non-defensively.
- Create a team atmosphere or culture that is informal, comfortable, and personally non-threatening of others.
- Encourage team participation, joint decision-making, and consensus-seeking.
- Be open to planned change, risk-taking, and innovation.
- Value listening and circular communication.
- Be concerned about strengthening team morale and commitment.
- Clarify roles, relationships, and responsibilities.
- Foster trust, supportive norms, and shared leadership.
- Resolve conflicts and use this energy constructively.
- Promote cooperative and collaborative relations or synergy among members and with other work units.
- Be a team, goal-oriented, self-evaluating, and linked to other organizational groups.

Such approaches not only improve organizational relations, but a company or agency's effectiveness as an enterprise. A culture that is permeated with people applying these approaches encourages positive social exchange and interpersonal interactions. The very differences in the perceptions of team members then becomes a source of strength for the team, enriching the mix of the inputs and insights. Realistically, individuals may disagree on such issues as team strategies, problem-solving, accountability, resources, scheduling, and numerous other items that make up the group's life. But when they start with synergistic attitudes, such differences can be resolved and built upon. As Andre Van Dam, director of planning for Corn Products Company–Latin America, once stated at an international conference:

> Admittedly, cooperation requires trade-offs between rival ideas or interests—trade-offs imply negotiation. Cooperation hinges upon the recognition of common as well as conflicting interests.

Those who would exercise organizational leadership need to remind themselves that *people* make up groups and institutions. However, it is management relationships that can either turn people on or off—people may feel they are being manipulated or imposed upon, or they may be inspired and energized. For truly high performance, leaders should give high priority to organizational and team relations that are positive and supportive.

Team management requires a manager or HR leader who is a facilitator—one who reflects on ideas or suggestions; clears up confusion, gives examples, offers alternatives; who provides synthesis and summarizes by pulling together ideas, restating, or articulating conclusions. Such a leader is not only concerned with task issues, like getting the job done, he or she also is effective at *group maintenance,* so as to promote group cohesiveness and morale of the working unit.

Team effectiveness can be increased when a facilitator or observer sits in on team meetings to evaluate the process underway, using some form of data-gathering instrument to record individual behavior and performance. A central issue in this regard is conflict resolution and utilization. This implies questioning how members handle conflict or differences with one another. Do they envision it as energy that can be constructively channeled? How open are members in giving and receiving feedback, and how sensitively is it handled? Again, how well do teammates deal with feelings and emotions? Effective team maintenance is evident by demonstrations of individual caring for each other, or the amount of encouraging offered. It is also manifested in supportive ways with warmth of feelings, friendliness, as well as the amount of acceptance, sharing, or recognition offered. Some group participants contribute to this maintenance process by being sensitive to each other's moods, by harmonizing or reconciling differences, by reducing tensions, or getting the members to explore positions and feelings on an issue. Others do it through negotiations and compromise, admitting errors, or practicing self-discipline in the interest of group cohesion.

It is useful to have an observer assess such matters by means of a data-gathering instrument, and then give feedback to the team on both the task and maintenance aspects of such behavior. To help in this process, behavioral scientists can provide team development assistance that ensures group productiveness and synergy. Successful management actively promotes not only a team spirit, but installs team mechanisms and the means to develop team skills.

Team building can be used to improve either intra- or intergroup relations. Functional work teams can be brought together, in the latter instance, to analyze each group's perception of the other unit, and how communication and cooperation between them can be promoted for the good of all. In the new work culture, we often establish task force teams that go beyond conventional lines in organizations. Because the composition of such problem-solving groups usually cuts across status, ranks, and organizational levels, the concern is to gather personnel with the expertise and diversity who will provide a variety of perspectives, (i.e., marketing, manufacturing, and management backgrounds or disciplines). Teams can be formed with people from a horizontal or vertical distribution of the work force. Teams in the forms of task forces or ad hoc groups can cut across organizational barriers and boundaries to create a talented mix of human assets that enhance problem-solving capabilities. A team strategy is standard operating procedure in the new work culture for more effective energizing of people, and for improving their interfacing. However, Wellins, Byhumam, and Wilson [14] maintain that such teams must be *empowered* by management.

In the emerging high-tech work environment, those in leadership positions will have to know more than finance, marketing, and technology application. They will have to lead workers into unchartered waters, which will require skills to transform the work culture. We have already indicated what some of these competencies will be. Team management dictates that a delicate balance between the independent action of individual members and the social influence of the group be developed.

To encourage peak performance, cooperative action and sharing of competencies is essential. The explosion of information today and the complexity of our times demand it. Team management, then, is vital to achieve and maintain high output amid fast growth. Thus, thinking managers are committed to learning the skills of group dynamics, including how to influence team processes and activities, norms and values, task and maintenance functions. Furthermore, they acquire new tools like the computer to control the diverse elements involved in matrix, project, or product management. Increasingly, they practice group leadership, which implies clarifying roles and relationships, sharing of unique talents, and decision-making. In such ways, an effective team culture can be created that improves performance beyond the sum of individual member efforts.

Thus, the HR leader seeks to create a new mindset, as well as mechanisms for facilitating collaboration at work in planning and problem-solving activities. The post-industrial scene and the demands of a global economy, make this necessary because our challenges and problems are increasingly complex. Cooperative efforts are needed within organizations, their divisions or subsidiaries, and also within industries and regions.

The spirit of competition is embedded in the American culture. New team-training involves a re-analysis of how we view and interact with each other; how we can learn from each other and gain more by working together rather than struggling and dissipating group energies. The metaindustrial work climate fosters more collaborative support of peers, mutual growth activities, and attitudes that enhance high team performance.

With the end of the Cold War, former adversaries like the Americans and the Soviets now can cooperate in democratic endeavors to improve their economies and the global environment, to foster world peace and resolve conflicts, to explore space and develop its resources. Similarly, in international business, former enemies enter into joint venture and promote free market enterprises. No wonder Parker [12] says team players and team work is the new competitive business strategy.

Examples of Successful Teamwork

Consider these several, diversified mini-cases on the importance of cooperation in team development.

Team Management in Japan. William Ouchi [11] predicted that teamwork can recapture the global competitive edge for America by using the Japanese style of cooperation and consensus through work groups. The flip-side is that cultural tradition dictates that an individual should be very cautious and respectful in a group, never speaking his or her mind openly. It is for such reasons that Link Consulting Associates of Kyoto recently contracted with The Executive Committee (TEC) of San Diego to introduce the American team approach to Japanese managers. In this cross-cultural transplant of an executive network, Japanese CEOs will be trained to be more candid, sharing, and authentic through the small group experience, something quite contrary to their natural cultural conditioning in business.

Digital Equipment Corporation. Because the new work culture often means cross-skills training and learning by teams, Digital uses this approach at their electronics plant at Enfield, Connecticut to replace the standard production assembly line. Each team member is trained to perform well twenty different job functions involved in producing circuit board modules. In this high-tech factory, there are three autonomous manufacturing groups, each consisting of four teams with eighteen members. To be fully certified to work on the total product, members undergo three months of team training for acquisition of both technical and group interaction skills. The pay system there reinforces learning because increases are tied to acquiring knowledge and competency. The plant manager, Bruce Dillingham, emphasizes that it takes a certain type of new manager to make the team strategy work—one who assumes a teaching or facilitating role, who knows when to step back and let people grow and develop. [Source: *Productivity,* Vol. 5, No. 11, 1984.]

Pilots in the Global Airline Industry. Advances in air transportation worldwide have not just been in technology, but in the training of airline pilots. Two characteristics of the training stand out—it is cross-cultural in practice and requires team development. The way pilots are recruited and trained to fly sophisticated jet airlines differ markedly by cultural or national group. Until recently, the United States has drawn most airline pilots from among experienced military flyers, while other countries employ a "made-to-order" system. Japanese Air Lines, for instance, recruits inexperienced youths in college who demonstrate ability and promise, sends them out-of-country to the JAL Flight Training Center at Napa County Airport operated by its California contractor, IASCO. For their national airlines, Saudi Arabia, Singapore, Egypt, Brazil, and others use the same type of procedure for future "747 captains." Whether using this approach, or one developed in conjunction with universities, as in Germany, the aspirants attain 300 to 500 flying hours before they are fully checked out as copilots. As part of their education in "cockpit resource management," the candidate learns not only how to fly, but to operate related technology, especially computers. Most particularly, they learn how to function and communicate as part of a *crew team*. In this new work culture, future pilots are oriented toward taking advantage of crew member's knowledge and abilities rather than "captain knows best." British Airways' experience has been that the self-reliant, jet pilot fresh out of the military does not necessarily make a good airline pilot—instead of making decisions on his own, the modern airline captain must function as part of a team.

Space Crew Systems. Expanding human presence in the high frontier is resulting from development of a space shuttle and station, and may eventually, lead to a lunar outpost and space colonies [4]. For this emerging work environment, NASA published a report [5] that examines everything from habitability and performance to organization and management. What concerns us here is the section on small groups. Space crews are becoming larger in number, more heterogeneous, with space missions lasting longer. Living together in a microsociety, astronaut survival depends upon cooperative performance within their group, and with ground control. Given the isolation and confinement of spacefarers, it is understandable why space scientists and engineers are beginning to review the behavioral science research literature of the past forty years on group process, performance, and foreign deployment. The issue has increasingly cross-cultural implications—crews from the U.S.A. and other countries are no longer just white males from the military—there are increasing numbers of civilians, women, minorities, and internationals on board the spacecraft.

HRD Strategies

A major study [6, pp. 318–322] examined international cooperation projects and determined that cross-cultural team members have a special need to

- Think in multidimensional terms while considering different sides of issues.
- Deal with ambiguity, role shifts, seeming lack of structure, and diversity in personal/professional styles, as well as in social/political systems.

- Facilitate cross-cultural communication and positive interactions, especially by sensitivity to language difficulties with colleagues from varied macro/microcultures.
- Cope with unfamiliar/uncertain situations during accelerating change in life/work styles/environments.
- Negotiate acceptable working arrangements with personnel of differing cultural backgrounds and expectations.
- Recognize and overcome national/international differences in problem statement and procedures for solutions that will create appropriate organizational responses.
- Become comfortable with informality, feedback, results-oriented performance.

Obviously, Western approaches to team development must be adapted considerably if such methodology is to prove helpful with international teams. Similarly, those from Second and Third World economies and bureaucratic organizations require specialized training if they are to contribute to a work team that includes representatives from First World countries, and vice versa.

Team Building

Among the many group process opportunities for improving organizational relationships, team building is among the most valuable. It is an essential process with international teams requiring cross-cultural sensitivity. Team building is most effective when it uses an internal or external consultant familiar with the process. A concerned manager who is a good facilitator can conduct such sessions with the help of management development texts, instruments, and films.* Team building

---

* Books and learning materials for this purpose are available from Pfeiffer & Company, International Publishers (8517 Production Ave., San Diego, CA 92121, U.S.A.—Tel 619/578-5900—e.g., *The Encyclopedia of Team Activities Set,* "Team Development Inventory." Films or videotapes on the subject from producers, such as, CareerTrack Publications, (P.O. Box 18778 Boulder, CO 80308, U.S.A.—Tel. 1-800/334-1018, e.g. "Team Building" videocassettes). CRM Films (2215 Faraday Ave., Carlsbad, CA. 92008, U.S.A.—Tel. 1-800/421-0833), e.g., films *Team Building, Group Productivity,* and a learning package, "Task-Oriented Team Development." Multinational Team Building/Project Consultants—Mel Schnapper Associates, Inc., 2522 West Fitch Ave., Chicago, IL 60645. (313/262-2133); Woodrow H. Sears, Ed.D., 2160 Plaza del Amo #123, Torrance, CA 90501 (310/320-2948)

can be employed to improve team relations among group members, or to improve intergroup relations among various teams or work units. Team building meetings aim at group maintenance, and can consider these performance issues:

- How do we work together, including how we resolve conflict?
- How do we solve problems and make decisions?
- What are our roles and relationships on this team?
- What are our relationships with other groups?
- What changes are needed in how we function?

Team Building Conference

Who. Members of a work unit or teams who must relate to each other along with an external facilitator. For example, in a global corporation, cross-cultural team building might involve peer representatives of the same function, such as marketing, from divisions or subsidiaries around the world.

What. Series of intensive learning experiences about team structure, process, and relationships as previously described.

When. With the start-up of a team; when a group's performance level drops; when a cross-functional task force is being established; or the group is having difficulties with other teams.

Where. This might begin away from the work site, in a conference center, hotel, or resort for a weekend; then continue with monthly meetings on-site in a company meeting or training facility.

Why. To improve team collaboration and performance by

- Clarifying team expectations, goals, resources, and potential.
- Analyzing interpersonal dynamics and relations.
- Confronting and clarifying issues that block mission accomplishment.
- Examining team interfaces and relations with other work units or external groups.
- Developing leadership skills in communication, cooperation, problem-solving, and conflict resolution.

How. By structured exercises, role playing, data-gathering, analysis, as well as problem-solving, the group learns how to work together more efficiently and effectively. Members are urged to

- Be experimental—test out new styles of behavior, communication, participation and leadership in this human relations laboratory.
- Be authentic and open—in one's communication by telling it like it is and avoiding game playing with people, while considering others' viewpoints.
- Be sensitive—express feelings, while being conscious and empathetic to the other person's feelings and attitudes, particularly when giving feedback. Also be attuned to non-verbal cues and communication.
- Be spontaneous and helpful—respond creatively to here and now data shared in the group, warmly receiving people's revelations of themselves, and sharing yourself in the process of assisting other members.

The team building conference not only develops meaningful relations among members, but enables them to become more trusting and congruent (comfortable with themselves and their capacities). It is a challenge for participants to revise their self images and to actualize their potential through personal and group change. The learning experience aids members in gaining control over their own team space and risk becoming what they are capable of becoming. If a company or agency does not have a competent facilitator on its staff to conduct the team building, external consultants in organizational development or transformation are available.

Team Building Through Simulations

Simulations are powerful training tools. Participants may play themselves or assume roles, or the roles may be played by actors and then discussed. The technique may be in the form of a game and performed live, or be undertaken through a computer. The simulated experience condenses what might happen on the job during the course of a day, week, or month. Simulations usually reflect behavior as practiced on the job, as pilots in training do with aircraft simulators.

These learning experiences may be originals, customized by a trainer to deal with organizational problems or to prepare personnel for new challenges, such as a more diverse work force. Or, they may be purchased, as in the case of *Bafa Bafa,* one of the most famous simulations designed by Dr. R. Garry Shirts to prepare persons to deal with individuals from a different culture. These and other of Shirts' participatory training games have been translated into twenty languages and are used in sixty countries. Now his company, Simulation Training Systems, has issued his latest creation on team building entitled *Pumping the Colors*. It aims to develop healthy, high-performance teams for the global marketplace. Six to ten trainees learn teamwork through hands-on tasks that simulate real world jobs. One or more teams engage in the exercise with a time framework of three to five hours (Simile II 218 Twelfth St., Del Mar, CA 800/942-2900).

Team Building with Computers

Another useful management tool for managing the diverse elements involved in project or matrix management is the personal or microcomputer. To make a complex project more manageable, a computer can assist in planning, monitoring and tracking. It can aid project teams to identify tasks and sequences to be performed, establish and follow a schedule with its milestones and deadlines, and estimate resources as to what and when they will be needed and how much they will cost. It can even be used to manage accountability, using the computer to analyze, clarify, and evaluate roles and relationships. Dauphinais and Darnell [3] make an interesting distinction between project tracking and monitoring—the former is more recordkeeping and historical, while the latter is more subtle, forward-looking in nature, and considers unexpected changes. Project monitoring is real-time planning that alters the project in progress and observes changes in plans. The information collected via the computer is a compilation of team history and can be used from project to project to improve team performances.

Different software packages are now available to assist team leaders with the variety of project functions: maintaining the calendar, task definition and sequence, resource and cost definitions, charts and reports. Software companies like Digital Marketing, Earth Data, Harvard, North America Mica, Omicron, Primavera Systems, Scitor, VisiCorp, and Westminster all have such programs and can offer descriptive catalogues on their distinctive features. Whether small or large projects, the software packages are becoming more sophisticated and helpful to team leaders.

Intercultural Team Building

Many companies have "off-shore or twin plants"—out-of-country operations to which they ship materials and know-how because the cost of labor abroad is less and enables them to stay economically competitive. Control Data Corporation of Minneapolis has one such plant in Tijuana, Mexico. When American and Mexican managers were brought together in Tijuana for intercultural training, many insights were discovered. One of the main problems of cross-cultural communication was with the headquarters staff in Minnesota who made telephone calls directly to the Mexican plant causing confusion by their lack of intercultural communication skills.

Another insight occurred through use of a group technique called "inner/outer circles." American managers were put in an inner circle and discussed what they liked/did not like about the Mexican managers' style; the Mexican managers were observers in the outer circle. The roles were reversed and the Mexicans discussed the same questions about their colleagues from the United States. The ground rules permitted no interruptions of the inner circle conversations. Later, a cluster was formed for both groups to analyze together the significance of the feedback received. The Americans were particularly upset by the Mexican comments that they were "cheap." The "gringos" inquired as to the meaning and proof for that statement. The Mexican managers replied:

> Every Friday afternoon you Americans ask us to go out after work for a drink in the cantina. That is very nice and we appreciate your interest in us. But when we get there, you say, "Remember, this is Dutch." That is why we think you are cheap. What is this "Dutch" business? In my country where you are visiting, if someone invites us out to socialize, then the person who issued the invitation pays!

There was much laughter, a collective sigh of relief came from the Americans, and another cross-cultural misunderstanding was cleared up.

Data-Gathering Instruments

Such questionnaires or inventories can be used for individual or group analysis. These instruments can be used for self or team improvement purposes; for use during performance evaluation between a leader and team member; or for group discussion during team building. They may be used to raise awareness in group members, or to collect information on feelings, opinions, and insights that is then processed by the team, or used by a professional consultant or behavioral scientist, for diagnosis and to provide management briefings. These instruments may be homemade or purchased commercially. Exhibit 3-1 is an example of such an instrument.

Exhibit 3-1
Cross-Cultural Team Performance Survey

CCTPS can be used as a pre/post instrument for data gathering in conjunction with a team building session. Members of project teams or other work units can use the survey to evaluate a group's progress and problems from an individual perspective. Then the participants can compare their selection on the 25 items for further discussion, clarification, and learning.

To record total group scores on the CCTPS, a matrix can be drawn on a blackboard or flip chart with the four columns on which the headings or choices are written horizontally across the top of the sheet— "Yes," "Sometimes," "No," "Uncertain." Next, vertically along the left side, number from 1 to 25 representing each item. Each team member would then be invited to place their personal response for all items on the display matrix for other members to see. By tallying up the results for the group on each item, one may quickly identify trouble spots in team relations. For example, with reference to item #1, in a team of 8 persons, if 4 of them marked "No" and 1 checked "Uncertain," the consensus is that the group's goals are uncertain. In this way a leader and team can diagnose the healthiness of the group's development and where improvements are desirable for increased performance.

Directions: Please consider each item relative to a specific work team or unit with which you are associated (e.g., a project or product team, or a task force). Name of the group you are describing: Date:

_____   _____ 19__

Kindly describe how your cultural background is uniquely different from other members in this group, and whether this team values that uniqueness.

_____

_____

_____

_____

_____

_____

_____

_____

_____

_____

_____

Please check each item that best describes your feelings or opinions about this group at this moment:

	Yes	Sometimes	No	Uncertain
1. This group's goal or mission is quite clear to me.	—	_____	—	_____
2. The group's charter in terms of mandate, parameters, and time frame is evident to me.	—	_____	—	_____
3. My role and relationship to team members and other functional units is clearly understood by me.	—	_____	—	_____
4. The team shares with me a sense of being accountable individually for the group's results.	—	_____	—	_____
5. From my perspective, the material and human resources available to accomplish the group's tasks are adequate.	—	_____	—	_____
6. My competencies are sufficient to help this team accomplish its goals.	—	_____	—	_____
7. In my opinion, this team lacks some members from the organization who are vital to its success.	—	_____	—	_____
8. The team works well together and has cohesion.	—	_____	—	_____

	Yes	Sometimes	No	Uncertain
9. The members of this group do feel free to level with one another, sharing true opinions and feelings.	—	————	—	———
10. Some members of this team seem to be psychologically threatened or intimidated by me.	—	————	—	———
11. To be effective, this group deals with the differences within it, instead of ignoring or smoothing over them for task accomplishment.	—	————	—	———
12. This group has the skills within it to deal effectively with its differences and disagreements.	—	————	—	———
13. This group communicates at both the cognitive (I think) and affective (I feel) levels of interaction.	—	————	—	———
14. This team provides individual support to members when needed.	—	————	—	———
15. This group regularly gives recognition and encouragement to me.	—	————	—	———
16. This team facilitates member involvement and seeks their opinions.	—	————	—	———
17. This group fosters my participation and positively reinforces my contributions.	—	————	—	———
18. The leadership in this team is shared.	—	————	—	———
19. Members play a variety of roles in this group, and no one person dominates.	—	————	—	———
20. This group welcomes my input and feedback.	—	————	—	———
21. This team is committed to cooperation and collaboration among members and with other groups.	—	————	—	———
22. This group values competence and high performance.	—	————	—	———
23. This team inspires my best effort.	—	————	—	———
24. Our members work well together.	—	————	—	———
25. This team pauses occasionally from pursuit of its tasks to improve group maintenance and functioning.	—	————	—	———

Exhibit 3-2 lists several useful learning instruments and simulations and the phone/fax numbers of the sources that offer them.

Exhibit 3-2
Team Instruments and Simulations

1. **Culture and Value Analysis Tool (CVAT)**—Reed Nelson, 1025 Kenwood, Ruston, LA 71270; Phone: 318/257-2473.

2. **Employee Opinion Survey**—Measures employee satisfaction of jobs, work environment, management and supervisory practices; Phone: 904/241-1721, Fax: 241-4388.

3. **Survey of Organizational Effectiveness**—Evaluates those conditions that are critical to the process of organizational effectiveness, identifies organizational strengths and weaknesses; Phone: 904/241-1721, Fax: 241- 4388.

4. **Participative Climate Diagnosis**—Determines whether or not your organizational climate will support participative management and employee involvement programs; Phone: 904/241-1721, Fax: 241-4388.

5. **Team Climate Survey**—Gives managers the information needed to make teams as supportive as possible and to increase employee participation in decision making and problem solving; Phone: 904/241-1721, Fax: 241-4388.

6. **Team Performance Survey**—Uses a team-building session to evaluate a team's progress and problems; Phone: 619/453-2271.

7. **Intercultural Relations Inventory**—Improves cultural awareness and sensitivity; Phone: 619/453-2271.

8. **Team Effectiveness Profile**—Identifies major issues impeding team work; Phone: 215/279-2002, Fax: 215/279-0524.

9. **Group Maturity Analysis**—Employed by team members to evaluate themselves as a group; Phone: 619/453-2271.

10. **Team Synergy Analysis**—Self-assessment of synergistic attitudes and skills within a work unit; Phone: 619/453-2271.

11. **Individual Behavior Analysis**—Diagnosis of the level of an individual's interpersonal performance skills with a work unit; Phone: 619/453-2271.

12. **Communication Effectiveness Scale**—Gives team members feedback on how others in an organization perceive their communication skills; Phone: 619/453-2271.

---

13. **Team Communication Analysis**—Improves awareness and understanding of communications between group members; Phone: 904/241-1721, Fax: 241-4388.

14. **Group Role Analysis**—Aids team members in understanding their perceptions and roles in teams; Phone: 904/241-1721, Fax: 241-4388.

15. **Group Participation Analysis**—Helps groups' facilitators observe and critique the group process skills of team members; Phone: 904/241-1721, Fax: 241-4388.

16. **Group Creativity Index**—Measures perceptions, creative characteristics, barriers to creativity and organizational impact on creativity in a team; Phone: 904/241-1721, Fax: 241-4388.

17. **Team Task Analysis**—Improves problem solving skills of team members; Phone: 904/241-1721, Fax: 241-4388.

18. **Acceleration**—Team member inclusion activity. Organizational design Phone: 215/279-2002, Fax: 215/279-0524.

19. **Group Process Questionnaire**—Analyzes group members' task and maintenance behavior after simulations; Phone: 215/279-2002, Fax: 215/279-0524.

Learning Materials
Simulations, Games, Videos, Cases

1. **Diversity: Making it work for you (video)**—Enhances participants cultural sensitivity; Phone: 215/279-2002, Fax: 215/279-0524.

2. **The Alien Encounter Exercise (simulation)**—Dramatizes the communication process, develops decision-making, strengthens team interaction, *increases intercultural awareness and sensitivity;* Phone: 904/241-1721, Fax: 241-4388.

3. **The Time Warp Exercise (simulation)**—Dramatizes time management principles, prioritizing, and team interactions skills; Phone: 904/241-1721, Fax: 241-4388.

4. **Hostage Rescue Exercise (simulation)**—Team members must not only sharpen their decision-making skills, but work together as an effective team, or else; Phone: 904/241-1721, Fax: 241-4388.

5. **The Hurricane Disaster Exercise (simulation)**—Develops planning and organizational skills, builds team skills, assesses leadership behavior, and ability to make decisions under pressure; Phone: 904/241-1721, Fax: 241-4388.

6. **Trapped Underground (simulation)**—Develops listening skills, improves interpersonal communication, decision-making ability, and teamwork; Phone: 904/241-1721, Fax: 241-4388.

7. **Team Building: An Exercise in Leadership (cases)**—Uses cases and step-by-step plan to transform groups into teams; Phone: 904/241-1721, Fax: 241-4388.

8. **Games Teams Play (game)**—Helps groups discuss and reach consensus on desired behaviors and accepted norms; Phone: 215/279-2002, Fax: 215/279-0524.

9. **The Jungle Escape (game with audio cassettes)**—Identifies key teamwork concepts and skills; Phone: 215/279-2002, Fax: 215/279-0524.

10. **Whitewater (simulation)**—Aids teams in developing synergistic team building skills; Phone: 215/279-2002, Fax: 215/279-0524.

11. **Earthquake (simulation)**—Used for team building, decision-making and problem-solving; Phone: 215/279-2002, Fax: 215/279-0524.

12. **The Five Star Team Builder (video)**—Explains the team concept and the nature of superior work teams; Phone: 904/241-1721, Fax: 241-4388.

13. **The Diversity Task Force Exercise (case study)**—Helps one to better understand how attitudes influence an organization stance on diversity and how to better manage diverse work forces; Phone: 215/279-2002, Fax: 215/279-0524.

References

1. Adler, N., *International Dimensions of Organizational Behavior,* Boston, Mass: Kent Publishing Co., 1986.

2. Connors, M. M., Harrison, A. A. and Atkins, F. R., *Living Aloft Human Requirements for Extended Spaceflight.* Washington, DC: U. S. Government Printing Office, 1985 (NASA/SP-483).

3. Dauphinais, W., and Darnell, L., "Project Management: One Step at a Time," *PC World,* Sept. 1984, pp. 240–250.

4. Harris, P. R., *Living and Working in Space: Behaviour, Culture and Organization,* Chichester, UK: Ellis Horwood (USA—Prentice Hall, Englewood Cliffs, NJ), 1992.

5. Harris, P. R., *Management in Transition—Transforming Managerial Practices and Organizational Strategies for a New Work Culture,* San Francisco: Jossey-Bass, 1985.

6. Harris, P. and Moran R. T., *Managing Cultural Differences.* Houston: Gulf Publishing Company, 1991.
7. McClenahen, J. S., "Not Fun in the Sun," *Industry Week,* October 15, 1990, Vol. 239 #20, pp. 22–24.
8. Miller, J. G., *Living Systems,* New York: McGraw-Hill, 1978.
9. Miles, R., Snow C., and Coleman, H., "Managing 21st Century Network Organizations," *Journal of Organizational Dynamics,* Winter 1992, Vol. 20, pp. 4–20.
10. Moran, R. T. and Harris, P. R., *Managing Cultural Synergy,* Houston, TX: Gulf Publishing, 1982.
11. Ouchi, W., *The M-Form Society,* Reading, MA: Addison-Wesley, 1984.
12. Parker, G. M., *Team Players and Teamwork—The New Competitive Business Strategy,* San Francisco, CA: Jossey-Bass, 1990.
13. Senge, P. M., *The Fifth Discipline—The Art and Practice of Learning,* New York: Doubleday, 1991.
14. Wellins, R. S., Byhuman, W. C. and Wilson, J. M., *Empowered Teams—Creating Self-Directed Work Groups,* San Francisco, CA: Jossey-Bass, 1991.

CHAPTER 4

SOLVING CONFLICTS IN A MULTICULTURAL ENVIRONMENT

Introduction

Each person operates within her or his own private world. Psychologists call it our perceptual field or life space. From that base we view others, interact, and sometimes conflict with one another. Our unique view of the world is influenced by the input we received from our families and friends, school and work experience, etc.

In the process of communication, we attempt to share our worlds, to enter into the life space of the other person. During this exchange, each participant receives (decodes) information, interprets (analyzes) it, and replies (encodes) to the other. This can be a complex process and may lead to conflict in viewpoints, especially when there are profound cultural or generational differences. Exhibit 4-1 summarizes some insights on conflict and its management.

Exhibit 4-1
Behavioral Science Research on Conflict*

The following ideas are presented to stimulate small group discussion about the subject of conflict, whether it is between individuals or groups.
1. *Conflict Is a Relationship:* It takes at least two persons, groups or even nations to have a conflict. Do we permit the experience to develop so that issues, not personalities, can be confronted? Exploring differences can result in useful insight and information IF we do not cut off the relationship before data is sufficiently generated for analysis.
2. *Conflict Is Energy:* Human effort is necessary to maintain it, so the critical question is whether we can use this energy constructively or permit it to be wasted. Conflicts cannot always be resolved when their source, for example, is a sick sense of self. Sometimes

---

the individuals have to be honest with one another and "agree to disagree" while respecting one another.

3. *Conflict Can Be Defused or Unfused:* If we do not deliberately seek and promote conflict, there are strategies which a leader can pursue to minimize unnecessary conflict in the organization or community. When the situation that can lead to conflict is not yet critical, when it is still simmering, an innovative supervisor can "head it off at the pass!" Like the bomb detection squad that deactivates weapons of potential destruction, a manager can confront or resolve situations that might end up in serious conflict. He or she can keep combustibles apart and can deal with differences of opinion before they get out of hand.

4. *Conflict Is Aided by Hardening of Positions:* When people become inflexible and rigid out of a sense of fear or threat, they tend to set hard boundary rules, to draw lines and dare anyone to step over, to polarize in their positions. In periods of profound transition, like today, conflict seems to be growing as people experience "future shock." Pluralistic societies require cooperation rather than dogged adherence to past traditions and positions.

5. *Persons Are in Conflict:* Human relationships are strained, tension is increased and emotions run high during conflict situations. Reason can work only when the situation is "cooled," objectivized rather than subjectivized. Keep in focus that "feelings" are involved, and try to shift discussion to the issues. Yet it is just as bad to over emphasize the interpersonal elements in conflict as it is to de-personalize intergroup conflict.

6. *Conflict Involves Perception:* The apparent conflict may sometimes be caused by misunderstanding or misperception of the situation. Clarify each person's true position, and you might discover that there is no real conflict, or at least it is not so great that it cannot be handled.

7. *The Opposite of Conflict Is Collaboration:* One way to reduce undesirable conflict in organizations is to encourage team building, consulting skills and the development of a "helping relationship" among staff.

8. *Conflict Happens Because People Are Different:* People come from different cultural, social, and educational backgrounds, which form or condition their unique viewpoints and opinions.

* From *High Performance Leadership* by P. R. Harris, Glenview, IL: Scott Foresman/Harper Collins, 1989. Reprinted with permission.

The important insight to remember is that the other side of conflict is collaboration. When people share their private worlds, their cultural backgrounds, they are more apt to cooperate than dispute or avoid each other. To assist the reader in developing cross-cultural management skills, this chapter examines unconventional and traditional ways of coping with conflict within one's self or with others. To further enhance human resource leadership, alternative methods of conflict resolution are analyzed and appropriate resources are identified.

Traditional Methods of Conflict Resolution

The last half of this chapter is devoted to creative methods of cross-cultural conflict resolution that are interesting, exciting, and worthwhile. However, they may not be appropriate in all circumstances. Human resource professionals will have to use their own best judgment on whether or not to use these techniques.

Many corporations will prefer that their human resource departments stick with traditional methods of conflict resolution. In evaluating traditional methods, *negotiation* should be placed at the top of the list. Chapter 8 presents an in-depth examination of cross-cultural negotiation.

Litigation is another traditional method of conflict resolution. When American business persons are unable to reach a negotiated settlement, they often resort to litigation. This approach has benefits and shortcomings. On the plus side, litigation may be the only way to definitively establish the rights and obligations of the disputing parties. Additionally, and contrary to popular belief, disputants can usually expect courts to render fair and reasoned judgments.

On the minus side, the legal process is expensive and time-consuming. Rigid rules of procedure necessitate the hiring of expensive attorneys. Judges are imposed upon the disputants and may not have any specialized expertise in the subject matter of the dispute. Often the court's decision will be unsatisfactory to everyone concerned.

Many legal systems suffer from cultural lag. For example, in the United States, court administration and practices are often obsolete (e.g., jury selection and orientation; inadequate use of computers and telecommunications); justice facilities are insufficient, staffs are usually undermanned and undertrained. As a result court dockets are overcrowded, frequently clogged with frivolous and misdemeanor cases. Plea bargaining by lawyers and judges abound in questionable attempts at settlement and punishment. Until the criminal justice system is updated and renewed, "justice" is not well served and conflicts are better resolved outside the courtroom.

When a cross-cultural conflict involves people from different countries, with another type of legal system, going to court becomes even more expensive, more time consuming, and more complicated. Business persons cannot rely on "international law" as a means of enforcing international business contracts. Nations are often unwilling to accept the decisions of an international or foreign tribunal regarding business matters. For this reason, many attorneys argue that there is no such thing as international law. In their view we only have domestic laws that may be applied internationally if certain complex criteria are met.

Furthermore, it is very difficult to successfully conduct international civil litigation in American courts. Corporations and their attorneys must wrestle with issues such as service of process abroad, personal jurisdiction over foreign defendants, international forum selection, extraterritorial discovery, foreign sovereign immunity, and the act of state doctrine. Even if these issues can be favorably resolved, a foreign government may choose to neither recognize nor enforce the judgment.

Frustration with American Litigation

Despite the complexities of international litigation, many American business persons are quick to sue their foreign counterparts, earning Americans the reputation around the world as being "sue happy" and legalistic. This has caused a lot of hard feelings, especially in Asia.

Japan is representative of this view. The Japanese concept of *wa* (harmony) is one of conflict avoidance. It is difficult to reconstruct harmony after a legal confrontation. Therefore, it is shameful to take someone to court. Japanese judges recognize this and purposefully hesitate to render a decision that would terminate a relationship. They prefer that the disputants settle their own differences.

The need for harmony is also reflected in the strong power of the bureaucracy. The government is held in high esteem. Its decrees are traditionally accepted without question. No one challenges them. Traditional Japanese deference to authority has resulted in the effective use of "administrative guidelines." Although the guidelines are technically non-binding, most Japanese strictly adhere to them.

The traditional Japanese notion of contracts also reflects a basic need for harmony. Historically there were no written contracts in Japan. It was felt that there was no need for a contract if you trusted your counterpart, and no one would do business with someone they did not trust. Any difficulties were worked out without resorting to a court of law. Contracts were merely a framework for ongoing relations. Terms were vague and ambiguous to allow for future negotiation. The contract was only meant to be tentative and was re-negotiated if conditions changed.

Everything changed with the globalization of Japanese business. Major Japanese companies were increasingly exposed to American style contracts. They began to have bitter experiences with American firms and had to pay significant damages because they didn't closely examine their contracts. This has made Japanese companies very cautious. They now often require detailed contracts and have their attorneys review everything.

Nevertheless, Japan has not increased its number of attorneys. Japan has 20,000 attorneys, compared to 650,000 in the U.S.A. Less than 2% of applicants pass the Japanese bar exam every year. Most law graduates enter government or business. The minimal number of Japanese lawyers and the need for harmony has led to fewer lawsuits. Per capita lawsuits in Japan are less than one tenth of the commonwealth countries.

The Cultural Defense

Increased dealings with Japanese and other foreign business persons has forced American attorneys to realize that cultural differences must be considered. The concept of culture has added a new complex variable to the process of international civil litigation. Creative defense attorneys have introduced the "cultural defense" in American criminal cases. In cases involving rituals as diverse as the Japanese tradition of parent-child suicide (*oyako-shinju*) and the Laotian Hmong tradition of marriage by capture (*zij poj niam*), American courts have had to wrestle with defenses based upon cultural background.

The cultural defense is based upon the observation that "persons raised in other cultures, who are subject to influences that inculcated them in a different set of norms, will likely feel morally obligated to follow those norms." The cultural defense recognizes that "a person's cultural background represents a relevant individual factor that a just legal system should take into account."

Application of the cultural defense in criminal cases is extremely controversial. Understandably, American courts have been reluctant to apply such a concept when dealing with murders and rapes. It is felt that deterrence, fairness to the majority, and upholding the principle of legality all require a rejection of the cultural defense. However, a strong argument can be made that the cultural defense should be applied in civil cases.

It is well-recognized that cultural differences have a great influence on international business transactions. Therefore, an attorney or business person involved in international transactions is negligent if he does not factor cultural differences into the contractual equation. For example, when considering the inclusion of a clause that includes the concept of "reasonable time," an attorney would be well-advised to consider the differences between "monochronic" and "polychronic cultures." In monochronic cultures, like the United States, people compartmentalize time by adhering to a set schedule. In polychronic cultures, like Egypt and Mexico, appointments and schedules are not taken seriously and are frequently broken.

Business people who have interacted with people from polychronic cultures are aware of their nonchalant attitude towards time. Seemingly simple projects often take inordinate amounts of time due to local customs and trade practices. In determining what constitutes a "reasonable time" when a business person from a monochronic culture has entered a contract with a business person from a polychronic culture, the cultural defense can be used by either side. The polychronic person can argue that it is common knowledge that time is unimportant in the local community. On the other hand, the monochronic person can argue that it is common knowledge that international business transactions depend upon strict scheduling.

Alternative Dispute Resolution

When the concept of culture is factored in with the other complex variables involved in international civil litigation, most attorneys will agree that global business persons should consider using methods of "alternative dispute resolution" (ADR). ADR is a relatively new field of study, so there is a significant amount of debate over what should and should not be included within the field.

Alternative dispute resolution techniques include:

- Negotiation (discussed in Chapter 8)
- Dispute resolution contract clauses

- Neutral lawyering; early neutral evaluation
- Neutral expert fact finding; joint fact finding
- Ombudsmen
- Conciliation
- Mediation
- Arbitration
- Private judging
- Private mini-trials
- Private dispute resolution services

All of these ADR techniques work, but they do not work in all cases. If a good ADR technique is misapplied to a cross-cultural dispute, it can actually be counterproductive. The task facing the human resource professional is to pick the ADR technique that is most appropriate for resolving the particular cross-cultural dispute. The technique can then be fine tuned or customized to fit the specific situation.

We will begin with a model case involving a contractual dispute between American and Saudi business persons. Readers should consider how to resolve the dispute using various ADR techniques. We provide a brief description of each ADR technique, a resource that can be contacted for further information about that technique, and some training suggestions.

HR professionals can use actual legal cases in their cross-cultural conflict resolution training programs. Workshop participants can read a case and then consider how the dispute could have been better resolved using ADR techniques. Recent cases can be easily accessed through the computerized legal services.

- Westlaw (West Publishing Company, 610 Opperman Drive, St. Paul, Minnesota 55123; Telephone: 800-937-8529)
- Lexis (Mead Data Central, 9443 Springboro Pike, Miamisburg, Ohio 45342; Telephone: 800-543-6862).

As an example, we will use WEIDNER COMMUNICATIONS, INC. v. H.R.H. PRINCE BANDAR AL FAISAL, (7th Cir. 1988) 859 F.2d 1302; (N.D.Ill. 1987) 671 F.Supp. 531. The case states the plaintiff's allegations and the defendant's response.

A Model Case Study—A Dispute in the Desert Kingdom

The Saudi Group (SG) is a joint venture, existing under Saudi law, comprising H. R. H. Prince Bandar al Faisal, H. H. Princess Basma Bint Majid bin Abdul Aziz, H. R. H. Prince Saud Abdullah al Faisal, and others. In July of 1984, SG hired an agent, Rittenberry, to find an English-to-Arabic computer-aided translation system. Later that summer, Rittenberry visited the offices of Weidner Communications Corporation (WCC) in Northbrook, Illinois.

WCC is in the business of developing computer-aided systems for translating languages to and from English. Accompanied by a computer expert, Rittenberry visited with WCC's president, Garrett, and observed a demonstration of a computerized English-to-Arabic translation device that WCC was developing. As a result of Rittenberry's report, in October of 1984, Prince Bandar sent three experts from Saudi Arabia to WCC's offices to look at the translation device. Rittenberry and the Saudi experts spent three days at WCC's offices examining the source code, discussing the system with WCC's staff, and putting many pages of text through the system.

After receiving a favorable report from his experts, Prince Bandar entered into a "Letter of Intent" with WCC on October 30, 1984. The letter provided that WCC and SG would form a new company in Saudi Arabia called Saudi Computer Aided Translation, Ltd. (SCAT). SCAT would be in the business of selling and leasing computer-aided translation systems and software and operating translation service bureaus.

According to the letter of intent, SCAT's stock was to be owned by SG (51%) and WCC (49%). SG would provide $510,000 as working capital and WCC would provide $490,000. Additionally, SCAT was to borrow $2.5 million at the current U.S. prime rate from SG. The loan was to be repaid from the initial profits of SCAT prior to the payment of any dividends. SCAT was to pay the $2.5 million to WCC to acquire the marketing rights to the English-to-Arabic translation device.

The letter of intent also provided that SCAT would immediately begin to market the translation device. WCC would work closely with SG in Riyadh to establish and manage SCAT, to provide necessary software and updates, and to train SCAT personnel. WCC would be paid for any new software conversion or development.

The letter of intent included a schedule that required SG to pay WCC $100,000 when the letter of intent was signed. SG was required to register SCAT in Saudi Arabia. WCC would hire and train technical and administrative personnel, purchase computer hardware and software, and step up development of the English-Arabic dictionaries. Upon Saudi registration of SCAT, SG would pay $2.4 million to WCC, which would then pay $490,000 for 49% ownership of SCAT.

After signing the letter of intent, SG and WCC continued to meet to discuss the terms of the joint venture. Garrett met with Prince Bandar, Princess Basma, and other Saudis in Aspen, Colorado, Paris, France, and Riyadh, Saudi Arabia. At the meetings Garrett was told of the great Saudi need for the translation device. Prince Bandar and Prince Saud stated that their family, personal, and political connections would enable SCAT to bring in revenues of $22 million per year. They told Garrett that the entities that would provide business to WCC were currently spending $90 million per year in manual translation. The assurances of future income were made to induce WCC to enter into a business relationship.

On February 22, 1985, WCC and SG entered into a joint venture agreement that largely embodied the terms of the letter of intent. However, there were some changes. The division of ownership was changed, giving 51% to SG, 43% to WCC, 5% to Rittenberry, and 1% to a man named Abadullah. WCC would pay $430,000 for its share. The $2.4 million would not be paid to WCC until it had delivered the translation device to the company offices in Saudi Arabia and received written confirmation from SCAT that the system was delivered, installed, and operating. Garrett signed for WCC and Princess Basma signed for SG.

After signing the agreement, WCC devoted substantial efforts and incurred significant expenses in developing the translation device, installing it in Saudi Arabia, and training SCAT personnel in its use. WCC completed its obligations under the agreement by September 5, 1985. About a week later, Prince Bandar invited Garrett to his palatial home in Saudi Arabia for a meeting. Garrett was led to believe that the meeting was to be a celebration of the successful development, delivery, and installation of the computer translation system.

Prior to the meeting Prince Bandar had his servant take Garrett to the town square in Riyadh, where punishment was being publicly inflicted upon criminals. Prince Bandar's servant made numerous statements to Garrett about the power possessed by the prince to imprison and punish foreigners at his whim. Afterwards, Prince Bandar began the meeting with a discussion of the recent beheading of three persons. He then threatened and intimidated Garrett, insisting on a renegotiation of the joint venture agreement. Garrett was asked to accept a drastic reduction in the monies and compensation to which WCC was entitled. When Garrett refused, Prince Bandar flew into a rage.

Garrett felt extremely threatened by Prince Bandar's actions and his references to punishment and imprisonment. Perceiving a threat to his own personal safety and well-being and feeling that it would be useless to further demand the agreed compensation or the return of the computer source code and components, Garrett left Prince Bandar's palace and immediately flew to the United States. Garrett refused to return to Saudi Arabia.

WCC repeatedly demanded payments and threatened to bring a lawsuit, but SG refused to answer. Finally, SG offered to pay the remainder due under the agreement if WCC would perform additional services, including the task of interfacing a new Wang computer. On October 15, 1985, SG's attorneys paid $700,000 to WCC. On October 16 Garrett signed a "clarification agreement" with Prince Saud, which referred to the past agreements. It stated that WCC believed it had performed its obligations and was due $1.7 million, while SG believed WCC had not so performed but was willing to pay $700,000 to induce WCC to comply with its remaining obligations.

The clarification agreement provided that SG would acquire a Wang processor and Fortran compiler, and that WCC would develop an interface from its system to the Wang system. All of this was to be done within four months, as "time was of the essence." The $1.7 million that SG owed to WCC would be secured by an irrevocable letter of credit to be paid in two installments. The first installment of $570,000 would be delivered to WCC's attorney, when it notified SG that it had completed its preparations and was prepared to make final delivery. After receiving this amount, WCC would deliver and install the equipment at SCAT's offices in Saudi Arabia. Upon written verification from SCAT's general manager that the interface was operating satisfactorily, the remaining $1.13 million would be paid to WCC's attorney. WCC would use $430,000 of the money to purchase a 43% interest in SCAT.

On December 5, 1985, WCC certified completion and received $570,000. On February 4, 1986, Prince Saud wrote to Garrett, stating that SCAT received a $430,000 capital contribution in WCC's behalf that entitled WCC to 43% equity. In the latter part of February WCC sent an employee to Riyadh and successfully installed the interface. The interface and translation device have operated satisfactorily ever since.

Beginning on March 10, 1986, WCC made repeated demands for payment and its stock certificate showing 43% ownership in SCAT. SG refused both demands. On April 16, 1986, Prince Saud refused to sign a certificate of satisfactory operation.

Weidner Communications Inc. and the Saudi Group wound up in litigation in the United States federal court system. Cases similar to this one, involving litigation between American corporations and foreign counterparts from most countries in the world, can be found. The fact patterns in these cases can be used to explore alternatives to litigation. What ADR techniques can be used to prevent cross-cultural disputes from winding up in court? The following is a discussion of contractual protections.

Dispute Resolution Clauses

It is extremely important for HR leaders to emphasize that cross-cultural disputes are a common occurrence. Business persons must anticipate disputes and take preventive measures before a dispute occurs. One of the best ways to prevent destructive disputes is to include a dispute resolution clause in the contract. By spending the time to create a dispute resolution clause, the parties are acknowledging that problems may occur, but that the problems will be resolved in an amicable, orderly manner.

The dispute resolution clause should be as specific as possible. The contract should explicitly state what method of dispute resolution will be used. For example, contracts can provide for "best efforts" mediation, to be followed by mandatory arbitration in the event that mediation is unsuccessful.

If the ADR method requires the intervention of third parties, such as arbitrators or mediators, the contract should state how they will be chosen. The contract should also specify what *language* will be used during the proceedings, where meetings will be located, and what procedural rules will be followed. Standardized rules of procedure, which should be acceptable to most business persons, are available. Both the American Arbitration Association and the International Chamber of Commerce have developed highly regarded rules of procedure.

Choice of law is another important consideration. The terms of the agreement will have to be evaluated according to some standard. Substantive law defines and determines the rights and obligations of contracting parties. The dispute resolution clause should explicitly state which country's substantive law will govern the terms of the contract.

Another area of concern is *enforceability* of the ADR agreement. Business persons may believe that they have resolved a dispute, only to find that their counterparts are not complying with the new agreement. Rather than going to court and determining the parties' rights and obligations all over again, business persons should ensure that the ADR agreement is enforceable. This can be done by including a clause in the contract that states the award or consensual agreement may be confirmed and entered directly as a judgment by a court of competent jurisdiction.

Human resource professionals should contact their corporate legal department or a private law firm for information on developing dispute resolution clauses in cross-cultural contracts. For example, twin plant activities on both sides of the U.S. and Mexican border are causing increasing conflict and legal problems. An interesting presentation or case might center on the fact that the U. S. legal system is based on English Common Law (e.g., you are innocent until proven guilty), while the Mexican system is based upon the Napoleonic Code (e.g., when arrested or charged, you are guilty until proven innocent.) HR professionals may wish to ask an attorney to come and speak at a training session.

Neutral Lawyering

The United States District Court for the Northern District of California has developed a new conflict resolution approach called "Early Neutral Evaluation" (ENE). To reduce the cost of litigation, the parties to a lawsuit attend a two-hour case evaluation session. The session is hosted by a neutral, lawyer-mediator, who is appointed by the court. It is essential that the lawyer-mediator be well grounded in the subject matter of the dispute, for example contract law.

During the ENE session, the parties to a lawsuit have the opportunity to confront and analyze the problem. Each litigant and their lawyer listens to the opposing side's presentation of its case. The lawyer-mediator helps the parties isolate the center of their dispute and identify the factual and legal matters that will not be seriously contested. Then the lawyer-mediator offers all counsel and litigants a confidential, frank, thoughtful assessment of the relative strengths and weaknesses of their positions and of the overall value of the case. After receiving the neutral assessment, the parties have the opportunity to try to negotiate settlement.

Human resource professionals can simulate the ENE program by having attorneys from the corporate law department attend the training session as a lawyer-mediator. To find out more about the ENE program, trainers can contact:

- Director, ADR Program, U.S. District Court for the Northern District of California, 450 Golden Gate Avenue, San Francisco, CA 94102; Telephone: (415)556-2117.

Neutral Expert Fact Finding

Another ADR technique is the use of a neutral expert fact finder to narrow or resolve differences through the research process rather than through adversary processes. Neutral experts are often used in cases involving complex technical or scientific matters. Often scientific and technical contracts are so complex that misunderstandings arise between the parties. Experts are brought in to reliably determine what the facts are. The experts can be hired by private parties or by a court of law.

Normally, the disputants choose a third-party neutral with specialized subject matter expertise, such as market research or chemical engineering. The expert investigates the facts of the dispute and presents a report to the disputants. The report may influence the parties to reach a voluntary settlement.

For example, the Federal Trade Commission used joint fact finding to answer a critical question that was the key issue in litigation with Yamaha International Corporation. Yamaha had been advertising that, with proper instruction, a Yamaha motorcycle could be "just as safe as an automobile." The FTC and Yamaha jointly designed a market research study to determine what the advertisement would lead consumers to believe. When the findings of the market research study were presented, the case settled out of court. The total cost of the study was less than the base daily rate of one of the attorneys involved in the case.

Trainers can design simulations in which a cross-cultural dispute has resulted from different understandings of the facts. Workshop participants can be divided into three teams. Two teams will act the part of the disputants, while the third team acts as the neutral fact finders. Team members and trainers can evaluate the usefulness of the technique for various fact patterns.

Ombudsmen

An ombudsman is a third party who investigates complaints made by constituents, clients, or employees against an organization. Traditionally, ombudsmen were public officials who investigated the activities of government agencies that were accused of infringing on the rights of individuals. Today, ombudsmen also investigate problems within private organizations.

The ombudsman has the responsibility or authority to represent the complainant. In doing so, the ombudsman may take actions such as bringing an apparent injustice to the attention of public officials or private executives, advising the complainant of available options and resources, proposing a settlement of the dispute, or proposing changes in the organization.

Ombudsmen are appropriate in cases in which an individual has a dispute with a private organization or with a government entity or officer. Typical cases involve corporations, hospitals, universities, professional associations, and municipalities. Organizations usually agree to sponsor or cooperate with the ombudsman. An organization may refer a complainant, or the complainant may approach the ombudsman directly.

Human resource professionals can develop cross-cultural conflict resolution training programs that use ombudsmen to investigate complaints and propose settlements. To find out more about ombudsmen programs, trainers can contact the following resources:

- Chairperson, Ombudsman Committee, Society of Professionals in Dispute Resolution, 815, 15th St. N.W., Suite 530, Washington, D.C. 20056-3169; Telephone: (202) 783-7277 or (617) 253-5921.
- Ombudsman Research, School of Education, 4407A Tolman Hall, University of California, Berkeley, California 94720; Telephone: (510) 642-7984.

- President, Organization of News Ombudsmen, c/o Ombudsman, *Boston Globe,* 135 Mornissey Boulevard, Boston, Massachusetts 02107; Telephone: (617) 929-2000.

Conciliation

Conciliation is similar to the ADR techniques of neutral lawyering and ombudsmen. Rather than being a judge, a conciliator is similar to a neutral lawyer who is consulted by the disputing parties as to the chances of success of a lawsuit and the advisability of a compromise. The conciliator clarifies the disputed issues, reconciles the parties, and propounds the terms of settlement.

The object of conciliation is to obtain the consent of the disputants to the solution proposed by the conciliator. The chances of success are greater if the disputants' consent can be obtained at every stage of the proceedings. If the disputants have played an active part in the effort to reach agreement, they will understand the reasoning and grounds on which it is based. Disputants will be more inclined to accept the results of an effort in which they have shared, than a solution dictated by the conciliator, whether it is reasonable or not.

Secrecy must be strictly enforced during the conciliation procedure. None of the conciliator's declarations or written statements may be divulged at any time, either during or after the proceedings. Conciliators should obtain a written statement from the disputants, which renounces any right to make use of the material discussed during the course of the proceedings.

One consequence of strict secrecy should be the frankness of the disputing parties. Protected by the rule of secrecy, the disputants should divulge any material in their possession, either in the initial phase when both sides are heard, or in separate interviews with the conciliator. Unfortunately, in practice this does not often occur.

The conciliator and the disputants must collaborate to ascertain the facts of the dispute. The main burden falls on the disputants. To prove their allegations, the disputants must aid the conciliator with the investigation. If the disputants do not cooperate with the investigation, then the conciliator is faced with an insurmountable problem and should withdraw.

After investigating the facts, the conciliator writes a report. A written document is essential for the disputants to form their own opinions on the nature of the conclusions arrived at by the conciliator. The report contains two main sections, the terms of the settlement and the conciliator's main reasons why the disputants should accept the settlement.

The disputants evaluate the report and send their reply to the conciliator. If the parties accept the report, the conciliator draws up an agreement stating the terms of the conciliation. If one party rejects the report, the conciliation procedure is considered to be null and void.

Human resource professionals should use cross-cultural conflict situations from their own experience to create training models. During the workshop, participants can take turns acting out the role of disputants and conciliators.

Mediation

Mediation is very similar to conciliation. Many ADR professionals use the terms interchangeably. The distinction we make is that, while a conciliator proposes a solution based upon the conciliator's analysis of the facts, a mediator facilitates a solution by influencing the disputants to come up with their own proposals for a voluntary settlement. Another distinction is that in conciliation the disputants do not necessarily have to meet face to face. Everything can be done through the mail. In mediation the importance of developing a good relationship necessitates face-to-face interaction.

The personality of the mediator plays an essential part. Mediators cannot rely upon power, because they don't have any. Their authority is purely charismatic and moral. If one of the parties doesn't like the mediator, then the mediator should be replaced, or the mediation should come to an end.

Mediators strive to create an intimate, informal atmosphere. The emphasis is on the disputants' relationship, not on adherence to or development of consistent rules. There are no rules of evidence, and no stenographer. The disputing parties are obligated to conduct a friendly discussion, using moderate tones.

Typically, a mediator gathers the disputants in a single room, listens to their arguments, then meets privately with each side, looking for common ground. A favorite tactic of mediators is to create doubt in the minds of each side about the strength of their position. This often stimulates a settlement.

If the parties cannot agree on a solution, mediators normally give a non-binding opinion on who they think would prevail if the case went to arbitration or trial. The parties are then given the opportunity to meet again to see if they can resolve their dispute with the added information. If they cannot reach a mutually agreeable settlement, the mediation ends and the disputants are free to pursue other methods of dispute resolution.

Studies have found that mediation resolves employee disputes more quickly and less expensively than traditional arbitration. One estimate puts the average cost of mediating a grievance at approximately ¼ to ⅓ the average cost of arbitration.

For further information on mediation training programs, human resource professionals can contact the following organizations:

- Director, New Mexico Center for Dispute Resolution, 510 Second Street N.W., Suite 209, Albuquerque, New Mexico 87102; Telephone: (505) 247-0571.
- President, American Mediation Resources, Inc., 2344 Perimeter Park Drive, Atlanta, Georgia 30341; Telephone: (404) 455-4455.
- President, U.S. Arbitration & Mediation, Inc., 300 Two Union Square, 601 Union St., Seattle, Washington 98101; Telephone: (206) 467-0794 or (800) 933-6348.
- President, Judicate, Inc., 1500 Walnut Street, Suite 1300, Philadelphia, Pennsylvania 19103; Telephone: (215) 546-6200 or (800) 473-6544.
- The International Chamber of Commerce, 1212 Avenue of the Americas, New York, New York 10036; Telephone: (212) 458-1534.
- International Centre for the Settlement of Investment Disputes, World Bank, 1818 H Street, N.W., Washington, D.C. 20433; Telephone: (202) 477-1234.

Arbitration

Private arbitration is a consensual process in which a neutral third party arbitrator hears arguments by both parties to a dispute, considers evidence, and issues an award. The award is binding, enforceable, and not subject to review except for gross error in the conduct of the arbitration process.

Arbitration has no set, definite process, but there are certain commonalities to most arbitration procedures. The disputants choose a private individual or individuals to serve as arbitrator. Normally, arbitrators are chosen because they have technical expertise in the subject matter of the dispute. This saves a great deal of time over litigation, during which both the judge and the jury must be educated in the subject matter before they can render a decision. If the arbitrator is an expert in the field, then the disputants can get right to the merits of the case.

Disputants can choose arbitrators on their own or with the help of a professional organization. The American Arbitration Association has over 60,000 arbitrators on its rosters and more than 45,000 matters are referred to it annually for resolution. The association normally assigns three arbitrators to resolve cases involving amounts greater than $100,000. Each side gets a list of five arbitrators with their biographies. They then strike two unacceptable choices and rank the other three in order of preference. The arbitrators are chosen based upon the rankings.

The disputants get to decide what standard the arbitrator will apply. It may be the law of some jurisdiction, the rules of an organization, or the ethics of a profession. If the disputants trust the arbitrator, the standard may be left to the arbitrator's personal view of justice and fairness.

Because arbitration is a private dispute resolution process, the disputants can design the procedure. Disputants who do not have the time to establish their own rules, may adopt the rules of established arbitration groups. Organizations that provide model procedural rules include the United Nations Commission on International Trade Law, the Arbitration Court of the International Chamber of Commerce, the American Arbitration Association, the Inter-American Commercial Arbitration Commission, and the London Court of Commercial Arbitration.

In normal arbitration proceedings the disputants submit evidence and arguments to the arbitrator. The arbitrator evaluates the evidence and comes to a decision. Typically, the decision is only an award, without elaboration on the facts found or the resolution of the individual issues presented. Sometimes, the decision is supported by a brief recitation of the facts and conclusions. In either case, the decision is final, with only a limited amount of review available.

Arbitration is useful when the disputants want to save time and money. It is also a private process, so that secrecy can be maintained. However, there are certain drawbacks. Arbitration is not particularly appropriate if the disputants want to establish uniform rules to be followed in the future. To establish a precedent that can be looked to as a guideline, the disputants will be required to go to court. Of course, litigation is time-consuming, expensive, and open to public scrutiny.

For more information on arbitration, trainers should contact the following organizations:

- President, American Arbitration Association, 140 West 51st Street, New York, NY 10020; Telephone: (212) 484-4100.
- Inter-American Commercial Arbitration Commission, 1889 F Street, NW, Washington, D.C. 20006; Telephone: (202) 458-3444.
- International Chamber of Commerce, 1212 Avenue of the Americas, New York, NY 10036; Telephone: (212) 354-4480.
- Asia/Pacific Center for the Resolution of International Business Disputes, 417 Montgomery, 5th Floor, San Francisco, CA 94104; Telephone: (415) 981-3901.
- Center for International Commercial Arbitration, One World Trade Center of Greater Los Angeles, Suite 295, Long Beach, CA 90831; Telephone: (310) 495-7071.
- Center for International Commercial Dispute Resolution, 810 Richard Street, Suite 641, Honolulu, Hawaii 96813; Telephone: (808) 531-0541.
- World Arbitration Commission, 140 W. 51st Street, New York, NY 10020; Telephone: (212) 484 4000 (or call any regional office of AAA).
- British Columbia International Commercial Arbitration Center, World Trade Center, Suite 670, 999 Canada Place, Vancouver, Canada V6C 2E2; Telephone: (604) 684-2821.

Private Judging

Similar to arbitration, private judging, or "rent-a-judge," permits litigants to have their case heard privately and quickly by a third party of their own choosing. In certain states, trial court judges have the statutory authority to refer a case to a privately selected referee. The referee listens to the evidence and makes a decision that is entered as the binding decision of the trial court. Unlike arbitration, once the referee's decision is entered as a judgment, it may be appealed for errors of law or on the ground that the judgment is against the weight of the evidence.

At least 48 states in the U.S.A. permit some form of private judging. The type of cases that can be referred and the powers of the private judge vary from state to state. California allows the most expansive version of private judging.

The California procedure allows the court, upon agreement of the parties, to appoint qualified private judges ("referees") to try a case, report a finding, and make a judgment. The disputants may choose to have a panel of up to three judges try their case. Once appointed, the referee has all of the powers of a trial judge except the contempt power and the power to appoint another referee.

The procedure at the trial may range from traditional court procedures to the more informal procedures of arbitration. Witnesses are sworn, but if the parties desire, the evidence taken need not be reported, or even recorded. The referee is directed to make a written report to the appointing clerk within twenty days of the close of testimony. Generally, this report consists of findings of fact and conclusions of law, which must be stated separately.

The finding of the private judge stands as the finding of the court. Unlike arbitration, however, appeal rights are fully preserved, just as with any judgment. Costs, including the referee's fee, are chargeable to the disputants, who may stipulate to any fee sharing arrangement they desire.

Proponents of private judging point to many advantages over traditional adjudication. First, the litigants choose the party who will decide the dispute, rather than trusting to the luck of the draw in the assignment of a trial judge. Second, it is fast and convenient. Third, the rules are flexible. Fourth, it is private. The only thing which becomes public is the referee's findings of fact and conclusions of law.

Private Mini-trials

Private "mini-trials" are not trials at all. They take problems out of the lawyers' realm and place them back in the laps of business persons. Rather than making presentations to a court of law, lawyers present their case to the disputants, who then decide what they want to do.

After a short period of pre-trial discovery, the disputants' lawyers develop their best case. The lawyers then appear before the disputants and make informal, abbreviated presentations of their arguments. The presentations are designed to give the disputants a clear, balanced conception of the strengths and weaknesses of the positions on both sides. Settlement negotiations begin immediately after the presentations.

No judges or arbitrators are involved. Generally, a jointly selected neutral advisor is present at most mini-trials to moderate the proceedings, pose questions, and highlight crucial facts and issues. If the disputants do not reach an agreement, they may ask the neutral advisor to give an opinion about how a judge, jury, or arbitrator would decide the case. The opinion is totally non-binding, private, and inadmissible at any later trial.

Trainers should work with their corporate legal departments to develop simulations of cross-cultural mini-trials. Fact situations from actual cases can be used.

Private Dispute Resolution Services

There are several private, for-profit businesses that provide dispute resolution services for a fee. Some of these businesses are very specialized, offering a very limited array of dispute resolution services. Others can provide specialists in any kind of ADR. A few of the services are very creative and are willing to customize techniques to fit unusual fact situations.

A general directory of ADR organizations is available by writing or calling:

- American Bar Association Section of Dispute Resolution, 1800 M Street, N.W., 2nd Floor Smith Lobby, Washington, D.C. 20036; Telephone: (202) 331-2258. The entire booklet costs approximately forty dollars, but the ABA will send the pages for your city free of charge.

HR professionals should feel free to contact the following businesses for more information on their ADR programs:

- President, Dispute Resolution, Inc., 179 Allyn Street, Suite 508, Hartford, Connecticut 06103; Telephone: (203) 724-0861.
- President, EnDispute, 1201 Connecticut Ave. N.W., Suite 501, Washington, D.C. 20036; Telephone: (202) 429-8782.

We have presented different conflict resolution techniques that can be used to develop innovative programs in cross-cultural conflict resolution training. There are many training programs in basic arbitration, mediation, and conciliation. However, an emphasis on cross-cultural variables allows trainers to distinguish the innovative from the standard programs. New niches can be found by moving across disciplinary and industry lines.

Innovative Methods of Cross-Cultural Conflict Resolution

Cross-cultural training is as much an art as it is a science. Trainers can use their imaginations to develop innovative and effective cross-cultural conflict resolution training programs. From the non-traditional perspective art, music, and dance can be used to explore possible methods of cross-cultural conflict resolution. Two examples of creative and innovative techniques follow that the HR specialist may find helpful in developing programs that are different and stimulating.

Musical Strategies for Conflict Management

Music to Soothe the Savage Subway

No environment is more multicultural and more conflict-ridden then the New York City subway system. Millions of inhabitants in the metropolitan area ride the underground rail system and are dependent upon it for transportation. The vast majority of its users are civil to one another and respectful of the municipal taxpayer's property. But the sheer mass and diversity of riders, age of the facilities and breakdowns in that subterranean system contribute to hostility, suspicion, and frustration. Normal passengers may be subject to a minority of deviants who abuse the public subways to deface and soil, to hustle and threaten, to assault and batter, to rob and harm, even murder. Thus, this environment below the streets of a great city becomes an arena for conflict.

The subways are necessary as a mode of transportation, even if they are sometimes conflict-ridden. So, most New Yorkers are stuck underground. However, they are not without remedies. The New York Transit Authority has decided to use music to calm riders' nerves and uplift their spirits.

Music will only be played in subway stations, not on the trains. The music will vary from station to station, depending upon the preference of individual communities. For example, they are playing classical music at the 59th Street station at Columbus Circle and jazz at the 149th Street and Third Avenue station.

Subway riders have said that they like the idea, but are concerned about the type of music that will be played and the quality of the sound equipment. One rider complained that a piano concerto sounded terrible through the station's raspy speakers. Another suggested that the Transit Authority play the hip-hop music of Big Daddy Kane, Heavy D, and Queen Latifa. Different cultures have different musical tastes and appreciation. Will rider complaints and suggestions improve the subway experience, or lead to further conflict? Or will music soothe the savage subway beast? Only time will tell, but one point is clear—music can be a means to reduce stress, calm fears, and even curb conflict.

Take Two Arias, and Call Me in the Morning

Music is a part of all of our lives. Beginning with our mother's heartbeat, we become accustomed to it. It lifts us when we're down, calms us when we're excited, moves us to tears, and gets us in the mood to eat, study, work, or make love. The right music at the right time brings a joy and serenity that can be acquired in no other way.

Medical studies have shown that music influences the respiratory rate, blood pressure, stomach contractions, and the level of stress hormones in the blood. The brain's electrical rhythm is altered, and the hypothalamus releases endorphins, the body's natural opiates. The heart rate synchronizes with music, speeding up or slowing down accordingly.

Music played before, during, and after surgery has been found to reduce anxiety, lessen pain, reduce the need for pre- and post-operative medication, and speed recovery. Patients in Japan listen to music before and after surgery to reduce stress hormones in the blood.

The two cases just presented illustrate that human resource professionals should consider using music as a cross-cultural conflict resolution tool. Music can calm, reorient, and motivate conflicting parties. Through the use of familiar music, an unfamiliar or seemingly hostile environment can be made to feel safe and secure, with the result that conversation and interaction are less threatening and more easily initiated.

There are other good reasons to use music. It meets with little or no intellectual resistance. It doesn't need to appeal to sound judgment to initiate action. It promotes social interaction. It removes barriers that often divide one person from another. It promotes a feeling of union among listeners. Sometimes when people are in conflict within themselves, music therapists employ music to calm the mentally ill. But music has broader applications as a conflict management strategy and should be considered as a means to reduce stress and conflict in the workplace.

Another area in which music can be helpful in conflict management is that of national anthems. Understanding and perhaps even singing the national anthem of an opposing country can help managers understand their opponents' point of view.

Human resource professionals can use music as a tool for reducing unhealthy cross-cultural conflict. Many conflict situations are created through miscommunication and misunderstanding. Music allows people to express feelings that they can't put into words. It can be used to discern the common ground as a starting point for discussion. Music is a means of expressing our unique cultural contribution to the human family.

Dance Therapy

Dance is another innovative training tool for cross-cultural conflict resolution. Dancing is easy, fun, and educational. Managers learn how to dance, how to see the world in a new way, how to coordinate themselves cross-culturally, and how to interact with people from diverse environments. It is also a great way to learn how to resolve cross-cultural conflicts. To develop dance programs, trainers should gain a general understanding of dance therapy and international folk dancing.

Dance therapy can provide innovative training techniques for human resource professionals who are interested in cross-cultural conflict resolution. A dance therapy program can help managers discover the source of their intercultural conflicts. Upon learning why the conflict occurred, managers can take steps to improve their cross-cultural interactions.

Trainers who are interested in dance therapy can contact the American Dance Therapy Association (2000 Century Plaza, Suite 180, Columbia, Maryland 21044; Telephone: 410-997-4040.)

International Folk Dancing

Dance therapy can be combined with international folk dancing to develop effective cross-cultural conflict resolution training programs. Folk dancing is a great way to have some fun and learn about other cultures at the same time. By watching folk dances, listening to international music, wearing ethnic clothing, and moving to the rhythm, managers begin to understand how other cultures see the world.

The dance movements are as varied and unique as the cultures that perform them. They can be merry and spontaneous or melancholy and measured. Often the movements are symbolic, representing nature, people, birds, and animals. Some of the movements are permeated with foreign influences, reflecting the cultures of invaders and conquerors.

Those who would demonstrate human resource leadership can develop training programs that include visits to ethnic dance performances, followed by a discussion of how dance relates to cross-cultural methods of conflict resolution. Training programs centered around folk dances from Africa or Eastern European countries, such as Russia, Poland, Hungary, and Czechoslovakia, would be especially interesting.

Business persons can learn a great deal about Japanese methods of conflict resolution by watching Japanese dance performances. Trainers should arrange for workshop participants to attend performances of one or more dance styles. Japanese dance is interesting, educating, and aesthetically pleasing. Workshop participants will have much to talk about afterwards.

The dance performances should be followed by discussion sessions. Trainers can portray conflict resolution as a form of dance. They can analyze the history and style of Japanese or some other country's dances, pointing out those characteristics that are present in other aspects of Japanese life: simplicity; economy of movement; a highly developed symbolism in the gestures; beauty in line and posture; harmonious sequencing; restraint of expression. Trainers can then ask participants to relate the dance performance to an American versus Japanese conflict that they have either been involved in or heard about. This should lead to a broader understanding of Japanese methods of conflict resolution.

Cross-cultural trainers can receive training in international folk dance at seminars and workshops held throughout the U.S.A. The Folk

Dance Federation of California (1020 B Street, Hayward, California 94541; Telephone: 510-581-6000) is a good resource. FDFC sponsors teacher training seminars each year, with college credit available for those who desire it. Their summer seminars and workshops normally last for a week to 10 days. The training programs are intense. Each program has a faculty of 8 or 10 international folk dance experts.

Art Therapy

In addition to music and dance, human resource professionals should consider using art to train managers on how to resolve cross-cultural conflicts. Art has a great power to alter emotions, relieve stress, and heal the body. The reduction of stress and the creative surroundings of an art studio can influence managers to try innovative cross-cultural problem-solving techniques.

Human resource professionals can contact the American Art Therapy Association for help in developing a training program.

If art, music, and dancing aren't appealing, trainers should try something else. They can organize walking tours through local ethnic grocery stores, and discuss cross-cultural conflict resolution as they stroll along. They can lead bicycle trips down the Baja peninsula, and conduct Latin American mediation programs around campfires on secluded beaches.

The point of this overview is that conflict between and among peoples of different cultural backgrounds can be prevented or reduced by innovative interventions. Even competitions in music/dance/art, just as in sports, are positive symbolic ways to involve people from differing cultures.

One way to better understand new arrivals, minorities, or ethnic groups is to mutually share cultural heritages. Recently, media reports told of a small, rural Michigan college where all 80 of the African-American students withdrew from that institution because of racial slurs and conflict with the majority white student body. Speculate how this unfortunate affair of minority harassment might have been countered if the student personnel services had invited these urban black collegians to produce a cultural festival of African art, music, and dance.

Creating Cultural Synergy

Cultural differences may sometimes exacerbate a situation and result in conflict. Obviously, it is better to capitalize on the differences and create cultural synergy that will minimize conflict and promote collaboration [4]. Apart from the conflict management techniques of human relations trainers, we have reviewed both traditional and innovative methods for reducing and resolving misunderstandings between and among persons, groups, and organizations. In creating cultural awareness and knowledge, human resource leaders would be well advised to learn about how conflict is dealt with in other cultures and how harmony is preserved among them.

References

1. Baggett, E., "Cross-Cultural Legal Counseling," *Creighton Law Review,* 1985, pp. 1475–1501.
2. Baxter, I. F., "International Business Disputes," *The International & Comparative Law Quarterly,* April 1990, pp. 288–299.
3. Breese, C. R., "Some Considerations for International Negotiating,"*International Law Practicum,* Spring 1990, pp.12–16.
4. Harris, P. R. and Moran, R. T., *Managing Cultural Differences,* Houston: Gulf Publishing, 1991.
5. Hillman, R. W., "Providing Effective Legal Representation in International Business Transactions," *The International Lawyer,* Winter 1985, pp. 3–28.
6. Kessler, J. B., "The Lawyer's Intercultural Communication Problems with Clients from Diverse Cultures," *Northwestern Journal of International Law & Business,* Spring 1988, pp. 64–79.
7. Kolkey, D. M., "Fora for the Resolution of International Business Disputes When Doing Business with the People's Republic of China," *Loyola of Los Angeles International and Comparative Law Journal,* December 1989, pp. 102–114.
8. Lecuyer, T., and Thieffry, C. P., "Negotiating Settlement of Disputes Provisions in International Business Contracts: Recent Developments in Arbitration and Other Processes," *The Business Lawyer,* February 1990, pp. 527–623.
9. Moran, R.T. and Stripp, W. G., *Dynamics of Successful International Business Negotiations,* Houston: Gulf Publishing, 1991.
10. Ribicoff, A., "Alternatives to Litigation: Their Application to International Business Disputes," *The Arbitration Journal,* December 1983, pp. 3–8.

11. Sams, J., "The Availability of the 'Cultural Defense' as an Excuse for Criminal Behavior," *Georgia Journal of International & Comparative Law,* 1986. Vol. 16, pp. 335–354.

12. Sandrock, O., "Arbitration between U.S. and West German Companies: An Example of Effective Dispute Resolution in International Business Transactions, " *University of Pennsylvania Journal of International Business Law,* Winter 1987, pp. 27–66.

13. Sherman, S., "When Cultures Collide," *California Lawyer,* January 1986, pp. 33–36, 60.

14. Sheybani, M.-M., "Cultural Defense: One Person's Culture Is Another's Crime," *Loyola Los Angeles International & Comparative Law Journal,* 1987. Vol. 9, pp. 751–783.

CHAPTER 5

CROSS-CULTURAL TECHNOLOGY TRANSFER

Introduction

Silvere Seurat, a French engineer and technology transfer consultant observed that [20]

- Technology transfer is the capacity to store and transmit to people the accumulated experience and understanding of others.
- Meticulous analysis of knowledge, skills, and perceptions that make for success in any task and operation must be combined with advanced methods of motivation and positive reinforcement to effect this transfer.
- The process also requires sensitive adjustment to different cultural and work values on the part of the transferee.
- The focus should be upon accelerated development of local managers and instructors, so dependence upon expatriates can be reduced.
- The transfer necessitates close linking with community educational systems, as well as assistance to their efforts in technical education.
- Early planning of human and managerial aspects of the project is preferable to "crash" programs—such planning should gradually introduce a systems approach that includes task analysis, organizational design, recruitment, training, control, feedback, and dynamic development.
- Competence in large-scale project management also must be supplemented by dedication to human development and cost effectiveness.

Universal Cultural Lag

American business people used to laugh over anecdotes about Asians who didn't know how to use American toilets. For example, many Laotian refugees in America were confused by sit-down, porcelain toi-

118

lets. They had never seen them before. Some of them began to use the toilets as wash basins. Others, who were informed of the toilet's function, would stand on the toilet seat, and squat down to urinate.

Many Americans laughed because the Laotians didn't know how to use a simple piece of technology. Now the situation is somewhat reversed. Americans have become the subject of toilet jokes in Japan, because they don't know how to use the new Japanese high-tech electronically controlled, all-in-one, toilet/bottom-washer/bidet. Both cases represent classic examples of "cultural lag."

Cultural lag results when one culture falls behind in the use of new technology. Technology comprises all useful knowledge. It includes all technical methods and devices for achieving any practical purpose. It is the totality of the means employed by mankind to provide the objects that are necessary for human sustenance and comfort. Technology encompasses systems of knowledge, such as civil engineering and financial accounting, and artifacts of civilization, such as toilets and computers.

Technology transfer occurs when people, information, and technical artifacts move from one culture to another. If a culture considers the new technology to be useful, then the technology will be adopted. This adoption may spur a process of modification and invention from which new technologies emerge.

The invention of new technologies has increased phenomenally in recent years. As a result, a universal cultural lag has developed. Not only is it impossible for individuals and businesses to keep up with all of the latest technological developments, it is impossible for nations to keep up.

Many people suffer from cyberphobia—fear of new technology—and need training to accept the changes inherent in technologies' adoption. The problems most users have in operating video recorders should prove the point. Furthermore, people, especially in less-developed nations, need training in maintenance and steps to follow when high-tech devices fail.

Balanced Technological Leadership

Many Americans fear that the United States is in a period of inexorable decline, because it doesn't dominate every technology in the world. Yet thousands of American firms, both big and small, dominate many critical technologies, including computer software and hardware of all types, microprocessor chips, aerospace, pharmaceuticals, biotechnology, new materials, energy, and environmental control.

It is no longer possible for any one nation to dominate every critical technology in the world. There is currently a balance in technological leadership among two nations and one region: the United States, Japan, and Europe. When the Japanese Economic Planning Agency surveyed 110 critical technologies in 1991, it concluded that American firms dominated 43 of them, Japanese firms dominated 33, and European and other miscellaneous firms dominated 34.

The conclusion of the Japanese survey is that America dominates more critical technologies than any other country or region. One of the reasons why America remains dominant in so many areas is its strong scientific community. The United States has more scientists and engineers, spends more money on scientific research, and publishes more scientific papers than Great Britain, France, Germany, and Japan put together.

At the same time, there is a serious decline in scientific and technical competency in American schools and their students. It may explain in part, the "brain drain" of scientific personnel from other countries to the U.S. making up for the deficiencies. The future may lie in the sharing among nations of both new technologies and the talents to apply them. Today, many Western nations are going to Russia not only to purchase or use their space technology, but to form joint ventures with emerging Russian companies so they may use the formidable talent of Russian engineers. To promote democratization within the Commonwealth of Independent States, Western investment is helping to underwrite scientific projects and personnel within these countries transitioning to the free enterprise system.

The need and value of transcultural technology exchanges may be appreciated in the following analysis of the Japanese.

The Japanese Approach to Technology Transfer

Japan recognizes the value of American scientific research and has taken steps to gain access to it. One method the Japanese use is the systematic farming of the wide-open American university system. American universities provide Japanese corporations with new technology for a fraction of what it would cost the Japanese if they had to develop it from scratch. As a result, American politicians are beginning to complain that American taxpayers are subsidizing Japanese industry.

Japanese initiative in scouring the American university system for new ideas is representative of its strategic approach to technology transfer:

1. The Japanese view technology transfer as a strategic weapon.

2. The Japanese government predicts what technologies will be the most valuable in the future, and suggests technology development strategies to corporations.

3. Japanese personnel policies, such as lifetime employment, a relatively flat compensation structure, and bonuses tied to corporate financial performance, are aimed at encouraging a strong sense of loyalty and cooperation among employees. This promotes internal technology acquisition and transfer between various functional areas.

4. Japanese managers are trained in all aspects of the business. Promotions are based upon seniority, the ability to work with others, and demonstrated technical competence. These qualities are of great help in implementing effective technology transfers.

5. Japanese companies use experienced "executive technologists" to act as internal consultants and business developers. They give reports on new technologies to groups of executives from the various functional areas. The reports are a strong influence on the future direction of the company.

6. Management ensures that communication occurs by giving executive technologists access to substantial resources.

7. The Japanese feel that direct person-to-person contact is the most effective means of transferring technology. The Japanese make extensive use of face-to-face meetings. They also frequently move people from research & development to other organizational units.

8. Employees are not punished for failure. Instead, failure is viewed as an opportunity to learn.

9. Japanese companies carefully control the movement of new technology through the product development chain. Manufacturing processes are only changed to improve quality. Changes are only made after consulting knowledgeable people within the organization.

Gaining Access to Japanese Technology

While Japan is quick to take new ideas from America, it is slow in giving other countries access to its new technology. One reason for this is the complexity of the Japanese language. A recent study estimates that fewer than 1,000 American scientists are fluent in Japanese.

Another reason for the inaccessibility of Japanese technology is the closed nature of the Japanese university system. The big national Japanese universities that have reputations for research are part of the Japanese civil service and do not admit foreigners as faculty members. As a result, more than ten times as many Japanese scientists leave Japan to teach and study in American universities, than vice versa.

Research departments in Japanese corporations are also tight-lipped. Although many Japanese firms send staff overseas to pick up expertise at the research departments of foreign companies, few foreigners are allowed to penetrate the laboratories of Japanese corporations.

The American government has been taking suggestions on how it can help American corporations gain access to Japanese technology. Dr. Christopher Hill of the United States Congressional Research Service recommends the following:

1. Japan publishes approximately 10,000 technical journals. The American government should subscribe to every one of them. This program would cost approximately $1 million per year.
2. All Japanese technical journals should be translated into English. The cost of this program is approximately $80 million per year. (Unfortunately, America presently does not have enough translators to do this.) The journals could then be made accessible to American corporations.
3. The American government should send 2 engineers in each of 20 specialties to visit 5 locations abroad. They will be required to publish reports of their observations. The cost of this program is approximately $2 million per year.
4. The American government should send 100 researchers to Japanese universities and labs. They will be required to publish reports of their observations. The cost of this program is approximately $5 million per year.
5. The American government should give tax credits for Japanese translation services and Japanese consultants. This program would cost approximately $50 million per year.

6. The American government should set up 10 automatic Japanese-to-English translation research programs. The cost of these programs would be approximately $10 million per year.

Strategies for Acquiring Foreign Technology

American corporations are beginning to press the American government to adopt proposals such as those suggested by Dr. Hill. However, corporations realize that they cannot afford to wait for the government to act. They must move quickly to develop their own strategies for obtaining new technology.

To remain competitive in the expanding global market for hi-tech products, American corporations must gain access to foreign technology. The quickest way to do this is through international technology transfer agreements. There are many types of technology transfer agreements, but the most popular fall under the heading of "strategic alliances."

Strategic alliances are partnerships between firms that work together under a cooperative agreement to attain some strategic objective. Corporations that want to gain access to advanced technology are often well-advised to enter into an alliance to offset the immense expense that research and development entails. Allies share costs, establish a pool of joint resources, and create a synergistic effect in the problem-solving process.

The success of an alliance depends upon the compatibility of the partners. A company must take the time to find a partner with a cooperative business philosophy, a complementary mission, compatible managerial capabilities, and the resources necessary to acquire and develop new technology.

A checklist for establishing such a strategic alliance would include the following steps:

1. Choose your partner carefully.

- Research the company thoroughly.
- Make sure that you have the same goals.
- Make sure that your technological capabilities match up.
- Understand cultural, corporate, and legal differences.
- Tailor the agreement to meet your objectives.

2. Make a long-term commitment.

- Design agreements for long-term flexibility.
- Invest in human capital.
- Be patient, avoid shortcuts.
- Get experienced help to handle business and legal details.

3. Set market-oriented objectives.

- Focus on the market, not the money.
- Establish clear and explicit objectives.
- Let the venture fail if it doesn't meet objectives.

4. Keep control of your technology.

- Minimize the risk of theft, but assume that it will happen anyway.
- Control the evolution of your technology.
- Strengthen your position on intellectual property protection.
- Control the marketing of your technology.

In developing alliance strategy, the partners must avoid "niche collision." Alliance members may be involved in other partnerships that are conducting business in the same or similar markets. This puts corporations in the position of both cooperating with and competing against their partners. It also increases the risk that a partner will use information gained through the alliance to betray the partnership.

To avoid potential losses, corporations should consider strategic alliances to be a new form of competition. The objective is to gain a form of strategic synergy where the corporation gains the benefits of cooperation without forgetting that the partner is an actual or potential competitor.

One scholar advises corporations to run the alliance like a marriage. A corporation must find a "dancing partner" who can complement the corporation's technology acquisition strategy. If the partners "marry," they must create a nurturing environment or risk a messy "divorce." Offspring of the alliance, such as a joint venture, need as much attention and support as a baby.

Alliances face many barriers to success, ranging from antitrust laws to cultural attitudes. One major problem area is the difficulty that many firms have in giving up total control. The alliance board must clearly establish which managers have the authority to make decisions. Once decision-making authority has been granted, alliance management must decide who has access to information, who has the authorization to release plans and specifications, and who will get new products which are released from the manufacturing division.

Selecting alliance representatives is another critical problem area. Human resource professionals must give careful attention to evaluating and selecting potential candidates. The alliance board members must be functionally matched to the mission and be willing to support it. Project managers must be willing to share selected expertise and organizational resources. Team members must be willing to cooperate in joint R&D efforts. Generally, there must be total commitment to a true team effort.

The changing interests of alliance members may also create problems. The life of the partnership depends upon the ability of members to sustain their commitment because of mutuality of interest. Partners will leave if they lose interest or the venture appears unsuccessful. A corporation must be sure that a potential partner will remain interested in the alliance or be prepared to go through a costly divorce.

The biggest internal struggle in an alliance is the conflict between corporate cultures. Cultural chemistry is the most important factor in the endurance of the alliance. Cultural incompatibility can lead to complete shutdown of partnership operations. The partners must be willing to create an "alliance culture" while retaining their corporate identities.

Identifying Corporate Culture

Whether a strategic alliance is being formed with a domestic or international partner, the issue of organizational culture must be addressed. Before the human resource department can work on plans for developing an alliance culture with strategic partners, it must identify its own corporate culture. Corporate culture is derived from the cultural problem-solving maps that managers use in attempting to run a company, and the actual experiences that people in the company have had in resolving problems. Corporate culture arises from the interaction of old cultural maps with new learning experiences.

To identify corporate culture, the human resource department must perform an internal audit. The auditors should identify the values and problem-solving methods of owners, managers, and employees. Attention should also be paid to the following variables: corporate decision-making systems, organizational structure, formal procedures, reward systems, compliance with organizational requirements, regulation and control processes, the accuracy of communication, the makeup and support of dominant coalitions, and responsiveness to change.

The internal audit will result in an outline of the corporate cultural philosophy. Companies involved in world trade and investment have four cultural philosophies: ethnocentrism, polycentrism, regiocentrism, and geocentrism. Each philosophy can be linked to an organizational type and a strategic process:

Cultural Perspective	Type of Company	Strategic Process
Ethnocentric	International	Internationalization
Polycentric	Multinational	Multinationalization
Regiocentric	Multiregional	Transnationalization
Geocentric	Global	Globalization

Human resource professionals should use these descriptions to identify the corporation's cultural philosophy.

Ethnocentric Corporations

These corporations are home-country oriented. Ethnocentric managers believe that home-country nationals are more intelligent, reliable, and trustworthy than foreign nationals. All key management positions are centered at the domestic headquarters. Home-country nationals are recruited and trained for all international positions. Foreign managers and employees are second-class corporate citizens. When rewards are distributed, home-country nationals receive the lion's share.

The ethnocentric approach is fostered by many internal and external influences. The CEO may be limited by the biases of the owners and stockholders. Labor unions may impose intense pressure in favor of domestic employment. Home government policy may force emphasis on the domestic market.

The ethnocentric philosophy is exhibited in many international companies. The standard international company finds great difficulty in communicating in different languages and in accepting cultural differences. International strategic alternatives are limited to entry modes such as exporting, licensing, and turnkey operations because "it works at home and will work overseas."

Polycentric Corporations

These corporations are host-country oriented. Profit potential is seen in a foreign country, but the foreign market is too hard to understand. The polycentric firm establishes multinational operations on condition that host-country managers "do it their way." The polycentric message is: "Local people know what is best for them. Let's give them some money and leave them alone as long as they make us a profit."

The polycentric firm is a loosely connected group with quasi-independent subsidiaries as profit centers. Headquarters is manned by home-country nationals, while local nationals occupy the key positions in their respective local subsidiaries. Host-country nationals have high or absolute sovereignty over the subsidiary's operations. There is no direction from headquarters and the only controls are financially oriented. No foreign national can seriously aspire to a senior position at headquarters.

The polycentric approach often results from great external pressures. Foreign laws may require managers to be citizens of the host-country. Engineering standards may have to be determined locally. The host-country government may be a major customer and force emphasis on local ways of doing business.

The polycentric philosophy is often exhibited in multinational corporations. MNCs face a heterogeneous environment where product needs and preferences are diverse. In addition, governmental restrictions may be severe. Strategically, the MNC competes on a market-by-market basis because it believes that "local people know what is best for them."

Regiocentric Corporations

These corporations capitalize on the synergistic benefits of sharing common functions across regions. A regiocentric corporation believes that only regional insiders can effectively coordinate functions within the region. For example, a regiocentric organization might select a Japanese subsidiary to manage its Asian operations and a French subsidiary to manage its European operations. The regiocentric message is: "Regional insiders know what neighboring countries want."

The regiocentric firm is highly interdependent on a regional basis. Regional headquarters organize collaborative efforts among local subsidiaries. The regional headquarters is responsible for the regional plan, local research and development, product innovation, cash management, local executive selection and training, capital expenditure plans, brand policy, and public relations. The world headquarters takes care of world strategy, country analysis, basic research and development, foreign exchange, transfer pricing, intercompany loans, long-term financing, selection of top management, technology transfer, and establishing corporate culture.

Geocentric Corporations

World-oriented, a geocentric corporation's ultimate goal is creation of an integrated system with a worldwide approach. The geocentric system is highly interdependent. Subsidiaries are no longer satellites and independent city-states. The entire organization is focused on both worldwide and local objectives. Every part of the organization makes a unique contribution using its unique competencies. The geocentric message is: "All for one and one for all. We will work together to solve problems anywhere in the world."

Geocentrism requires collaboration between headquarters and subsidiaries to establish universal standards with permissible local variations. Diverse regions are integrated through a global systems approach to decision-making. Good ideas come from and flow to any country. Resources are allocated on a global basis. Geographical lines are erased and functional and product lines are globalized.

Within legal and political limits, the best people are sought to solve problems. Competence is what counts, not national origin. The reward system motivates managers to surrender national biases and work for worldwide objectives.

The geocentric firm overcomes political barriers by turning its subsidiaries into good citizens of the host nations. It is hoped that the subsidiary will become a leading exporter from the host to the international community. Furthermore, the geocentric organization will provide base countries with an increasing supply of hard currency, new skills, and a knowledge of advanced technology.

Technology Transfer Training Programs

The human resource department must develop training programs that match the corporation's cultural philosophy. If a training program violates the corporation's culture, it will fail. Employees have been known to resist and actually sabotage operational changes that are opposed to traditional ways of conducting business.

If the internal audit shows that corporate culture will impede the acquisition of new technology, then trainers must develop programs that will help change the culture. Change will not occur by sending someone to school, hiring new staff, or acquiring new businesses. Even inspirational speeches by the CEO won't work. Change must be backed up by building new structures, creating new role models, and doling out rewards and punishments.

The human resource department's task is to develop and maintain a culture that (1) promotes and sustains efficient performance of the highest quality and quantity; (2) fosters and uses creativity; (3) stimulates enthusiasm for effort, experimentation, innovation, and change; (4) takes advantage of interaction situations; and (5) looks for and finds new challenges.

To help manage necessary changes, trainers should remember to follow certain broad maxims. First, recognize that managers and employees will be more willing to accept change if they are included in the decision-making process. Second, establish open communications to reinforce trust that will be shaken by the change. Third, provide training and counseling for managers and employees who don't have the required skills and abilities to carry out the new plans. Fourth, allow enough time for the change to take hold. Fifth, emphasize that the purpose of the change is to implement a new strategic vision.

Technology Transfer Training in International Companies

International companies are engaged in a wide range of global business activities, including exporting, licensing, franchising, manufacturer's contracts, technical agreements, turnkey operations, and joint ventures. All of these activities are consistent with an ethnocentric cultural philosophy, i.e., "it works at home and will work overseas."

Most American international companies do not prepare their executives for cultural differences that will be encountered overseas. International executives are chosen for technical proficiency, rather than language skills or cultural knowledge.

An international company's training department tries to teach foreign associates to operate as much like a domestic corporation as possible. Typically, this is accomplished by shipping domestic training programs overseas without making any changes in content or delivery. Sometimes, materials are not even translated into foreign languages.

Training departments in international companies often use behavior modeling as a large part of the training program. The idea is that by modeling existing domestic practices, foreign associates will be able to perform just like their more experienced American brethren.

Transferring Ethnocentric Accounting Systems

Technology encompasses both "hard" artifacts, such as computer disk drives, and "soft" systems, such as financial accounting. International companies often want to apply soft technology from the home-country throughout their international operations. One of the most important home-country technologies is the national accounting system. Accounting controls are a virtual necessity for the effective operation of large international corporations. They are used to measure performance, keep track of taxes, etc.

Cosmopolitan executives need to recognize also that American accounting systems

1. Suffer from culture lag—practices established for the industrial organization are often inadequate for the metaindustrial environment with the emphasis on high technology business. For example, we now live in an information society where knowledge is the new wealth. Traditional accounting principles treat intellectual property as intangible and invisible—thus, the balance sheet of IBM does not reflect the value of its 30,000 patents.

2. Under-utilize human resource accounting systems that place a capital value on personnel that is equal or more than buildings and equipment [6]. When employees go away for specialized training, accountants treat this as an expense, rather than capitalizing a human asset. Until intellectual and human assets are properly valued on the organizational balance sheet, global competitiveness is undermined and the conventional financial reporting is unreal.

American accountants have developed standardized accounting practices. These practices often conflict with foreign laws regulating financial reporting and bookkeeping. As a result, international implementation of American accounting techniques may require revisions of foreign law. This is a significant barrier to change.

There are also cultural barriers to change. Accounting systems are ethnocentric. They are based on cultural assumptions about human behavior and managerial goals. For example, American managerial accounting techniques, such as responsibility accounting, are based on the assumption that the desire for personal achievement and advancement will push employees to accept increased amounts of individual discretion and responsibility. However, in highly paternalistic business environments, such as the Middle East, the inherently competitive aspects of decentralization and responsibility accounting are undesirable. Advancement requires employees to risk the loss of a part or all of what they have gained. Employees may not want additional responsibilities at the price of possible failure.

Accountants are conditioned to respond to problems by following a nationally determined program. American accountants develop an instinctive ability to evaluate the "quality" of the reported earnings of American corporations, but lack the perception to view the statements of foreign companies with equal acuity. Similarly, while the cost accounting system of a manufacturer in a developing country may be antiquated or inaccurate by American standards, the foreign manufacturer may feel that it is a comfortable and effective system. Introduction of a new system may involve a painful relearning process.

Another barrier is that many accounting skills can only be taught through direct face-to-face interaction between student and teacher. This makes international training difficult. Language is also a problem. Accounting terminology is difficult to translate, not only because many languages lack an accounting vocabulary, but more importantly, because accounting terminology is a type of shorthand for complex concepts. Translations must be made by a person who is fluent in both languages and in the accounting skills of both countries. Such translations are extremely time-consuming. By the time a translation is complete, the accounting concepts may be outmoded.

Due to difficulties in transferring technology that is inherently ethnocentric, many international companies rely upon international service firms for assistance. For example, large international accounting firms, such as Price Waterhouse, are the most effective vehicle for the transfer of American accounting skills to other countries.

Technology Transfer Training in
Multinational Corporations

Multinationalization is most appropriate in industries that are "country-based" by nature. Typically, a business in a country-based or multi-domestic industry faces a heterogeneous environment, lacks economies of scale, produces products that differ greatly among country markets, must pay high transportation costs, and doesn't have high internal resources. Examples of multi-domestic industries include retailing, consumer goods, hazardous chemicals, and metal fabrication.

Corporations become multinational for many reasons, including to adopt their products to local demands, avoid high storage and transportation costs, borrow at low interest rates, and reduce total corporate tax liability. Another major reason that a corporation becomes multinational is to monitor and gain access to foreign technological developments.

Most multinational corporations exhibit a polycentric cultural philosophy. An MNC's headquarters is manned by home-country nationals, while host-country nationals occupy key positions in their respective local subsidiaries. There is no direction from headquarters, and the only controls are financially oriented.

The natural tendency of an MNC's human resource department is to leave the foreign subsidiary alone. However, to keep track of new foreign technology the human resource department must develop a mechanism for monitoring the subsidiaries' R&D, engineering, and manufacturing departments. One of the best ways to do this is with a team of "cross-cultural interfacers."

The multinational headquarters recognizes that subsidiaries are culturally distinct. Host-country people solve problems differently than home-country people. They communicate differently. They have different attitudes and values. These cultural differences impede communication, which is required for technology to be properly transferred.

The human resource department must make sure that communications between headquarters and the subsidiaries are open, so that the internal flow of technology is not dammed up. "Cross-cultural interface management" is an effective way for multinational corporations to monitor developments of foreign technology.

Cross-Cultural Interface Management: An HRD Checklist

The following will help HR professionals better manage the human resource dimensions of technology transfer:

1. The human resource department is in charge of cross-cultural interface management. It must begin planning interface requirements early. Potential problems and solutions should be predicted and prepared for.
2. The human resource department should identify "cross-cultural interfacers" for the various functional groups. The department must assess the importance of the interfacers to the overall success of the technology transfer process.
3. Human resource personnel should meet with cross-cultural interfacers and make certain that they are well-informed about cultural differences.
4. The human resource department should prepare cross-cultural interface documents, including charts, checklists, schedules, and checkpoints. Tickler files should be set up to remind cross-cultural interfacers of important goals and dates.
5. All cross-cultural interfacers should be aware of all recent technological developments.
6. Human resource personnel should coordinate cross-cultural interfacing and check on its progress. This can be done by telephone. Meetings should be saved for key transition points.
7. The human resource department should only ask cross-cultural interfacers to keep records when it is important.
8. Cross-cultural interfacers should be required to be organized and have a consistent plan.
9. When cross-cultural interfacing problems arise, the human resource department should act rapidly and positively.

Attributes of an Ideal Cross-Cultural Facilitator

The best way to interface is to use people, not paper. The human resource department should appoint cross-cultural facilitators who will help integrate the functional areas by making bridges between different project groups.

Cross-cultural interfacers must be people oriented. An interfacer should be

- Well respected in the organization.
- Sensitive to the needs of others.
- Able to get people involved.
- A diplomatic salesperson.
- Assertive, rather than aggressive.
- Open to input from others.
- Skillful in human relations.

Functions of a Cross-Cultural Facilitator

Cross-cultural interfacers have a variety of functions to fulfill. They should be able to

- Establish clear and specific objectives for themselves and other interfacers.
- Establish an overview of both technical and nontechnical requirements for success of the project.
- Understand the capabilities, problems, and limitations of other interfacers in the organization.
- Maintain consistency in interfacing.
- Establish a regular awareness program to cover new developments.
- Develop sensitivity to weak interfaces.

International/Multinational Case Studies

McDonald's Two-Tiered Training Approach

McDonald's Corporation has been following a strategy of international expansion, that is, from McDonald's to McParis to McMoscow to McWorld. It currently has franchises in more than 50 countries. About 3,000 of its 12,000 restaurants are based outside the United States.

McDonald's is based upon Ray Kroc's simple creed of "QSC&V" (Quality, Service, Cleanliness, & Value). Every restaurant is required to become infused with McDonald's gung-ho culture and standardized procedures. Franchises that don't measure up are eliminated. Legend has it that Kroc eliminated a Winnipeg franchise after finding a single fly in their restaurant.

To ensure that franchises do things the McDonald's Way, the human resource department has developed a rigid management system. Rules are meticulously detailed in phonebook-like operating manuals, covering everything from how to clean bathrooms to the temperature of grease to fry potatoes. This approach has led one well-known management professor to accuse McDonald's of being "rules bound." He contends that McDonald's jobs are for the robots of yesterday, not the hi-tech leaders of tomorrow.

McDonald's definitely follows an ethnocentric approach in its international operations, i.e., "it works at home and will work overseas." However, it has faced great difficulties in international technology transfer. For example, McDonald's worked hard to maintain product consistency in Thailand, where farmers had to be taught to cultivate Idaho Russet potatoes. In Russia, McDonald's is building huge food processing plants, teaching Russians efficient food preparation, working with farmers to produce American-quality potatoes and beef, and setting up a huge distribution and supply network.

To accomplish international technology transfer, McDonald's human resource department follows a two-tiered training approach. The first tier is similar to what we have described as the international behavior modeling approach; the second tier is similar to the multinational cross-cultural interfacer approach:

Philosophy	Training Technique
Tier One: International/Ethnocentric	Behavior Modeling
Tier Two: Multinational/Polycentric	Interfacing

The first tier of McDonald's training system encourages international franchises to follow the American model. Each foreign operator is brought to one of McDonald's Hamburger Universities. The main campus is in Oak Brook, Illinois, but there are also campuses in Japan, Germany, Britain, and Russia.

Managers are brought to the various Hamburger Universities "to get catsup in their veins." An independent training department runs the program in Oak Brook, but human resource managers teach courses, devise curriculum improvements, and informally mix with international employees who are attending classes. After learning that "the secret to success isn't a milkshake, but a handshake," managers are granted a Bachelor of Hamburgerology degree.

The second tier of McDonald's training program is similar to cross-cultural interface management. McDonald's has five international personnel directors who work as traveling internal consultants. Each of the directors routinely spends 100 days or more abroad each year.

The international personnel directors keep foreign directors informed of McDonald's current status in several areas of human resource management, including international pay ranges, benefits, bonuses, stock option plans, performance review techniques, and employee incentive innovations. They also help foreign directors solve specific human resource problems that are impeding operations. Sometimes this requires the international directors to remain in a foreign location for several weeks or months.

Technology Transfer Training in Multiregional Companies

The development of economic blocs, such as the European Community and the proposed North American Common Market, has induced many corporations to look at regional strategies. This involves the use of regional strongholds to concentrate on markets within various blocs. Regional headquarters control local subsidiaries and collaborate with other regions to attain broad objectives.

A multiregional company (MRC) can be viewed as a natural step in the evolution of the multinational company. The MRC recognizes the commonalities of regions and the uniqueness of key marketplaces. It creates several regional headquarters and allocates global resources based upon perceived opportunities and threats. Regional headquarters share various functions to gain a synergistic advantage over competitors' quality and cost positions.

The MRC's human resource department must expose managers to regional issues. Training should be for both mid-level managers and senior managers. Seminars are most valuable when they concentrate on how regional issues affect the corporation.

Human resource professionals should draw on the expertise within the corporate strategic planning department and legal department to design the structure of the training seminar. A series of short seminars should be developed to concentrate on specific threats and opportunities that face the corporation.

A model training program is presented in Exhibit 5-1.

Exhibit 5-1
Keeping Managers Up To Date On Regional Issues:
A Model Training Program for the European Community (EC)

1. Begin the seminar with an overview of the importance of the European Community.
   - Point out that the EC represents a single market of 320 million consumers with a combined gross domestic product of nearly 5 trillion dollars.
   - Mention that the driving force behind the decision to formulate the EC was the realization that without the economies of scale that the larger market offers, western Europe would not prosper in a global economy.
2. Review the history of the European integration.
   - Evaluate the probability of success of the EC.
   - Assess the likelihood of the EC expanding to the east, to the north, and into the center of Europe.
   - Describe how your company can strategically place itself in the path of the EC as it expands.
3. Present a broad analysis of the threats and opportunities which the EC presents to your company.
4. Analyze your competitors' strategies for adapting to the EC.
5. Assess the impact of the EC on your primary customers.
6. Discuss how your company can best take advantage of opportunities and avoid threats in the new European market.
   - Assess your existing operations and exports to Europe. For example, ask: What is our exposure in Europe? Are our operations viable in face of the new European competition? Are we capable of assigning additional resources to further develop our European operations?
   - Discuss the "Europeanization" of your operations. For example, ask: Is our product/service marketed on a regional basis or country-by-country? Can we consolidate our country-oriented marketing, manufacturing, and distribution from a central European location? Are our information and telecommunications systems adapted to European operations? Can we take advantage of lower wage structures in eastern or southern Europe?
   - Discuss the potential expansion or contraction of your European operations. For example, ask: Should we expand our European operations through acquisition or internal growth? Should we seek European partners through merger or strategic alliance?

3M's Regional Training Approach

In February 1988, 3M started to set up a training team to help managers get ready to do business in the EC in 1992. 3M created European Management Action Teams (EMATs) for each of its 40 major product lines. Each EMAT was chaired by a product manager and made up of representatives from the "big four" countries in Europe (Germany, France, England, and Italy) as well as smaller European countries. When necessary, the groups called on experts from the manufacturing, technical, and finance functions.

Each EMAT had a mission, a charter, and a set membership. They were expected to help 3M become a more informal, flexible, and faster-reacting organization. The purpose was to boost product lines by sharing resources.

Training began in 1986. All 3M senior executives worldwide, along with the EMAT team leaders, participated in a communication course. All EMAT team members in Europe completed training on team development.

The training was ineffective. Senior managers in national subsidiaries worried about loss of power and influence. EMAT team leaders were given responsibility without the authority to push through decisions. Team members were uncomfortable with the reward system because it was still based upon the performance of individual subsidiaries.

Training had been mismatched to the challenge. The EMATs had been asked to help 3M increase its global success by becoming more responsive to individual markets. However, 3M's training was generic (more suited for ethnocentric-international trade.) Training had been given to EMAT members themselves, but not to the top managers who were expected to support their teams' efforts. Top managers were included only in regional communications training.

3M renamed the training program, "Leadership for Growth." The program brought together about 350 managers from 3M's European operations for two different rounds of training in 1989 and 1990.

The first sessions concentrated on personal change. In pre-session assignments, participants were encouraged to list the changes and difficulties they were experiencing in their jobs. One of the assignments asked them to list one example of how the organization was operating in the old way and another example to illustrate how it was starting to operate in a more regional way. The training also included a module on communicating with subordinates and bosses.

The second round of training focused on European business conditions. Some of it was informational, with experts relating what was happening in the marketplace. Most of the training was focused on discussing the company's mission and business strategies. As conflicts arose during those discussions, trainers asked participants to practice ways of resolving conflicts in group meetings. There were also modules on problem-solving and visioning.

To prepare the training program, 3M created a new position, manager of human resource development for 3M Europe. The new manager was based in 3M's Brussels office. Once he was in place, 3M deliberately avoided installing a strong American presence on the team; nor did the company assign a preponderance of English-speaking British trainers to the team. All the national 3M companies represented by the EMATs were urged to nominate possible team members. The final design team membership was German, Dutch, French, British and American, with seven more Europeans on the larger delivery team.

The design team members asked managers throughout Europe for their advice and recommendations for the training. This was not simply politically expedient. To adequately customize the program and make it pertinent to local needs, they had to ask questions at the local level.

During the design of the program, the key word was fluidity. In program delivery, team members made a point of mixing things up so that each team member worked with every other team member. It also used a Delphi process to combine individual work, input from international conference calls, and group meetings.

The first training sessions were held in January 1989. Trainers reported uniformly great sessions. Participants said they gained a sharper understanding of EMAT roles and responsibilities. Support from their managers increased and integration of teams in day-to-day operations improved.

Technology Transfer Training in Global Corporations

Globalization is most appropriate for industries that can gain significant benefits from worldwide volume in terms of reduced unit costs or increased reputation. Examples of such industries include automobiles, steel, chemicals, petroleum, cement, agricultural commodities and equipment, industrial and commercial construction, banking and insurance services, computers, semiconductors, publishing, transport, electronic instruments, pharmaceuticals, and telecommunications.

The global corporation operates as if the entire world is a single entity. It emphasizes global operations over the domestic market. It selects the best people available for management, regardless of nationality. It locates corporate headquarters anywhere in the world.

Training programs in global corporations are generally homogenous. The human resource department strives to develop global standards and practices. Training is designed to help the entire organization operate with one voice. By creating programs that are as applicable for people in Madrid as in Minneapolis, the organization gets the uniformity it prizes and gets more bang for its buck in the development process.

HRD departments in a global company spend much time and energy creating programs that translate well across borders. Foreign subsidiaries inform the central HRD department about training needs. Then a team tries to build a uniform training approach. Usually this means that the content stays the same no matter where it goes. Changes are mostly in language, location, and styles of clothing worn by trainers.

One of the most important functions of the human resource department is to develop a global corporate culture. International management consultant Stephen Rhinesmith [17] states that correct strategy formulation only accounts for 20% of globalization success. The other 80% lies in strategy implementation. To implement a globalization strategy, corporations must develop a global corporate culture. Rhinesmith says for a corporation to "go global" it must

1. Formulate a clear and simple mission statement. For example, the IBM corporation as a whole concentrates on 4 goals (profit, quality, efficiency, and growth). The IBM Human Resource Department is guided by 3 basic beliefs (attract, motivate, and recruit the best talent).
2. Have the systems and structures in place to ensure effective flow of information. These include cross-functional and cross-unit coordination councils; global, functional, and corporate meetings and conferences; global task forces and integrators; and clear decision-making criteria and information flows.
3. Create "matrix minds" to facilitate conflict management. Matrix minds are created by sending executives overseas on temporary

assignments of one to two years. This broadens corporate thinking and facilitates corporate decision-making.

4. Develop global career paths. The corporation must clearly communicate its values and tie those values to corporate promotion criteria. For example, Philips, the Dutch-based electronics giant, uses four criteria as the basis for assessing executive potential: (1) conceptual effectiveness (vision, synthesis, professional knowledge, business directedness);(2) operational effectiveness (individual effectiveness, decisiveness, and control); (3) interpersonal effectiveness (network directedness, negotiating power, personal influence, and verbal behavior); (4) achievement motivation (ambition, professional interest, and emotional control).

5. Use cultural differences among employees and markets for global competitive advantage. For example, Philips moved its technology center from the United States, where managers have a predominantly short-range strategic view, to the Far East, where managers have a long-range view; its R&D center to Italy, where the loose, free-flowing Italian approach to management allows for more creativity; and its manufacturing operations to Germany.

6. Implement worldwide management education and team development programs. Corporate global training programs must be used to establish corporate identity and image with employees, just as corporate advertising campaigns are used with customers. In global corporate training, a company selects a major value or competency and periodically trains its top 2,000 managers in internationally integrated groups of 20 to 40 people.

Before a corporation can globalize, management must acquire a geocentric view. To assist management in acquiring such a global mindset, the training department must develop programs that override national and cultural differences. This is not an easy task. People are reluctant to learn new problem-solving skills when they already have cultural maps that have proven effective in their local environments. Inexperience, mutual distrust, nationalistic tendencies, and immobility of top managers all play a part in impeding the development of a geocentric perspective.

Human resource professionals can use transition rituals to broaden middle managers' strategic vision to a geocentric perspective. Within this process, managers and employees mourn the passage of old ways and re-negotiate new values and relationships. This can help middle managers understand, accept and believe in the geocentric philosophy.

Human resource managers must emphasize that geocentrism requires total commitment by owners, managers, and employees. The greatest responsibility falls on the shoulders of the CEO who must visit as many markets and subsidiaries as possible. The CEO cannot go on whirlwind tours, but must have detailed meetings with middle managers, customers and government officials.

One of the CEO's primary tasks on the road is to assure each country's management team that they can meet the challenges of globalization and that they will be rewarded for doing so. The subsidiaries must make sure that the information given to the CEO does not reflect national bias. For globalization to work, the CEO must keep posted on critical world events and continually monitor subsidiary understanding of social, political, and economic objectives in the host countries.

This "globetrotting" often involves a brutal schedule that can take a heavy toll on the CEO's family life and personal health. The human resource department should offer counseling services to the CEO's family to explain the importance of the travel and present mechanisms for coping with the long absences. Cross-cultural trainers should also recommend a schedule of physical exercise for CEOs, so that their health doesn't deteriorate during the trips abroad. HRD professional should encourage wellness or fitness strategies suitable to global managers.

Technology Transfer in the People's Republic of China—A Case Study

The myth of the China market has been intriguing Western business persons for over 200 years. In the 18th and 19th centuries, English textile manufacturers believed that they could make enormous profits by convincing everyone in China to lengthen their shirttails by a few inches. There were so many Chinese that this simple change in fashion would result in the sale of enormous quantities of English linen. The plan didn't work.

In more recent times, American business persons began to look at China as "two billion armpits waiting for deodorant." If the Chinese could be convinced to use American deodorants, enormous profits could be made. The Chinese remain unconvinced.

Many American corporations tried to penetrate the Chinese market during the 1980s. They faced an extremely difficult task. Business persons were required to travel to China, where living conditions are very severe. Travel was arduous. Expenses were high. Negotiations were long and drawn out, and the Chinese played foreign corporations off against each other.

Those business persons who didn't get contracts often left China with a bad taste in their mouths. Corporations that did get contracts experienced higher rates of expatriate failure than in other areas of the world. After the Tianamen Square incident in 1989, many of the unsuccessful business persons and drop-out expatriates labeled China as a dangerous snakepit that should be avoided at all costs. Other business persons began to listen.

Nevertheless, the fact remains that China offers many companies a potential billion-dollar market and significant opportunities for foreign investment. The value of American high technology exports to China increased from $144 million in 1982 to $1.7 billion in 1991. Increasing numbers of American companies are interested in exploring opportunities for sales and investment in high technology businesses in China.

We will focus on China, because it exemplifies the problems that human resource professionals may run into while developing training programs on cross-cultural technology transfer. We will look at two areas. First, we will present training recommendations for expatriates, who will be required to live and work in China during the technology transfer process. Second, we will explore technology transfer training programs for Chinese workers.

Expatriate Experiences in China

Many American expatriates in China return home before their assignments are completed. One of the main reasons for expatriate failure is a lack of pre-departure training. Most business persons are unprepared for and ill-advised about the harshness of the Chinese environment.

If the corporation is willing to spend enough money, housing is not a problem. For several thousand dollars a month, expatriates can arrange for an apartment or hotel room. However, there is a serious lack of privacy. Many Chinese feel free to enter expatriates' bedrooms without knocking and use their personal belongings without asking.

Also, the cleanliness of rooms leaves much to be desired. One expatriate stated, "Anyone who is at all fussy about food and cleanliness of restaurants, hotels, and toilets should not consider a China assignment."

There is also a serious lack of activities and entertainment after working hours. Many expatriates take assignments to China with the hope that they will get to do some traveling both inside the country and around Asia. Unfortunately, making travel arrangements in China is extremely difficult. Flight schedules are inconsistent and confirmed tickets are often invalidated without explanation.

The lack of outside activities leaves expatriates with a lot of time to devote to work. This extra time is often necessary. Many expatriates cannot speak Chinese, so every small task takes longer than usual. This is compounded by Chinese temporal attitudes. One expatriate stated, "Westerners are time conscious. Chinese never bother about time and consume most of their time in lengthy, useless meetings without arriving at objectives or target accomplishment dates."

Americans are also frustrated by the Chinese work ethic. They feel that the Chinese take little pride in their work. One expatriate stated, "The dilemma we face is that the Chinese are intelligent and fast learning, but they are not independently motivated. It is the system as much as it is the individual. They have been conditioned to get paid whether they work or not." Another expatriate noted, "Chinese go to the work place to rest and go home to do housework."

Technology is the one area that Chinese workers are greatly interested in. The Chinese are highly respectful and desirous of gaining technical know-how. At the same time, they are fearful and suspicious of foreign ways. One expatriate expressed the prevailing view in his statement, "The Chinese are infatuated with science and technology, but no matter what you teach them, they will do it their own way when you're not around."

Preparing Expatriates for China

Expatriates have stated that their major problems in China have been due to a lack of preparation in terms of personal expectations, language skills, and how to communicate with the Chinese. Therefore, any training program must address these areas.

One of the most important portions of the training program is the selection of candidates. Experts have made the following recommendations:

1. The human resource department should select candidates with realistic attitudes and the endurance to bear the hardships of Chinese living conditions.
2. The human resource department should only select candidates who will be able to endure periods of alienation and isolation. The candidate must be willing to make personal sacrifices.
3. The human resource department should only select candidates who are versatile and sensitive to local cultural conditions.
4. The human resource department should select candidates who are open-minded and patient. Type-A personalities should be avoided.
5. The human resource department must only select candidates who are technically competent. Candidates also must be comfortable teaching in their area of expertise.
6. The human resource department should only pick candidates who can cope with cultural differences in temporal attitudes, views of privacy, and relationships.
7. The human resource department should only pick single employees or married employees without children. Newlyweds should not be sent. Spouses must be screened and trained before going to China.

Once candidates are selected, they must be thoroughly trained before being sent to China. The training program must include language training. General training should also be provided on Chinese culture, history, and politics. Experts have recommended the following training approach:

1. Trainers should use actual cases, vignettes, role playing, and critical incidents based upon actual expatriate living and working experiences. Workshops should include sessions in nonverbal communications, setting realistic expectations, and how to shop, travel, and entertain oneself.
2. Trainers should bring in expatriates who have recently returned from assignments in China. In addition to advising candidates on living conditions, recent returnees can screen the candidates and inform the human resource department of likely drop-outs.

3. The training program should include area briefings. Lecturers should review China's history, politics, and culture. However, the lectures should not be too academic.

4. Language training must be included in the program. At a minimum, candidates need to learn key words and phrases for eating, shopping, traveling, and working.

5. The training program should include a workshop on negotiating skills. Almost everything in China must be negotiated in one way or another.

6. Trainers should use short lectures and role plays on how to read Chinese nonverbal cues and mixed messages. Training should include quick, practical advice and experiential exercises with a lot of opportunity for feedback.

Before expatriates leave for China, corporations should take steps to make certain that their stay is comfortable. Expatriates should be provided with videocassette recorders and videotapes to reduce loneliness and cultural isolation. Once a week, the corporation should send a package of home country sporting events and current TV programs.

Expatriates should also be provided with detailed maps before they leave. Maps are a scarce commodity in China, and are difficult to obtain. The maps can point out possible recreational opportunities.

The corporation should also provide expatriates with local American contacts consisting of government officials, business persons, university students, or cultural groups. These people can be contacted for recreation and advice.

Training Chinese Workers

Many corporations have found that Chinese are more willing to enter contracts when training is offered as part of the technology transfer program. Corporations have the choice of training Chinese on the job or in the United States. By training Chinese workers in the U.S., companies help to provide technical and managerial skills that China lacks.

In return, the Chinese contribute information that is vital to a project's success, such as the quality of available materials or knowledge of Chinese regulations. Building understanding and honing technical skills also help ensure that American-made equipment is properly maintained and serviced in China and that jointly made products achieve quality standards.

Unfortunately, many corporations run into formidable obstacles when training Chinese workers. One trainer complained, "The Chinese don't understand how U.S. business works, and many still don't understand it even after being here." To ensure that training is successful, corporations must first evaluate who they will train and what type of training is appropriate to their project. Then, they should develop a well-organized program.

Training Contracts with the P.R.C.

Planning for the training program should begin during project negotiations. Presenting a comprehensive training plan from the beginning can enhance the company's negotiating position and lead to inclusion of a detailed appendix in the contract, setting forth the specifics of the program. If the contract specifies the training program, negotiators should be sure to include the number of trainees, the length of the program, the qualifications of the trainees, a description of the training program, and monetary arrangements.

American companies use different approaches in designating the number of trainees allowed. Some contracts stipulate a maximum number of trainees and duration of stay. Other contracts specify the total number of man-months of training needed. The duration of training varies with the type of project. A program designed to familiarize high-level joint venture management with the American corporation might last three or four weeks. Co-production training programs may last for over one year.

The contract should specify trainee qualifications, including English competency, education, and practical experience. If the project is a joint venture, the contract should insist that the trainee not be transferred to another facility without American approval. Some contracts require potential trainees to submit resumes, which specify the candidate's educational major, level reached, and number of years on the job.

American corporations may wish to leave the description of the training program vague. Some contracts are very specific, and include exact schedules listing five or six items to be covered each day, and the teaching materials to be used. It is better to leave trainers some leeway.

In the event that trainees are not comprehending the material, the training approach may have to be changed.

Monetary arrangements vary considerably from contract to contract. In most cases, the Chinese pay for airfare, room, and board. The Americans pay for cost of trainers, local transportation, work clothes, and tools. Companies should be prepared for extra expenses. The Chinese are often given such a frugal housing allowance, that the corporation may have to supplement it. Americans should also be prepared to host a variety of activities for the Chinese trainees.

Factors to Consider in Selecting Chinese Trainees

The human resource department should have some control over trainee selection. The corporation will want to ensure that it is training the people who will benefit the most. Training associated with licensing is an exception. Companies generally play little or no role in trainee selection. The training is considered part of the technology the Chinese are paying for.

Chinese and American partners often disagree over the scale of training programs. The Chinese are normally more concerned with the number of people trained than with the quality of the training program. The Chinese are especially prone to sending more trainees than necessary if the American corporation is bearing most of the cost. Americans can raise Chinese cost-consciousness by requiring the Chinese to bear at least half of the training expense. As living in the United States will require a sizable amount of scarce foreign exchange, the Chinese will be more judicious about who they send.

Typically, the Chinese will present a pool of candidates for consideration. The Americans will either pick the trainees or eliminate unqualified candidates from consideration before the Chinese make the final decision.

Companies involved in selection should interview potential trainees for language abilities and technical skills. Written English tests can be very useful. A documentable test score permits non-subjective comparison, taking some pressure off the corporation to accept unqualified trainees. One test already used in China is the test of English for International Communication (TOEIC). This multiple choice test evaluates the listening and reading comprehension skills of non-active English speakers who must communicate in English in a business, commerce, or industry environment. The test is put out by the Educational Testing Service (Princeton, New Jersey; Telephone: 609-921-9000).

One company tests candidates by asking them to discuss their proposals for improving the training program. This forces candidates to reveal their mastery of the English language, their technical proficiency, and their understanding of the job. Training content is debated until an agreement is reached. This also gives the candidate a preview of what is expected during training, so that fewer misunderstandings arise when trainees arrive in the United States.

In evaluating prospective trainees, human resource personnel should look for basic English competency, solid technical and educational backgrounds, and practical experience. If trainees lack these qualities, they may have trouble learning new techniques and adapting them for use in China.

Human resource personnel should also inquire about the candidate's employer. If candidates are not connected with the Chinese partner's work unit, they should be eliminated. Some companies have discovered that the Chinese government will send trainees who are from design institutes that are responsible for technical innovation within their particular industry. These "trainees" gain access to American plant and engineering departments, sometimes causing the loss of proprietary technology.

Legal Requirements for Chinese Trainees in the United States

Foreign trainees will be required to obtain visas before coming to the United States. Trainers can ask to arrange for visas for the foreign trainees. Trainers should familiarize themselves with general principles of immigration law, but should refer most immigration matters to a qualified attorney.

The immigration law of the United States was significantly changed by the Immigration Act of 1990, which took effect on October 1, 1991. Proponents of the law expect it to generate domestic economic growth and increased U.S. competitiveness in the global market. In fact, the Immigration Act of 1990 does appear to provide overall improvements for permanent business immigration, while somewhat restricting temporary workers.

Most foreign trainees will need to get an H-3 visa. An H-3 visa is commonly used to train foreign employees in established company training programs, including on-the-job and classroom training. The alien's time in the United States must be devoted to the training program. Any productive employment must be an incidental part of the program. The employer must also show that the training is unavailable in the alien's own country, and will benefit the alien in pursuing a career outside the United States.

To document the trainee's status as a non-immigrant trainee, the corporation is required to file the appropriate forms with the United States Immigration and Naturalization Service (INS). The form can be obtained from and filed with the regional immigration office nearest the location where the training program will take place. The INS will process the form, notify the company of approval, and forward the petition to the appropriate U.S. Embassy where trainees can obtain the visa.

Trainers should note that training foreigners in the use of restricted technology may be illegal. If the government requires exporters to obtain an export license before the technology in question can be shipped out of the country, then it is a good bet that training foreigners in the use of that technology also requires government approval. Trainers should contact the Department of Commerce's Office of Export Administration with any questions concerning restrictions on training foreigners in the use of technology.

Developing a Training Program for Chinese Nationals

The approach that American companies take to training programs often depends on the type of deal they are contemplating. Training programs for sales contracts may differ from training for joint ventures.

Surprisingly, Chinese have been able to convince many American corporations to provide gratuitous training. The training is supposed to enhance the foreign company's image in China by earning goodwill and creating product recognition among officials. Most corporations have given up on this approach. They have found that "giving away the farm" is not a good idea. Most often, the only result is that a new competitor is created.

High technology sales contracts often include training as part of the purchase price. Normally, several Chinese workers will visit the overseas supplier to be trained on the equipment purchased, such as computer-controlled machine tools or oil refining equipment. By the time the equipment arrives in China, there are employees waiting who know how to use it.

Co-production projects usually require Chinese trainees to spend several months in the United States gaining hands-on experience. These training programs have varied in size from three to ten trainees. The Chinese normally pay for the training when purchasing the technology or equipment, as part of the purchase price or as a separate training fee agreed upon before signing the contract.

The most complex training programs are usually for joint ventures. Programs begin with a high-level Chinese management team coming to the United States for a few weeks to familiarize themselves with their partner's operations. Although many of these managers are unwilling to get involved with the technical details, they become aware of the type of Chinese personnel who would benefit from the training. The managers then return to China and select a minimum number of highly skilled workers for training in the United States.

Trainers for joint venture projects have often included product planning, factory management, manufacturing techniques, commercial issues, scheduling, and customer service in the training program. Although these areas would not normally be considered as "technical training," trainers have found that exposure to Western management techniques increases business efficiency.

Most American companies provide on-the-job training. Trainees work closely with the lead engineer or foreman, who supervises their progress. Trainees may be hesitant to try new things, but working one-on-one with an American counterpart increases the probability that they will pitch in wholeheartedly. One-on-one training also eliminates the possibility that the trainee will "lose face" by making a mistake in front of other Chinese trainees. "Face" is an important consideration. Trainees may return to China fearful of putting their new skills into practice. One company found that trainees returned to their factory claiming that they had not learned various techniques. This can be avoided by specifying what trainees are taught, so that the American company is not blamed for failing to fulfill its training agreement. Another technique is to train Chinese on equipment that is more complex than their own. When they return to China, they will have fewer apprehensions, because the machines they will be working are simpler than the machines they trained on.

Chinese education is generally not participatory. Students are more willing to listen and absorb then to speak. The language barrier makes the classroom even quieter when Chinese come to the United States. In class and on the job, trainers must informally test trainees by asking them to repeat what they have learned. This helps prevent misunderstandings and indicates how much information is being absorbed.

One trainer recommends that Chinese trainees be given a lot of time to work by themselves, so that they can discuss and understand what has been taught to them. Another trainer begins each day by answering questions on material covered the previous day before moving on to a new topic.

Trainees are often more vocal during practical hands-on activities. Training coordinators must prepare trainers to answer many practical questions. Chinese trainees often ask about areas and details not directly related to successful completion of the project. One trainer recommends using a task force approach so that work is project-specific. Supplying project manuals and job-specific technical manuals also helps satisfy the trainees' desire for information. Manuals also provide a useful reference for trainees when they return to their homeland.

Foreigners trainees often have good technical skills, but are slow in project execution. In China, careful bureaucratic monitoring and numerous checks and balances permit projects to be revised even after they have been improved. This forces Chinese workers to be concerned with the manufacture of every nut, bolt or seal, in addition to the end product. Trainers should let the trainees learn at their own speed.

To conclude, many of the insights and tips provided for technology transfer with the Chinese can be adapted when dealing with people in other less-economically developed nations. For example, the reader is challenged to review the above analysis to discover what ideas can be applied to establishing a joint venture in Eastern Europe, Central Asia, Africa, or Latin America. Although each culture is unique, HR leaders will develop basic training strategies that are transcultural.

Effective Cross-Cultural Presentations

Making presentations to executives in one's own culture is relatively easy. In broad terms, they all speak the same language, have the same lifestyles, and recognize the same set of business norms. This all changes when trainers make presentations to groups of international executives or foreign employees. Many of those people attending the training session are likely to speak English as a second or third language. In addition, the trainees probably have markedly different lifestyles from those of their seminar colleagues and often work under completely different business systems. Chapter 9 will discuss this topic more fully.

Many foreign-born employees, especially those who are recent arrivals in the United States, feel uncomfortable about admitting that they do not understand an instruction. Trainers will encounter workshop participants who declare that they understand concepts when they obviously do not. This causes massive problems when the trainees return to the job and make mistakes.

The trainer must assess how well the foreign worker understands the material. Trainee understanding can be evaluated by noting subtle changes in trainee behavior such as:

- Facial expressions
- Excessive nodding and smiling
- Too many positive statements, such as "Yes, I understand"
- An absence of questions
- Rote repetition

Some experts estimate that 70 to 90% of face-to-face communication is nonverbal.

Trainers can facilitate understanding if they

- Start slowly. Warm up the audience.
- Speak clearly and distinctly.
- Communicate nonverbally. Smile!
- Use an appropriate tone of voice.
- Avoid slang, jargon, and acronyms.
- Repeat the information in several ways.
- Ask about comprehension frequently.

One of the most important things a trainer can do is to start slowly. The trainees have to become accustomed to how the trainer talks and sounds before they understand what the trainer is saying. Some studies estimate that intonation and tone of voice account for approximately 35% of face-to-face communication. Voice quality, accent, and speed of delivery all contribute to the level of comprehension of those listening. The trainer can communicate a great deal simply by using an appropriate tone. For example, an emphatic tone underlines the importance of a point.

HR professionals must also pay attention to nonverbal messages. The golden rule of international communication is "Smile!" Be careful, however, about telling jokes. Many jokes do not work cross-culturally.

HR managers should avoid the excessive use of technical jargon and acronyms. Any time such language is used, the trainer must explain its meaning. Trainees should be provided with a list of the company's particular jargon terms as part of the initial orientation session. One good approach is to write difficult words or acronyms on the blackboard. Leave them there for several days, until they are thoroughly understood by everyone.

Trainers must frequently ask about comprehension. However, they should be careful when quizzing foreign-born workers individually in front of their colleagues. It is essential that the trainer ensure that a trainee does not either "lose face" or get a reputation for "showing off." If a trainee appears to misunderstand the question, the trainer should ask the question in another way.

If it appears as though certain trainees do not understand a concept, wait until you can talk to them individually. Diplomatically ask them if they understand what you are talking about.

Pay attention to the trainees. A long training program can be exhausting, especially for people who speak English as a second language. Change the pace after a set time. Change to role-playing or teamwork exercises. However, don't use so many new techniques or trainers that the trainees have to continually get used to new voice patterns and concepts.

Preparing Company Employees for the Arrival of Foreign Trainees

Human resource personnel can avoid many problems by giving company employees an orientation program before trainees arrive. Employees should be sensitized to cultural differences. For example with reference to the previous analysis of the Chinese, the orientation should discuss the work style of Chinese factory workers, Chinese etiquette, Chinese diet, and gift giving.

Some companies ask Chinese-American employees to serve as interpreters, instructors in the training program, or "hosts" responsible for some of the trainees' after-work activities. If trainees are with someone who shares cultural or linguistic bonds, the company gets feedback and a better understanding of the Chinese trainees' concerns and difficulties.

A hospitality program should also be set up. Most trainees are first-time visitors to the United States and are eager to see the sights and observe American lifestyles. The corporation should not expect trainees to initiate these activities or to go out exploring on their own. The corporation should prepare a slate of activities, such as visits to local tourist sites, barbecues, and trips to sporting events.

Monitoring Trainees After They Return

Monitoring trainees' progress after they return to their homeland is essential. Job reassignment plagues training programs. Trained workers are often moved within the factory, promoted to jobs outside their specialty, or sent to new facilities. Sometimes this happens because a factory simply doesn't use its resources efficiently. In other cases, local labor bureaus or ministries responsible for highly trained technicians transfer workers over the objections of the factory manager. This is why it is important to include contractual provisions ensuring that the trainee will stay in the factory.

Foreign governments and the individual businesses may be less willing to transfer trained workers if they believe that the American company is willing to continue helping and advising those people who were trained in the U.S. Ongoing contact also helps build a loyal network of contacts abroad. For example, one company found that exchanges of Chinese New Year's cards and hosting reunion dinners was a good way to stay in touch with trainees. A framed diploma certifying graduation from the training program provides status and a tie to the company.

A Warning for Cross-Cultural Trainers

Human resource professionals should be aware that their technology transfer training programs may meet serious resistance both at home and abroad. There is a continuing debate over "appropriate technology." Many politicians feel that there should not be a free flow of technology throughout the world.

Certain technology, for example the machinery of chemical warfare, is not appropriate for any country. Nevertheless, there are many gross examples of multinational corporations exporting technology that is either not yet approved or is banned in their home country because of inherent dangers.

During the 1970s, a chemical company manufactured "Phosvel," an insecticide, in a plant near Houston, Texas. The company was in the process of testing Phosvel, but had not yet received approval for domestic use. Nevertheless, it sold 14 million pounds of the untested chemical to Egypt, Indonesia, and South Vietnam, where it was used on cotton and other crops. It turned out that Phosvel was extremely dangerous. The exact toll of environmental and health damage is not known, but in Egypt alone, the pesticide was implicated in the poisoning of 65 field workers and the death of several hundred water buffalos. OSHA later banned production of Phosvel in the United States when a large number of workers at the Houston plant showed evidence of neurologic disorders and the plant polluted the local area.

While Phosvel is a good example of technology that is inappropriate for everyone, there are examples of technology that is only inappropriate for some countries. "Appropriateness" in this sense refers to the type of technology in relation to the country's level of development.

For example, if a given product is produced capital-intensively at home, MNCs tend to build capital-intensive plants abroad using state-of-the-art technology that it knows how to work with and that will produce products of acceptable and uniform quality. However, when capital-intensive technology is brought into a developing country, it adds relatively few jobs, thus contributing little to the unemployment problem.

At the same time, new technology uses up plenty of capital, which is in scarce supply in developing countries. The host country will have to use what little foreign exchange it has to maintain the new machinery and repatriate profits, fees, and other charges.

Even worse, if the MNC's products are better than local products or its costs are lower than local firms, MNC production will gain in market share relative to local firms. If this happens, then the MNC technological infusion actually can make the employment problem worse. Competing labor-intensive firms will lay off workers, but these workers will not be hired by the new capital-intensive businesses.

This problem used to be limited to Third World countries, but it has recently hit home in developed countries. In 1992, the city of Los Angeles rejected a Japanese high tech, capital-intensive transit system as inappropriate. The Japanese transit system used fewer workers than the competing American system. In a period of high unemployment and recession, a capital-intensive, foreign technology was too politically risky in America.

Many developing country planners have proposed the creation of uniquely suited technologies of their own, particularly through national and regional research and development centers that would work on innovations specifically designed to meet local needs. But labor intensive technologies do not have significant markets in developed countries, so there is little incentive for MNCs to direct R&D money toward the kinds of technologies suited to conditions of economic backwardness.

Despite the fact that developing country labor is cheap, it may be very expensive to use in production because of low productivity, thus justifying labor saving technologies. Also, substantial amounts of R&D may be required to make established technology more labor intensive, and returns on the R&D may be small, zero, or even negative. In adapting production technology to local conditions, product uniformity and quality may be difficult or impossible to maintain.

As global competition increases, there will be increasing questions as to whether technology is appropriate or not. Human resource professionals must be aware of these issues, and incorporate them into their training programs.

The people involved in technology transfer in the 1990s will no longer have to be just good technologists. R&D, engineering, manufacturing, and marketing are blurring into one entity. New types of international corporate collaboration will be necessary.

This will result in an increase in "people exchanges." The frequency of short-term technical-learning exchanges will increase significantly. Effective sharing and transmission of technology among various corporate units will become vital. More employees will be sent to foreign environments on assignments in the three-month to one-year range specifically to learn about and absorb new technologies firsthand.

The human resource department will have to develop effective cross-cultural training programs to meet the increased need for technology transfer.

Many of the insights shared in this chapter relative to transferring technology abroad, also have domestic applications. The same sensitivities used to deal with foreigners and their cultures are also required for tech transfer within one's homeland. In the United States a case in point would be the New England industrialist or computer manufacturer who opens a plant in the South and can utilize some of the same strategies proposed. Similarly, the Eastern business person who establishes an operation on the West Coast is well advised to observe the cultural differences there and act accordingly. For the foreign firm who wants to be successful in establishing facilities in the United States, it would be most valuable to heed the guidance offered in the previous pages.

Human resource professionals involved in any "twin plant" agreements have the biggest challenges in helping technology transfer to succeed. With ecologists in different countries joining forces to combat cross-border pollution, for example, HR leaders should be educating their own top management and technicians about the importance of ecological controls and avoidance of dumping toxic wastes in less developed nations. Furthermore, they should help their own personnel to be aware of problems related to technological fads and gadgets that are too quickly adopted and abandoned.

Readers may wish to consult with the Technology Transfer Society in their own locality about their services and the international symposium which is conducted annually.

References

1. Badway, M. K., "Lessons to Learn," *Industry Week,* June 19, 1989, pp. 71+.
2. Brandt, E., "Global HR," *Personnel Journal,* March 1991, pp. 38–44.
3. Cook, B. M., "In Search of Six Sigma: 99.9997% Defect-Free," *Industry Week,* October 1, 1990, pp. 60–65.
4. Cook, B. M., "Flexible Manufacturing: Something That People Should Do," *Industry Week,* November 5, 1990, pp. 36–45.
5. Dunbar, E. and Katcher, A., "Preparing Managers for Foreign Assignments," *Training & Development Journal,* September 1990, pp. 45–47.
6. Flamholtz, E. G., *Human Resource Accounting.* San Francisco, CA: Jossey-Bass, 1986.
7. Foran, C., "Restaurant Chief Is at Home Under the Golden Arches," *The Business Journal-Milwaukee,* September 19, 1988, p. 10+.
8. Grunbaum, R., "Flushing Out a Market for the Paperless Toilet," *Puget Sound Business Journal,* June 17, 1991, p. 1.

9. Kim, W. C., and Mauborgne, R. A., "Cross-Cultural Strategies," *The Journal of Business Strategy,* Spring 1988, pp. 28–35.
10. Masterson, R. and Murphy, R., "Internal Cross-Cultural Management," *Training and Development Journal,* April 1986, pp. 56–60.
11. McEnry, J. and DesHarnais, G., "Culture Shock," *Training & Development Journal,* April 1990, pp. 43–47.
12. Miller, L., "How to Keep Managers Up to Date," *Training & Development Journal,* September 1990, pp. 35–37.
13. Moskal, B. S., "Supervision (or Lack of It)," *Industry Week,* December 3, 1990, pp. 54–59.
14. Oches, N. "Cross-Cultural Presentations—How to Make Them More Effective," 1989.
15. Randolph, B., "When Going Global Isn't Enough," *Training,* August 1990, pp. 47–51.
16. Reid, T. R., "Tokyo's Tech for Teeth and Toilets," *The Washington Post,* June 15, 1992, p. A12.
17. Rhinesmith, S. A., "Going Global from the Inside Out," *Training & Development,* November 1991, pp. 42–47.
18. Rohan, T. M., "In Search of Speed," *Industry Week,* September 3, 1990, pp. 78–83.
19. Sensenbrenner, J.S., "The Training Component," *The China Business Review,* November/December 1986, pp. 8–12.
20. Seurat, S., *Technology Transfer—A Realistic Approach.* Houston, TX: Gulf Publishing Co., 1979.
21. Shaikh, R. A., "The Dilemmas of Advanced Technology for the Third World," *Technology Review,* April 1986, pp. 56+.
22. Sheridan, J. H., "World-Class Manufacturing," *Industry Week,* July 2, 1990, pp. 36–47.
23. Sheridan, J. H., "Lessons from the Gurus," *Industry Week,* August 6, 1990, pp. 35–41.
24. Thiederman, S., "Training Foreigners," *Training & Development Journal,* November 1988, pp. 81–84.
25. "Translate Thine Enemy," *The Economist,* May 20, 1989, pp. 92.
26. Weiss, J. W., and Bloom S., "Managing in China: Expatriate Experiences and Training Recommendations," *Business Horizons,* May/June 1990, pp. 23–29.

CHAPTER 6

THE CROSS-CULTURAL EMPLOYEE

Introduction

"The most important challenge facing our company today is being able to integrate skillfully and manage effectively a rapidly changing work force," stated a senior E.I. DuPont executive in a private conversation with one of the authors (Moran).

Poverty and unemployment in their countries have brought millions of people to the United States both legally and illegally. The United States has always been perceived by others as a land of opportunity.

The Immigration Act of 1965 resulted in a large-scale immigration from Asia. The 1990 U.S. Census Bureau estimated there are now 7 million Asians living in the United States. This includes Filipinos (22%), Chinese (19%), Vietnamese (13%), Koreans (12%), Japanese (12%), Indians (10%), and approximately 12% from other groups. In the past decade people came to the United States from many other countries as well—the Punjab, Europe, the Caribbean, North Africa, the former Soviet Union, Hungary, France, Kuwait, etc. This enormous migration is changing and enriching the texture of the United States.

The metaphor of the "melting pot" never was accurate and certainly doesn't reflect the reality of the United States or any other country at present. One's cultural heritage and background is not lost or assimilated upon immigrating into the United States, where supposedly a new "American" cultural heritage is acquired, and shared by all who become citizens.

Diversity among ethnic groups of Americans is growing as well. In New Jersey the U.S. Census Bureau found these trends:

	1990	1980	% increase
Caucasian	6,130,400	6,127,400	insignificant
Afro-American	1,030,800	925,000	+12%
Hispanic	739,800	491,800	+50%
Native American	14,900	8,390	+78%

The complexity of our society is changing.

Large-Scale Movements of People

The movement of people from one country to another is nothing new, but the impact of such large-scale immigration and naturalization on the work force of a country merits attention. Findings contained in the recent 1990 U.S. Census confirmed what has long been known— minorities are gaining representation in the U.S. population with lightening speed. In March 1991, the U.S. Census Bureau released statistics that revealed four important facts. The white majority in the U.S. fell to 80.3% in 1990, the lowest this century. In addition, the Hispanic population grew 9 times faster than the majority white population grew since 1980; the Asian population grew 18 times faster; and the black population grew 2 times faster (*USA Today,* March 11, 1991).

In Canada, it has been estimated that by the year 2001, about 15% of the country's population will be members of a visible minority group. The Ontario provincial government, in an effort to promote employment equity, has begun to expand its annual internship drive by targeting the disabled, racial minorities, Francophones, and the aboriginal peoples for job openings (*Communication World,* July–August 1989).

In many European countries, minorities today make up a significant part of both the population and work force. For example, in Switzerland, a country with German, French, Italian, and Romansch as official languages, the Germans constitute 65% of the population, the French 18%, the Italians 10%, and the Spanish 2%. The population in Switzerland grew at a rate of 5.3% during the 1980s, but, incredibly, the native Swiss population only grew annually at 3.4% during this time while the foreign population grew annually at 15% (*The Economist* Intelligence Unit Country Profile Report, 1990–1991; and P.C. Grobe, 1990).

In tiny Luxembourg, which has a population of less than half a million people, the Portuguese, Italians, French, and Germans make up 22% of the population. One category of ethnic group in Luxembourg simply classified as "other" makes up 8% of the population. In January 1990, Luxembourg was inhabited by 377,000 people. Of this number, 26.39% or 99,500 were of foreign nationality. Statistics from 1987 indicate that 25,000 of the 159,200 strong Luxembourg labor force were foreign workers.

In France, Algerians make up the largest minority group, and the "other" category accounts for 17% of the population, which is primarily North Africans and other immigrants from France's former colonies. France's 1990 census contained some interesting statistics. In that year over 3.6 million immigrants resided in France. In the labor force, resident foreigners accounted for one of every ten workers.

Even the small European principality of Monaco has not escaped global multiculturalism. With a population under 30,000 Monaco has large minority representation in its population. The French in Monaco are 47% of the population, the native Monegasque make up 16% of the population, the Italians 16%, and an "other" category constitutes an astounding 21% of the population.

HRD Cross-Cultural Challenges

What does all this mean to the human resource specialist, the diversity trainer, and the employees of the future? Simply put, if an employee is to function effectively in a multicultural environment, one must learn to cooperate with, understand, and be tolerant of other cultures.

Many top multinational and national corporations have recognized the importance of multicultural relations to their future success. Xerox, Avon, Corning, Digital, and Procter and Gamble are just some of the major multinational corporations that have instituted programs to aggressively respond to work force diversity.

The U.S. hospitality industry received a boost when Florida International University developed a program in 1988 to train future hospitality workers to operate effectively in diverse multicultural environments. The course of study involves seven stages. The first teaches students the language of multicultural management. The second stage is that of discussion, in which the students talk about stereotypes and beliefs about other cultures inherent in U.S. society today. The third stage teaches competencies necessary to learn about ethnic groups. The fourth stage teaches awareness of one's self and of the cultures around him. In the fifth stage, students develop an awareness of the cultural values and behavior patterns held dear by different ethnic groups. The final two stages center on ethnic learning and communication styles.

As demographic differences are gradually combined with different rates of economic growth, companies around the world find that their work force is no longer made up of one dominant culture, but rather, several different cultures that must co-exist in often increasingly cramped work space.

As a result, every profession and occupation must consider how to reeducate their members to become transcultural employees. Colleges and universities have begun to tackle the challenge in two ways:

1. Revamp their curriculum to include themes on diversity, gender, and cultural understanding, as well as providing students with a global view of history and society.
2. Provide continuing and executive education courses on cross-cultural subjects from management to communications. The University of California-Irvine has a cultural diversity program offered through its extension service. The dean, Melvin E. Hall, explained it this way in a *Los Angeles Times* interview (April 15, 1992):

> No matter what field you are in today, whether it is emergency response, health care or engineering, anyone who is in a professional field that deals with people, either directly or indirectly, needs to have some appreciation of culture.
>
> Today's engineers, architects, computer software designers have to realize that they are creating products that will be used by people of different cultures. In the event of a toxic spill or disaster, hazardous materials specialists and public safety officers need to be able to communicate the dangers to people who speak different languages.

Even local communities are awakening to the problem as a means of promoting neighborhood harmony, as well as improving intercultural relations in the work place. In 1992, the Santa Clara Convention Center in northern California showcased a conference on the theme, "Bringing You Face to Face with Global Diversity." Presented by local volunteers, the sessions addressed everything from cross-cultural communications and multiple languages in the work environment, to supervising a multicultural labor force and doing business in centrally-planned economies. For information on how to organize such an event in your locality, contact Intercultural Resources Forum (760 Homer Ave., Suite 3, Palo Alto, CA 94301, (415) 322-6491).

It isn't easy to work in a multicultural environment. In an average size corporation with eight full-time employees (five Canadians, two Asians, and one Turk), tempers flared when the two Asians spoke to each other in Punjabi—a language the other six employees did not understand. "I always felt they were talking about me," said one employee. Another employee said, "When those two Asians spoke to each other in Punjabi, it made me nervous." This is just one example of how cultural mis-understandings can occur.

High context cultures can often conflict with low context cultures. A recent joint venture agreement that occurred in an Arab country between a Japanese firm and an American firm created difficulties when foreign workers could not get definite "yes or no" answers from their Japanese managers. The Japanese often remained silent when confronted with problems or questions requiring immediate attention. In addition, foreign workers felt "left out" when Japanese nationals socialized together without them (*Tokyo Business Today,* February 1990).

Often biculturalism and multiculturalism are confused. A bicultural environment is one in which two cultures are present. A group of Italians working in Japan for a Japanese company would be an example of a bicultural working environment. A multicultural environment is one in which three or more different cultures are present. A definition given by Beverly Beyette [1] of multicultural environment is

> A multicultural work environment is one in which the skills and talents of three or more people of different ages and/or ethnic and cultural backgrounds are directed towards achieving a common organizational goal.

An interesting aspect of this definition that HR managers should be aware of is that a multicultural environment can exist even when only one *nationality* is present. For example, an Hispanic, a black, and a Caucasian American are a multicultural work force even though all are American citizens. Similarly, Parisians, northern French, southern French, and Algerians, although citizens of France, have different cultural backgrounds and a multicultural work force results from their interaction.

Finally, another aspect of this definition addresses the issue of age. The generation gap caused by age difference that is perceived between parent and child is not exclusively part of the family arena. A multicultural environment can exist in an organization where the ages of some or all of the employees is very broad.

Case Study

The challenges inherent in employment across cultures becomes evident in the following case.

Daniel Montet is a thirty-four-year-old French citizen. Between 1984 and 1990, Mr. Montet worked for a U.S. company as a project system analyst in Atlanta, Georgia. Mr. Montet's primary duty was to design software by writing specifications and codes. After his writing was complete, the programs were tested and any problems or "bugs" were removed.

In the Atlanta headquarters, Mr. Montet worked with programmers from many different cultures; Indian nationals, Chinese nationals, Eastern European nationals, and Iranian nationals. Although many of the programmers were U.S. citizens, most had only recently immigrated to the United States.

Mr. Montet enjoyed his experience working in a multicultural environment. "I worked with all of these programmers on a project, and the way we worked together was interesting. The work atmosphere was very informal. People would often drop by your desk to chat and to socialize."

During Mr. Montet's term of employment many important political events occurred that had an indirect effect on some of his co-workers. The death of Ayatollah Khomeni in 1989, and the massacre of the Chinese students in Tiananmen Square by the Chinese government in the same year affected the Chinese and Iranian programmers, respectively. According to Mr. Montet, the affected group of programmers did not let their personal feelings or concerns affect their work. "Co-workers affected by events in their home country remained professional at all times at work, but after hours, in a private setting, they would discuss personal feelings with friends and or family."

Mr. Montet often had difficulty understanding the English of some of his co-workers because of strong native accents. Although co-workers of similar nationalities often spoke to each other in their native tongue, this did not bother Mr. Montet. What did bother him, however, was the Chinese programmers who spoke to each other in a loud tone. "The Chinese often seemed to be yelling at each other," he said.

Mr. Montet noticed that both the Chinese and Indian programmers tended to work as a group and socialize as a group. "The Indian programmers even lived in the same apartment building," he said.

Mr. Montet also realized a cultural problem. All the upper level managers were American. The Chinese, in particular, began to resent the fact that no Chinese programmer had yet been promoted to management even though some of them had seniority over other American programmers who had been promoted to managerial positions.

Finally, Mr. Montet recognized that Americans were often excluded from any discussions of current world events among the programmers. "The Americans never seemed to know what we were talking about. They never seemed up-to-date on world events," he said.

Testing and Interviewing in a Multicultural Environment

Today, with large numbers of people looking for work and with the number of jobs few and far between, companies can often have their pick of the "cream of the crop" of job seekers or students graduating from graduate schools. Although this may sound like an enviable position, corporations often have a difficult time choosing future employees simply by studying a résumé. One recruiter said recently, "When you've looked at over a hundred résumés, candidates begin to look the same." Some HR managers are now asking potential job candidates to submit videocassettes of themselves.

Promoting employees from within can also prove to be a difficult task, especially when seniority and competence levels among promotion seekers are relatively equal. One method companies use as an aid in making employment or promotion decisions is written employment tests. These tests can take many forms ranging from multiple choice questionnaires to full-length essay examinations. Other firms establish assessment centers where simulations, performance exercises, and case studies are given to those seeking promotion or employment.

In a multicultural work environment, written tests must be prepared differently and/or the results of existing company tests must be considered in the appropriate context. For example, graduate business schools around the world require applicants to take an admission test called the Graduate Management Admissions Test (GMAT). This test is administered in English. Results vary, but an average score on a scale of 200 to 800 is 500. In 1985, the Harvard Business School abolished the GMAT as a criterion for admission when their studies revealed that this test unintentionally discriminated against certain groups of people. Today Harvard's MBA application procedure is primarily a series of essay questions designed to learn more about the applicant, his achievements, and his philosophy toward life.

Tests must be designed for a multicultural work force in keeping with the knowledge that low context and high context cultures interpret the meaning of questions differently and that certain cultures may be more successful in written tests as opposed to being successful on the job. Standarized college entrance examinations are now being revised in an attempt to be less culturally biased.

Any employment test must be valid, that is, it must be a fair and appropriate measure of the characteristic(s) being observed. According to Ryan Kuhn of Reid Psychological Systems, the objective of any employment test should be to achieve high validity (the correlation between test result and actual performance) with low adverse impact (discrimination against foreigners or women, for example).

Sometimes a test that is effective in assessing actual job performance can discriminate against certain groups. For example, some tests merely highlight those employees who fit neatly into the existing work environment, i.e., white males, and fail to register attributes that make foreign or multicultural applicants potentially valuable employees.

One solution to discriminatory testing procedures was advanced by the U.S. Department of Labor in 1981, when the Labor Department promoted the adoption of a race-conscious way of recomputing test scores to avoid adverse impact. The procedure, called race-norming or "within-group-scoring," converts raw scores into group-based percentile ranks. In effect, race-norming gives bonus points to members of groups that tend to score lower than others.

Even with its numerous pitfalls, testing can be helpful in a multicultural work environment. Test results can aid promotion and demotion decisions and can measure attitudes and abilities. However, testing should only be used in concert with other employee evaluation techniques such as the traditional reference checks and interviews.

When interviewing prospective candidates for employment, what does one look for? Invariably, if a corporate recruiter is honest, the answer will be "I look for candidates who share the same values, beliefs, and attitudes that I possess." In a multicultural work environment, the interviewer must discard the practice of ethnocentrism. Instead of reacting negatively towards a candidate who shares different attitudes towards work as we do, we should, instead, look at diversity as a source of enrichment. Recruiters should include questions in the interview with the purpose of learning more about how a person's culture has shaped that person and about how the culture can and does play a role in the prospective employee's everyday life.

Recruiters may wish to involve a member of the multicultural work force in the interviewing process or may wish to have a second interviewer present because many times the way one person interprets an answer to a question will not mirror the interpretation of that same answer by a different person.

When recruiting, managers should look beyond cloning themselves and should attempt, rather, to recruit people who reflect the market. Managers should also be consistent across the board in a multicultural environment instead of overcompensating for cultural diversity.

To effect further change, managers and co-workers should stop judging minorities' efforts harshly and should question stereotypes and assumptions. (Further discussion on the diverse work force and how to empower these employees is contained in the *MCD* series companion volume *Transcultural Leadership*.) Finally, companies must adapt to the new realities of corporate life by reassessing existing company policies and procedures. Standards should be based on results, not on assumptions. Exhibit 6-1 cites some sources of such standards.

Exhibit 6-1
Sources of Guidelines and Standards on Leadership Diversity

Under the aegis of Ann M. Morrison [9], The Center for Creative Leadership (CCL) examined the issue of leadership diversity among women and people of color. The study contained interviews of 200 managers from 16 model organizations in business, education, and government. The report [9] examines benefits and challenges of incorporating diversity into the business agenda; the practices used successfully in the model organizations to develop leadership diversity; the specific steps and guidelines for an action plan. Conferences for professionals on the findings are being organized by CCL (P.O. Box 26300, Greensboro, NC 27438; 4250 Executive Square Ste 600, La Jolla, CA 92037; P.O. Box 1559, Colorado Springs, CO 80901, USA; or Avenue Moliere, B-1060, Brussel, Belgium).

The United States Commission on Civil Rights (Washington, DC 20425, USA) also sponsors studies, conferences, and publications related to multiculturalism in this country. One such recent report centered on *Civil Rights Issues Facing Asian Americans in the 1990s* (1992). Chapters are devoted to issues of prejudice, bigotry, violence, and discrimination and barriers to achieving equal employment opportunities in the workplace. One outcome is a series of annual National Diversity Conferences organized by Herbert Z. Wong & Associates (P.O. Box 978, Danville Square Station, Danville, CA 94526; Tel: (510)838-3028; FAX: 838-4412).

Performance Appraisal

To manage diversity effectively, an acute awareness of individual and cultural characteristics of specific segments of any society is necessary. If a business is to succeed, individual and cultural threads must be woven into the corporate fabric (*HR Magazine,* April 1991).

As the percentage of multicultural employees in the work force of a corporation grows steadily larger, a need will undoubtedly arise to reexamine the traditional ways the company appraises performance. Where there is evidence of strong cultural bias, performance standards must be redefined. Ultimately, substantive performance issues must be separated from stylistic preferences.

Every decision-maker in a corporation will, invariably, have a different attitude towards which performance standards are or are not important, so be prepared for a long review process. However, the performance standards decided upon by management should reflect the cultural diversity of the work force [8].

Majorie Derven [4] advocates using specific examples in discussing or evaluating an employee's performance to explain how conclusions were reached. Such specific examples, Derven argues, can be effective because they serve a developmental purpose by alerting employees to what behavior specifically to avoid or to continue in the future.

The Role of the HR Specialist and Diversity Training

Diversity in the work place is a topic that has been discussed by many authors and has come about as a result of changing work force demographics. It is a domestic as well as a global issue because work force demographics in all nations are changing. The HR specialist especially must understand what the work force diversity issues are.

Diversity in the work force should be seen as an asset; more often, however, it is viewed as a liability and weakness.

Lewan [7] cites leadership as the tool necessary for bridging diversity. It is the leadership that brings vision and value into the management process. Specifically, Lewan identifies three characteristics of excellent leadership:

1. Learning about and understanding the needs of the diverse people you want to serve—not boss, not control, but serve.
2. Creating and articulating a corporate mission and vision that your workers can get excited about, participate in, and be a part of.
3. Behaving in a manner that shows respect to and value of all individual workers and their unique contributions to the whole.

Because of the continuous globalization of the work force, what has become an important task of human resource managers is identifying and developing employees with these leadership skills. These leadership skills and management skills are not identical, although a clear distinction between the two is difficult to ascertain because they have usually been discussed at the same time. On one hand, management is a science with new methods emerging constantly that require certain skills; whereas leadership is something that has been observed but is not understood or adequately defined.

Lewan believes that leadership is a step beyond management because "leaders must understand, value, and practice management, but managers do not have to understand, value, or practice leadership." Leadership goes beyond management. And as work forces become more diverse, more leadership will be needed to lead and to manage the work force.

What can one do as a human resource professional? First of all review your organization's mission statement so that you have a clear, personal understanding of what it means. This will allow you to facilitate its meaning during your training sessions. This is especially important in diverse work forces because it gives every individual a common belief and is central to all activities of the organization. Individuals will see value in their efforts if they can see where they contribute to the organization's mission.

Every industry, professional, and occupational group should reexamine its policies and practices for recruitment, selection, training, and promotion of personnel in terms of gender, and minority or ethnic groups. Obviously this means, diversity and education programs for the existing work force, especially the majority representatives.

One Solution to Diversity Training

Dr. Bob Mezoff, president of ODT Associates, trains managers to perform the subtle art of managing a culturally diverse work force. He cites the challenge to professionals as "aspiring to flexibility, the ability to shift behavior culturally to whomever we are communicating with," and he proposes the following four-step model to meet that challenge:

1. Understand that cultural differences exist.
2. Develop self-acceptance of your cultural background and style.
3. Learn about other cultures.
4. Aspire to flexibility.

Mezoff believes that by changing yourself instead of trying to change the other person you don't make yourself powerless over diverse situations. He continues, "A lot of synergy takes place when managers acknowledge differences and help employees bridge the gap."

Few employers or managers are prepared to face the challenge and opportunity of increasing diversity in the work place. The U.S. Department of Labor projects that 75% of those entering the work force within the next ten years will be minorities and women. This creates a problem for most managers who have not dealt with culturally diverse employees and who haven't acquired the necessary skills. The traditional models of human behavior and management methods are based on implicit assumptions of a homogeneous white male work force. Exhibit 6-2 cires some opportunities for overcoming such assumptions.

Exhibit 6-2
Opportunities for Expanding the Horizons
for Leadership Diversity

Growing cultural awareness should cause HR leaders to recognize the under-representation of talented, minority men and women in many professions and trades. A unique strategy to remedy this situation is occurring within the National Science Foundation, which has established a Research Center for Minority Scholars. The Center publishes an *RCMS Directory* of its programs and directors, as well as the minority summer interns who are working with a Ph.D. level industry mentor. Two national newsletters are also provided; *RCMS LINKS* is an organ of communication for Research Careers for Minority Scholars. This program is intended to identify and support high-achieving minority and undergraduates in engineering, mathematics, and the sciences who clearly have the potential, interest, and determination for advanced degrees in those fields. RCMS scholars are teamed with faculty mentors, who participate in faculty research, receive research stipends, and are eligible for internships.

Interface is the second newsletter which joins together the RCMS institutions participating in the project. For further information, contact RCMS, Texas A & M University (EAPO 204, Zachary, TX 77843; Tel: (409) 847-8886; FAX: 847-8654). Obviously, this strategy could be replicated in other fields through schools of architecture, business, law, medicine, nursing, et al.

Training Programs

Effective multicultural training programs are a fundamental responsibility of management. According to Sondra Thiederman, a cross-cultural consultant, there are three issues that generate the greatest confusion and frustration for managers and employees in a multicultural work environment. The first is the hesitance to ask questions or admit a lack of understanding of instructions, policies, or procedures. People, by human nature, don't want their peers to think they can't follow simple instructions or directions, and this holds especially true in a multicultural work environment where native speakers may grasp concepts quicker than non-native speakers. If a non-native speaker doesn't understand a company policy, for example, he may be less willing to ask for clarification or guidance from co-workers or supervisors to avoid embarrassing himself.

The second is a general reluctance to make negative statements or provide constructive criticism. Some minorities in the work force fear that by making negative statements, they could risk losing their jobs. They believe that their bosses are just looking for an excuse to get rid of them or that their supervisor will delay that much wanted promotion if the employee doesn't "tow the company line." Furthermore, some minority employees don't make negative statements because they have been brought up to respect authority. These employees would never dare to question or offer constructive criticism to a higher ranking official. Although Americans tend to be authentic, direct, even confronting in their communications, people in some cultures are conditioned to smile, be indirect, and never offer feedback, especially to those in a higher social or supervisory position.

Finally, the third is the occasional unresponsiveness of foreign employees to respond to conventional incentives.

Incentives

Different things motivate different people. This holds especially true in a multicultural work environment. Latin American cultures, for example, place great importance on family. As such, performance incentives like longer vacation time as opposed to a cash reward could be more highly valued. North American cultures, on the other hand, although placing some importance on family, tend to be more materialistic. North American employees may be more motivated to perform if a cash incentive is offered. How can a trainer of a multicultural work force ensure that all the different cultures have some incentive that will motivate them to perform?

There is no easy answer. However, one solution can be found by offering a "cafeteria-style" incentive program. Such a program occurs when employees are allowed to freely choose from among a wide range of incentives or benefits. A cafeteria-style incentive program can be very successful in a multicultural work environment because an employee can tailor his benefits to satisfy the needs or wants of his particular cultural background.

An Arab employee of a major multinational firm located in France benefitted from a cafeteria-style incentive program: "My father was very ill when I began working in France. When he died, as the oldest son, I felt obliged to be with my family. I took one week's bereavement leave from work, which was a benefit *I* chose from among the wide range of benefits I was offered under the cafeteria-style incentive program."

To recap, traditional incentives used to motivate a homogeneous North American or European work force, for example, may not be considered favorably by Mexican workers. Non-traditional incentive plans which offer flexible benefits based on employee needs can be a solution.

Supervising a Multicultural Work Force

People, by human nature, don't like change, and employees who find themselves surrounded by "foreigners" or different cultures in the work place may have difficulty coping with the situation. To help these employees overcome any insecurities, supervisors should ensure that they are properly introduced to their new work environment. Often, longer term workers are left out of this kind of orientation, but they must be included if the orientation is to be a success. Supervisors must demonstrate patience, too, in working with employees who are experiencing work-initiated insecurities [13].

In any corporation, supervisors and managers must treat all employees equally to avoid charges of favoritism or bias. In a multicultural work environment, this is especially true as favoritism may be viewed by some as racism.

Often, supervisors try to protect minorities by not delegating challenging and important tasks to them for execution. Frequently, managers believe that if the minority employee fails to properly execute an assignment, he or she will be resented or ridiculed by the other employees, thus damaging the synergy of the group and creating tension. This, of course, is absurd, and managers must realize that they cannot protect their minority employees from the real world.

Minority or immigrant employees often crave challenging assignments so they can prove to doubters that they, too, have the "right stuff" to be successful. How can respect be earned if the minority employee is always sheltered from challenging assignments? Managers, if they treat every worker equally and fairly, regardless of race or gender, will find that the work atmosphere will be positive.

Shames' theory [11] on intercultural training nicely complements the work of Parnell and Vanderkloot [10]. Shames believes that successful intercultural management involves skills in such areas as cross-cultural communication, the ability to suspend judgement and have a multiple perspective, and the patience to find the inherent logic in each different culture. Shames' training program for employees in a multicultural environment would include such elements as an area-specific briefing, basic language instruction, and generic cultural training. Either outside or in-house trainers would be suitable for Shames' training program.

Other training programs combine role playing, exercises, lectures, discussions, and group experiences. An effective training program for employees who work or who will work in a multicultural environment will offer educational courses on political issues, geography, culture, and history of the countries represented in the work force. These may be short in-house seminars or self-learning opportunities or provisions for external learning (e.g., tuition subsidy in local extension or adult education programs).

Insensitivities of the Majority Supervisor Force

Copeland [3] cites the following examples of how cross-cultural insensitivity, especially by white male workers, occurs in the diverse work force.

- A manager, thrilled with a new technique developed by one of his American Indian employees, regarded her with great fanfare and congratulations in front of her peers—just as the management books suggest. Humiliated, she didn't return to work for three weeks.
- After learning that a friendly pat on the arm or back would make workers feel good and motivated, a manager took every chance to pat subordinates. The Asian employees, who hated being touched, avoided the manager. Several asked for transfers.
- Fresh from a course on delegation, a production supervisor asked her primarily Filipino staff to alert her to any problems with some new equipment. When a problem arose, they used masking tape and other makeshift remedies to get the machines working because they perceived the solution as part of their delegated responsibility.

- A manager patronizes Asian technicians with inadequate English speaking skills, forgetting that many of these knowledge workers have had a better general and scientific education than he or she possesses.

The first and urgent need of managers today is to acquire the skills that will allow them to deal effectively with their increasingly diverse work force. The management of diversity is thought by some to be a competitive edge for companies that are able to effectively manage their diverse work forces—"To value work force diversity in a way designed to seize the benefits that differences bring."

Copeland [3] identifies skills revolving around four problem areas when dealing with diversity:

1. Stereotypes and assumptions—Stereotypes hurt people if invalid conclusions about them are reached. Observations leading to invalid assumptions only reinforce a bias previously held. It is therefore necessary for managers and employees to learn how to prevent stereotyping and coming to these invalid conclusions.
2. Unwritten rules and double standards for success—It's important for all employees to know what the organization values are because they define the rules for success.White male managers have to learn to identify their organization's culture and rules as well as how to pass on that information to women and minorities.
3. Membership to "the club"—Being a member of "the club" or ruling group is as important as hard work and competence, because it provides associated access to important information and relationships. Learning to include everyone in work-related and social events can help in this area.
4. Actual cultural differences—Cultural differences affect the values people bring to the work place. Managers must take an active role in learning about such cultural differences and use this knowledge to change their old habits of thinking about the treatment of employees.

The Hudson Institute [5] cites the following trends in the U.S. work force:

- The American economy should grow at a relatively healthy pace.
- U.S. manufacturing will be a much smaller share of the economy in the year 2000, with service industries creating all the new jobs over the next thirteen years.

- The work force will grow slowly, becoming older, more female and more disadvantaged.
- The new jobs in service industries will demand much higher skill levels than the jobs of today.

Five demographic facts will be important to the work force and how it will perform in the future:

- The population and the work force will grow more slowly than at any time since the 1930s.
- The average age of the population and the work force will rise, and the pool of young workers entering the labor market will shrink.
- More women will enter the work force.
- Minorities will be a larger share of new entrants into the labor force.
- Immigrants will represent the largest share of the increase in the population and the work force since the First World War.

On a global scale, W. B. Johnston [6] identified the key trends occurring in the world labor force:

- Gender—More women will enter the work force, especially in developing countries.
- Age—The world's work force is aging, especially in the developed countries.
- Education—Individuals all over the world are becoming increasingly well educated and it's expected that developing countries will contribute a greater number of educated workers.

Managing these trends will create political and social tension in many countries. However, all countries can expect to gain from the globalization of the work force

Training and Development for Diverse, Multicultural Work Forces

When conducting training sessions, it is vital to remember that not everyone learns the same way. The complexities of learning increase when cultural factors are included in the learning process.

Several factors identified by Buckley and Caple [2] affect the success of training programs on the learning process by participants. A brief overview of these factors follows:

1. Sequence of the training material—Appropriate sequencing of material contributes to the ease and enhancement of learning.
2. Readiness of the learner—How ready the individual is to learn, intellectually, motivationally, emotionally, attitudinally, and physically will affect how well the individual learns. One question you must ask in this regard is, has the trainee been required to attend or requested to attend the program. The answer will surely dictate the individual motivational level and you can adjust your training accordingly.
3. Ways of learning—Consider the mental and physical activities that cause people to change their behavior. Such activities include (a) trial and error, (b) perceptual organizational (mapping), (c) behavior modeling, (d) mediation, and (e) reflection.

HR leaders appreciate that people learn differently because of their cultural conditioning. Thus, Iranians prefer aural learning—listening over written material; Indians are more used to rote and numerical learning—memory and quantification rather than abstraction. Many peoples, especially in developing economies, learn better through visualization, which explains why some international trainers use animated cartoons and films.

4. General conditions of learning—In addition to motivational considerations several other conditions must be considered that will promote the learning by participants:
   - The training environment must be arranged in such a way as to keep participants alert throughout the program
   - The trainer must stimulate interest during sessions, keeping participants' attention through visual aids, varying pitch and tone of voice, changing physical position, introducing humor (with caution in multicultural groups), and varying activities of the group.
   - Provide a climate and atmosphere conducive to learning.
   - Control competition between participants.

A caveat—In some cultures, individual competition is frowned upon, but group competition is accepted; in other cultures, cooperation, not competition is the norm. People from such backgrounds must be acculturated to Western-type competition, whether in business or in training sessions.

In addition to these general guidelines, Buckley and Caple [2], identify two actors in the process of learning: the trainer and the participant.

It is the interaction of the activities of both actors that affects the learning process.

1. Actions by the trainer—Trainers can use one or more of the following actions to facilitate the trainee's learning:
   - Setting sub-goals with participants
   - Directing attention towards specific issues
   - Pictures and demonstrations
   - Human modeling
   - Verbal instructions
   - Guidance, prompting and cuing
   - Feedback results and reinforcements

2. Trainee activities—Most effective learning by trainees must involve active participation in the learning process. Activities that facilitate the trainees' participation include the following:
   - Practice and rehearsal including the element of active recall
   - Imagining and reflection—engaging in mental practice
   - Distribution practice—spreading the learning over several sessions
   - Discovery learning and exploration—enabling learning from their own understanding of a subject.

Individual Differences

It is important for HR leaders to remember the individual differences of employees that go beyond culture-general distinctions. This is a complex situation that requires skill to accommodate these differences as much as possible. It is impossible to accommodate all differences, but understanding them will allow flexibility in introducing and applying the principles being taught. Appreciating individual uniqueness allows one to explain why individuals don't react in the expected manner and need to be challenged in a creative manner.

Recommended Strategies

HR specialists must prepare for the tasks of managing cultural diversity. In conclusion we propose three steps that will facilitate the consideration and preparation of training:

1. Preliminary research—To avoid any problems that may affect the participant's understanding of certain topics as well as aiding in one's understanding about cultures.

2. Solicit participation—Dialogue with participants about the training before hand to find out any specific cultural aspects that will assist in the training.

3. Solicit co-workers—Talk to co-workers who are of the same nationality as participants. They should be able to provide some "hands-on" experience that will be helpful in preparations.

References

1. Beyette, B., "Setting the Stage for Corporate Change," *Los Angeles Times,* March 14, 1991.

2. Buckley, R. and Caple H., "Learning Principles and Conditions," *The Theory and Practice of Training,* London: Kogan Press, 1990.

3. Copeland, L., "Learning to Manage a Multicultural Work Force," *Training,* May 1988, p. 48.

4. Derven, M. G., "The Paradox of Performance Appraisals," *Personnel Journal,* February 1990, Vol. 69, Iss. 2, pp. 107–111.

5. Johnston, W. B. and Packer, A. E., "Work Force 2000: Work and Workers for the 21st Century" (Executive Summary), Indianapolis, IN: Hudson Institute, 1987.

6. Johnston, W. B., "Global Work Force 2000: The New World Labour Market," *Harvard Business Review,* March–April, 1991, p. 115–127.

7. Lewan, L. S., "Diversity in the Workplace," *HRMagazine,* June 1990, p. 42.

8. Loden, M. and Rosener, J. *Work Force America! Managing Employee Diversity as a Vital Resource,* Homewood, IL: Business One Irvin, 1991.

9. Morrison, A., *The New Leaders—Guidelines on Leadership Diversity in America,* San Francisco, CA: Jossey-Bass, 1992.

10. Parnell, M. and Vanderkloot, J., "How to Build Cross-Cultural Bridges," *Communication World,* July/August 1989, Vol. 6, Iss. 8, pp. 40–42.

11. Shames, G., "Training for the Multicultural Workplace," *Cornell Hotel and Restaurant Administration Quarterly,* February 1986, Vol. 26, Iss. 4, pp. 25–31.

12. Thiedermann, S. *Bridging Cultural Barriers for Corporate Success,* Lexington, MA: Lexington Books, 1990.

13. Mondy, W., Premeaux, S., and Comish, C. R. "Supervising Employees with Job Insecurities," *Management Solutions,* June 1987, Vol. 32, 6, pp. 28–30.

CHAPTER 7

THE CROSS-CULTURAL MARKETEER

Introduction

By 1990, the writing was on the wall. Russia's future had been determined. In a survey of local Muscovites, McDonald's had replaced Lenin's Mausoleum as the most popular place to visit in Moscow by a ratio of 3 to 1.

By 1991, the Russian people had given up on tanks and missiles. They wanted to beat their swords into plowshares. One emerging Russian advertising agency offered to pay $6,000 per year to display its name and telephone number on twenty Soviet tanks. A local general rejected the offer as inappropriate, but it showed where the Russians were headed.

In 1992, President George Bush declared that communism was officially dead. If that is true, PepsiCo helped kill it. During the failed Soviet coup attempt in 1991, PepsiCo's Pizza Hut in Moscow delivered 260 pizzas and 20 cases of Pepsi Cola to the barricades at the Russian Parliament Building. Sixty of the pizzas went to Boris Yeltsin and his supporters inside the building.

The rest is history. The Soviet Union has disbanded and new nations have been created in Eurasia. Big markets have opened. Citizens are clamoring for Western goods and services. The potential in Russia and the other republics is extraordinary. Amazing opportunities await businesses that are willing to make a long-term commitment.

Old Russia Hands

One of the best ways for cross-cultural marketeers to learn about opportunities in Russia is to track the path of "Old Russia Hands," businesses that operated in the Soviet Union prior to its dissolution. By the end of 1991, foreign businesses had entered into 3,400 joint ventures with the Soviet government. American firms with Soviet joint ventures included Honeywell, McDonald's, PepsiCo, and Polaroid.

Most of the joint ventures were small. Fifty-four percent employed less than fifty workers, while only 1.7% employed more than 1,000 workers. General Motors entered into a relatively large $1 billion deal with Volga Auto works to provide the Soviet car maker with necessary equipment to meet toughened Western European emission standards. Colgate-Palmolive and the old Soviet government were involved in a medium-sized joint venture for making and marketing toothpaste. Procter & Gamble signed a joint venture agreement with Leningrad State University to market and distribute consumer products in Russia.

The dissolution of the Soviet Union has put the future of some joint ventures on shaky ground. Other joint venture arrangements were very farsighted. Philip Morris agreed to provide the Soviet government with 20 billion cigarettes by the end of 1991. Soviet citizens had been smoking 400 billion cigarettes annually, so the deal amounted to 5% of the total market. With the breakup of the Soviet Union, Philip Morris would have been left in a quandary, if they hadn't looked ahead. Philip Morris's deal also included an arrangement with Boris Yeltsin to continue supplying cigarettes to Russia until 1995.

IBM also took a long-range view. IBM has been in the Soviet market since 1972. During the ten-year American trade embargo of high-tech computers and equipment that began in 1980, IBM was restricted to selling and servicing typewriters and photocopiers. It wasn't very profitable, but IBM stuck it out and made connections throughout Russia. In 1991, IBM opened up a new office in Moscow and prepared to move forward.

Other companies with operations in Russia include Johnson & Johnson, Eastman Kodak, Holiday Inns Worldwide, Kellogg, and Xerox. Xerox took a creative approach to entering the Soviet market. In 1991, Xerox brought its "We taught the world to copy" campaign to Moscow by placing experimental signs on five buses. It planned to place advertisements on 200 buses in 1992.

Russian Cola Wars

Two of the most interesting corporations to initiate cross-cultural marketing programs are PepsiCo and Coca-Cola Company. Both had the foresight to make early inroads into the Soviet market. Today, they are both jockeying for position in Russia and the other nearby republics to see who can gain pre-eminence.

PepsiCo entered the Soviet Union first, and has been very effective in capturing the market. PepsiCo promotes Pepsi Cola around Moscow by using a series of outdoor advertisements. It reaches Russia as a whole through television ads. Pepsi Cola is sold at Moscow's Pizza Hut and in kiosks throughout the city. It has become a very popular beverage. To overcome currency exchange problems PepsiCo signed a major trade agreement in 1990 whereby the Soviet government agreed to trade freighters and vodka for increased production of Pepsi.

Coca-Cola Company is not taking PepsiCo's Russian success lightly. Coca-Cola entered the Soviet Union with Fanta Orange Soda in 1979, and added Coke in 1985, nearly fifteen years after Pepsi established a beachhead. To combat Pepsi, Coca-Cola entered into a joint venture with Svyatoslav Fyodorov, a Russian doctor and entrepreneur who owns 2.3% of the operation. Coke also opened an office in Kiev, capital of the Ukraine.

Coca-Cola Refreshments—Moscow plans to erect 2,000 stands to sell Fanta and Coke around Moscow. It will begin with 400 kiosks, which will double as outdoor advertisements. Coca-Cola will import whatever supplies are needed until local plants can supply the kiosks.

The battle between Pepsi and Coke for the Russian market is only one theater of a larger global "marketing war." In 1992, PepsiCo and Coca-Cola entered into a worldwide advertising war against each other. One commentator wrote: "Coke Plans the Real Thing: Global Attack." Coca-Cola created new global image spots and planned on running at least seventeen global commercials in 1992.

Pepsi's global approach is to use "music marketing" to appeal to young consumers. Their former slogan, "The Choice of a New Generation," has been replaced by "Gotta Have It." To spearhead their global campaign, Pepsi signed singer Michael Jackson to tour the world under the Pepsi logo.

For those engaged in transcultural marketing, there are many new challenges and opportunities both at home and abroad. Because of its sudden transitioning from a centralized planned economy to a more market-oriented one, we have chosen Russia as a target of opportunity within the global marketplace. Obviously, the same marketing prospects may extend to other newly independent states in Eastern Europe, Central Asia, the Pacific Basin, as well as Latin America where free enterprise are on the rise.

Cross-cultural marketeers can track the path of these corporations and others by researching the *Business Periodicals Index* and other business indices. The indices will lead marketeers to articles in journals and magazines such as *Advertising Age* and *Sales & Marketing Management*. The articles often contain thorough descriptions of a corporation's marketing approach in a foreign country. They can be quite helpful in learning what has worked and what has failed overseas. Human resource professionals can use magazine and journal articles as an effective resource for designing training programs on cross-cultural marketing. *The Economist* and the reports of its Intelligence Units are particularly helpful, as well as the *European Business Review*.

Global Marketing Program

In the worldwide battle between Coke and Pepsi, Coke has been the clear winner. The Coca-Cola Company gets more than 60% of its soft drink sales and 80% of its operating income from abroad. Its marketing program is looked upon as the purest example of global marketing in existence today.

One of the main reasons Coke has been so successful is its view of the world. Coca-Cola truly believes in the global marketplace. Its board of directors recognizes that 95% of the world's population lives outside the United States and "that's where the money is."

Coke's economists are also "gung-ho" on globalization. They have come up with projections that point to a climate favorable for global expansion.

- Disposable income is rising around the world. Coke estimates that the GNP of the Pacific Basin is growing at a rate of $3 billion a week. At that pace, the region will account for nearly a quarter of the world's gross national product by the turn of the century.
- Outside the United States and Europe, the world's population is getting younger. Half of Indonesia's 180 million people are under 20, as are half a billion Chinese. The average age of Brazilians is only 17.
- The world's markets are becoming easier to reach. The European Community will be a market with a population one-third larger than the United States, a population density greater than China's, and a Gross National Product greater than the United States and Japan combined.

These projections have influenced Coke to continue down the path of globalization. Nearly half of all soft drinks sold around the world are products of Coca-Cola Corporation. Five hundred and sixty million times a day, consumers in more than 160 countries drink Coca-Cola, Diet Coke, Fanta, Sprite, and other products of the Coca-Cola Company. No other soft drink company sells even half of that amount.

On its path toward becoming a global corporation, Coca-Cola faced a lot of pitfalls and learned a great deal. Based on their experiences, Coca-Cola has developed the following rules for success in the global marketplace:

1. Successful global companies must develop single and relentless strategies for attacking and conquering new markets. Companies that want to globalize should take a very pragmatic approach. Management should do whatever it takes to globalize, countering excuses and reasons for not globalizing. A successful global company must develop a single and relentless strategy for attacking and conquering new markets.

2. A company that wants to go global must have, or build, or buy, a powerful trademark. The best example is Coca-Cola. In an international survey, Coca-Cola was the most well-known, most highly respected, and most powerful brand name in the world. IBM finished second.

3. Effective global marketing requires a highly coordinated, global distribution system. Coke's success is tied to the efforts of more than 1,000 bottling partners, and multitudes of salespersons who work long, hard hours to sell Coke products. In Australia, one father and son sales team drives 7,000 kilometers through the Outback every week to deliver Coke to isolated pockets of consumers. In the Philippines, one 75-year-old salesman sells Coke for twelve hours every day, refusing to leave the marketplace until he has sold at least fifty cases. Dedication like this results in global success.

4. Global companies should live by the simple code, "Think globally, act locally." You don't necessarily need a global product to be a global competitor. It is more important to have a global state of mind.

5. Global companies should tailor their messages to the local market. Before introducing its "You can't beat the feeling" campaign, Coca Cola determined that the message had wide universal appeal. However, the message was adapted and localized in many countries. In

Japan, the theme became "I Feel Coke"; in Italy, "Unique Sensation"; in Chile, "The Feeling of Life."

6. The global marketing department must be extremely careful with translations and cultural differences. When Coke re-entered China in 1979, it discovered that the literal representation of Coca-Cola in Chinese characters meant "bite the wax tadpole." Coke engaged an Oriental language specialist to experiment with alternatives. The final choice was four Mandarin characters sounding very similar to Coca-Cola and meaning, "Can Happy, Mouth Happy."

7. Global companies should adjust their products for local tastes. Germans prefer a tart orange taste, while Italians prefer a sweet orange taste. Coca-Cola adjusts the sweetness of Fanta orange soda in those markets. In some markets, local fruit is used to make Fanta.

8. Global companies should concentrate on a central theme, idea, or symbol to bind together their business system, brands, and consumers. Advertising and marketing is designed to encourage consumers to associate Coke with their best feelings and memories, such as their friends and families, moments of joy and laughter, and sporting events and musical concerts. The worldwide system is designed to ensure that wherever consumers travel, they will find one friendly point of reference—a can of Coke.

Multinational vs. Global Marketing

Out of any American company, Coca-Cola comes closest to following a purely global marketing strategy. The transcultural marketeer bases the firm's marketing strategy on a few standardized world markets rather than on many customized markets. The corporation offers globally standardized products that are advanced, functional, reliable, and, above all, relatively low-priced. The corporation doesn't completely reject product customization and differentiation, but adjusts to differences in product preferences only after exhausting all efforts to retain standardization.

There has been a long ongoing debate over whether the proper approach to international marketing is a global, standardized approach or a multinational, localized approach. The answer depends upon the match between the firm's resources and the target markets.

The philosophies of multinationalization and globalization are based upon fundamentally different assumptions about the nature of the modern world. The multinationalists see a heterogeneous world where transportation and storage costs are high, technology is rapidly changing, governmental restrictions are severe, and product needs and preferences are diverse. To compete in such a marketplace the multinational corporation manages a portfolio of independent positions. The MNC evaluates each market as an independent entity and pursues high-profit markets more aggressively than low-profit markets.

The globalists see a homogeneous world where technological advances have reduced transportation and communications costs, softened governmental constraints, and narrowed national economic and social differences. To compete in such a world the corporation must take advantage of economies of scale to reduce costs and price. The focus on worldwide volume enables the global corporation to enter low-profit markets.

Human resource professionals can use Exhibit 7-1 to determine whether their company's philosophy and characteristics are suited to a multinational or global marketing strategy.

Exhibit 7-1
Multinational vs. Global Marketing Strategy

	Multinationalization	Globalization
Environment:	Heterogeneous	Homogeneous
Scale Economies:	Low	High
Type of Product:	Customized	Standardized
Transport Costs:	High	Low
Storage Costs:	High	Low
Communication Costs:	High	Low
Governmental Restrictions:	Severe	Soft
Company Resources:	Low	High
Industry:	Retailing, Consumer Goods, Hazardous Chemicals, Metal Fabrication	Automobiles, Steel, Chemicals, Petroleum, Banking, Computers, Publishing, Electronics

The globalization versus multinationalization debate influences all four areas of marketing strategy: product strategy; promotion strategy; pricing strategy; and distribution strategy. Human resource professionals should consider incorporating all these strategies in their cross-cultural marketing training program. We will touch upon all four areas, and include discussions of cross-cultural marketing strategies for products in terms of research and design, for promotion in terms of advertising and sales, for pricing in terms of price imagery, and for distribution in terms of selection and training of distributors.

Cross-Cultural Product Strategy

Product strategies specify the market needs that may be served by offering different products. Product strategies deal with such matters as number and diversity of products, product innovations, product scope, and product design. The primary emphasis in this section will be on product research and design.

The corporation must decide whether to take a global approach to product design, or to tailor its products to the preferences of an individual cultural group. The choice is crucial to the success of the marketing plan. It is also laden with concerns of multicultural and political correctness.

Coca-Cola's global success has led to charges of cultural imperialism. In the view of some artists and politicians, America is trying to "Coca-Colanize" the world. This is a highly emotional issue in many countries. Trainers must make sure that the issue is addressed during the training program.

In broad terms, corporations exhibit three product philosophies: (1) "We sell the same product to everyone, no matter where they live." (2) "We'll alter our products to sell them in other markets." (3) "We find out what customers want, and then we design products to meet their needs." Trainers should make sure that they spend some time on identifying the corporation's product philosophy.

"We Sell the Same Product to Everyone"

Corporations that follow a philosophy of "We sell the same products to everyone" don't change their products, no matter where they sell them.

Normally, these corporations begin selling abroad passively. Requests for information about their products appear from abroad like magic.

Blue Sky National Beverage Company of Santa Fe, New Mexico began its international sales this way. Blue Sky manufactures naturally-flavored sodas for the New Mexico market. Officials from New Mexico's Department of Agriculture went to an international trade convention and brought some Blue Sky with them. Blue Sky received some calls from "out of the blue," and began making international sales.

In 1988, Cheerio Kansai, an Osaka-based manufacturer and distributor of soft drinks, entered an agreement with Blue Sky to carry two of its six flavors. Mandarin-lime and lemon-lime were considered appropriate for Japanese tastes. Root-beer and cherry-vanilla ice cream soda were considered too bizarre. Today, over 10% of Blue Sky's total sales are to Japan.

Foreigners learn of products, like Blue Sky soda, through numerous channels, including developments reported in scientific and trade journals with international circulation, advertising that spills across national boundaries, and demonstration of products that consumers have bought in one country and transferred abroad. Foreign firms also may actively send out buyers to search for new products to sell.

"We'll Alter Our Products"

Corporations that follow a philosophy of "we'll alter what we make to sell it" alter products to fit various markets. There are many reasons to do this, including the legal, geographical, economic, and cultural factors.

One strategy for compromising between uniformity and diversity is to standardize many components, while changing the end characteristics. For example, Coca-Cola exports concentrate to bottling plants all over the world. Carbonation, sugar, and color are added at local bottling plants. The amounts may vary from one country to the next to conform with local preferences. This type of change is practically without cost, because standardization is achieved for the concentrate process, and because the finished product cannot feasibly be exported.

"We Sell First, Design Later"

Corporations that follow this philosophy do extensive research to discover what foreign consumers want. They establish good relationships by selling themselves to foreign manufacturers. Then they go home to design and manufacture marketable products.

Conner Peripherals, Inc., a Silicon Valley disk drive manufacturer based in San Jose, California, follows this approach. Conner's philosophy is "sell, design, build." Rather than creating a product and trying to sell it to computer manufacturers, Conner works to sell their disk drives by helping other companies design them into new products they are developing. Conner then uses the customer-specific design to build a drive that meets their exact needs.

To carry out its philosophy, Conner has concentrated on the Japanese market. Japanese manufacturers dominate 80–90% of the world market for laptop and notebook computers. To develop good working relations with these manufacturers, Conner has developed a direct sales force of twenty-three people in Japan, including customer liaisons, service technicians, quality assurance representatives, and administrators. All but three of the salespersons are Japanese nationals, and all speak Japanese fluently.

Conner's approach has paid off handsomely. By working closely with its Japanese customers on market development, Conner has earned a significant time-to-market advantage over its competitors. Conner now sells 75–80% of all 2.5-inch hard drives used worldwide.

Product Design

In designing products for the global marketplace, corporations must consider many factors (see Exhibit 7-2). In some countries, the level of technical skill is so low that products must be simplified to be useful to consumers. In other countries, climatic differences may require product adaptation. Trainers should review these factors during the cross-cultural marketing workshop.

The Future of Global Product Design

Product designers have been extremely tempted by the prospects of globalization. Designers have always sought universal solutions, hoping to develop products with powerful aesthetic and functional qualities that can transcend cultural differences. The global business environment gives designers the chance to become members of select teams that create products for the whole world. The acquisition of such employment is both lucrative and ego-boosting.

Exhibit 7-2
Factors in Designing a Product for
the Global Marketplace

Factor:	Possible Product Change:
Level of Technical Skill	Product simplification
Level of Labor Cost	Automation; Manual Labor
Level of Literacy	Remarking; Product simplification
Level of Income	Quality and price change
Interest Rates	Quality and price change
Maintenance Needs	Change in tolerances
Climatic Differences	Product adaptation
Isolation (difficult to access)	Product simplification; Reliability improvement
Differences in Standards	Recalibration; Resizing
Availability of Other Products	Greater or lesser product integration
Availability of materials	Change in product structure Change in fuel requirements
Power Availability	Resizing
Special Conditions	Product redesign or invention

The designers' dream of universal products is often unachievable. Manufacturers of products who sell in a variety of cultures usually cannot sell the same product everywhere. Even "global products," like Coca-Cola are altered to meet the tastes of local consumers. The best that can be hoped for in most situations is the development of products that are relatively easy to alter. For example, automobile manufacturers can design cars with readily changeable color, trim, and seats.

While the development and design of universal products is an interesting topic of discussion, the globalization vs. multinationalization debate may soon become moot. The world is rapidly entering an age of adaptive technologies. Computer-aided design, manufacturing and engineering (CAD/CAM/CAE), robotics, and new equipment and process technology (EPT) allow companies to use "economies of scope" in creating great varieties of relatively customized products at remarkably low prices. As this occurs, global products will be phased out. Consumers will choose to purchase products that specifically meet their needs, rather than products which fit some universal standard.

Cross-Cultural Promotion Strategy

Promotion is the process of presenting a message that will help to sell a product or service. It is extremely difficult to present messages that are effective across cultures. Trainers will want to spend a significant part of their training programs discussing and developing cross-cultural promotion strategies.

Cross-cultural promotion strategies are concerned with the planning, implementation, and control of persuasive communication with customers all over the world. In broad terms, there are two types of promotion strategies: "push" strategies and "pull" strategies. Push strategies involve face-to-face interaction with customers, such as door-to-door selling. Pull strategies involve non-personal communication transmitted through the mass media, such as magazine advertisements.

Most firms use combinations of the two strategies. The blend of the strategies is referred to as the "push-pull mix." For each product in each country, a company must determine its total promotional budget as well as the mix of the budget between push and pull. The push-pull mix is affected by several factors, including the type of distribution system, the cost and availability of media to reach target markets, consumer attitudes towards sources of information, and the price of the product relative to incomes.

Our discussion of push strategies will center around cross-cultural selling techniques and the need for language fluency. Our discussion of pull strategies will center around cross-cultural advertising and examples of marketing blunders.

Learning Foreign Languages

One of the most important things for cross-cultural marketeers to do is to learn the language of the countries where they want to do business. Marketing is communication! How can you communicate with someone if you can't speak their language?

The Japanese have learned English very well. They continually tell Americans that they don't need to learn Japanese, because Japanese business persons can speak English. Besides, the argument goes, Japanese is too difficult to learn. This argument is very beneficial for the Japanese, and very damaging to Americans. How can American marketeers communicate with Japanese consumers when American marketeers can't speak Japanese? They can't! What does that mean? It means that Japanese business persons can keep a hold on the Japanese market.

At a time when American salespersons should be knocking on doors from Moscow to Kuala Lumpur for new orders, foreign language skills are among the least important factors in decisions on executive advancement. When Moran, Stahl & Boyer polled fifty-one large U.S. multinationals about what they looked for in candidates for overseas postings, foreign language ability ranked tenth out of eleven categories. A spokesperson for Procter & Gamble Co. stated, "Another language is helpful, of course, but it's certainly never necessary."

Part of the argument against learning foreign languages is that English has become the universal language of the international business community. English is the native language of 400 million people in twelve nations. Another 400 million people speak English as a second language, and the numbers are growing. Over 250 million Chinese are currently studying English.

The fact that many people around the world speak English is no excuse for American business persons not to learn other languages. Marketeers are severely handicapped by their lack of language ability. Sometimes the inability to speak another language can be fatal to the cross-cultural marketing plan.

An old anecdote points to the value of language ability: Mommy Mouse and Baby Mouse were looking for some cheese when they were confronted by a big cat. As the cat raised its paw to strike, Mommy Mouse looked it in the eye and screamed, "BOW WOW WOW WOW WOW!!!" The astounded cat twirled around and ran away. Mommy Mouse looked at Baby Mouse and said, "Let that be a lesson to you. Always learn a second language!"

There are some excellent language programs available for business persons such as Berlitz Schools of Languages, Princeton, New Jersey, Dartmouth College's Language Outreach, and Middlebury College.

Another option is to attend a "culture camp." Culture camps offer language crash courses, and prepare people for the etiquette and business practices common to their new locale. International Orientation Resources of Northbrook, Illinois offers a language camp, as does Moran, Stahl & Boyer of Boulder, Colorado. Some organizations that can be of use in developing language and culture skills are listed in Exhibit 7-3.

Exhibit 7-3
Some Multicultural Resources

- American Graduate School of International Management, Thunderbird Campus, Glendale, Arizona 85306, USA.
- American Management Associations, 135 West 50th Street, New York, NY, 10020.
- American Society for Training and Development, 1630 Duke St., Box 1443, Alexandria, VA 22313 USA.
- Berlitz Schools of Languages of America, Building O, 1101 State Road, Princeton, NJ 08540, USA. For books of foreign phrases, Berlitz Publications, P.O. Box 506, Delran, NJ 08370.
- Business Council for International Understanding, (BCIU Institute) The American University, Washington, D.C. 20016. (202) 686-2771.
- Business International Corporation, One Dag Hammarskjold Plaza, New York, NY 10017, USA.
- Center for International Studies, (David M. Kennedy), Brigham Young University, 280 HRCB, Provo, Utah 84602.
- International Society for Intercultural Education, Training, and Research, 733 15th Street N.W., Suite 900, Washington, D.C. 20005.
- Moran, Stahl & Boyer, 366 Lexington Ave., New York, NY 10017. International Division, 900 28th St., Boulder, CO 80303.

Acquiring Translation and Interpretation Services

Executives who cannot speak foreign languages must rely upon translators and interpreters. "Translators" convert material that is written in one language into written form in another language. "Interpreters" work only with spoken words.

International businesses and organizations spend approximately $20 billion per year worldwide on translation and interpretation services. Interpreters usually charge for a minimum three-hour service, ranging in price from $85 to $250. Translators charge per word. Fair rates range from $.12 to $.35 per word.

Translation of business contracts is especially tricky. Being bilingual doesn't make a person a good translator. Many professional translators consider themselves expert at translating contracts from a foreign language into English, but not from English into a foreign language. In selecting a translator, business persons should consider the following:

1. Translators should be accredited by the American Translators Association in both the required language and the subject of discussion. For example, a corporation may require a translator who is proficient in Japanese and engineering terminology, or German and medical terminology.

2. Translators should understand the actual meaning and intent of any written material, not just its literal meaning.

3. Translators should have the proper equipment to provide timely, legible work. At a minimum, translators should have a personal computer, a fax machine, and a modem.

4. Translators should understand the particular industry or technical jargon of the material being translated.

One useful technique for checking on the accuracy of translations is to have one translator translate the contract into the foreign language and then have a second translator translate the contract back into English. If the second translator's version of the contract is significantly different from the original version, then the business must analyze why the discrepancies have arisen. It may be that certain scientific or legal concepts are not easily translatable. If that is the case, the business may want to insist that all contracts be written in English and governed by American law.

Human resource professionals can obtain a list of local interpreters through the American Society of Interpreters (Box 9603, Washington, D.C. 20016; Telephone: 703-998-8636). Information about local translators can be obtained through the American Translators Association (109 Croton Avenue, Ossining, New York 10562; Telephone: 703-892-1500). General information about translation and interpretation services can be obtained from George P. Rimalower (President, Interpreting Services International, Inc., 14402 Haynes Street, Suite 204, Van Nuys, California 91401).

The Cross-Cultural Salesperson

Selling is a form of communication. Salespersons must know their customers! Unfortunately, most American salespersons have not been willing to spend time learning about foreign cultures. Consequently, when international sales opportunities arise, most Americans are subject to a double whammy: (1) they can't speak the language, and (2) they don't know the customer.

Japan is a good example. Many American salespersons are complaining about their inability to penetrate the Japanese market. They are correct in their contention that Japan is a difficult market to enter. Japan displays an ingrained antipathy to anything from the outside. For many Japanese, buying foreign products is unpatriotic. This has resulted in a multiplicity of informal obstacles to selling in Japan. The tight-knit business system is inhospitable to all outsiders.

However, what steps have American sales representatives taken to overcome the inhospitality and penetrate the Japanese market? A senior official at Japan's Ministry of International Trade and Industry (MITI) said: "To really get access to this market, you've got to learn the language and drink sake in nightclubs for three to four years. Can you find many American executives interested in doing that? We have sent 100,000 businessmen to the U.S., and you have sent only 8,000 to Japan."

To sell in Japan, salespersons must learn the distinctive habits of Japanese consumers. For example, when Johnson & Johnson first introduced its baby powder into the Japanese market, it found demand to be very low. Then they learned that Japanese mothers use baby powder sparingly for fear that it might fly all over the place and get their spotlessly clean homes dirty. The Japanese consumer of baby powder requires a flat box and a powder puff, rather than a plastic squeeze bottle. When Johnson & Johnson changed its packaging, sales increased dramatically.

Betty Crocker cake mix is another example. In trying to adapt their product for the Japanese market, Betty Crocker designed the mix to be made in electric rice cookers. What Betty Crocker didn't realize is that the Japanese take great pride in the purity of their rice. Expecting Japanese consumers to bake cakes in their rice cookers is similar to expecting English consumers to make coffee in their teapots. It just doesn't happen.

The amount of time required to make a sale is an extremely important factor to consider in the Japanese marketplace. Japanese characterize the best salesmen of industrial chemicals as "wet." Wet salesmen are very traditional and are willing to spend hours cultivating personal relations. On the other hand, the best salesmen of high-tech products in Japan are characterized as "dry." Dry salesmen have a direct, businesslike approach. Buyers of high-tech products in Japan are young and possess advanced degrees. They don't have time for a lot of tea-drinking.

Given the unwillingness of many American salespersons to learn the Japanese language and culture, many corporations follow a multinational sales approach, relying on Japanese salespersons to sell American products in the Japanese market. The standard training approach is to bring Japanese salespersons to the United States for product orientation, not sales training. Salespersons are not allowed to sell the product until they are steeped in its features and armed with Japanese language sales brochures. After being sent back to Japan, salespersons meet once per week for two-hour sales meetings during which sales progress is checked and ideas for new products are reviewed.

Exhibit 7-4 presents three checklists that have been synthesized from the advice of leading international salespersons. Human resource professionals should customize and/or combine the lists as training guides for the cross-cultural selling workshop.

Exhibit 7-4
Checklists for a Cross-Cultural Selling Workshop

Five Tips on the Art of International Selling

1. Be prepared! The guidance of an experienced mentor is the most desirable way to learn about customers in a new market. International business persons should also read voluminously. Marketeers should read books on social and business etiquette, history, folklore, current affairs, cultural values, geography, sports, the arts, religion, politics, and practical matters, such as foreign exchange, time zones, transportation, and hours of business. The first thing that salespersons should do when they get off the plane is to read a local newspaper from cover to cover. It is an effective way to discover what is currently on customers' minds.

2. Slow down! International customers are usually on a different time schedule. Salespeople who are pressed for time often appear brash, arrogant, and untrustworthy.

3. Develop trust! Product quality, pricing, and clear contracts are often not as important as good personal relationships. International salespersons must establish that they are trustworthy.

4. Learn the language! How can salespersons expect to sell to customers if they can't speak their language!

5. Respect the culture!

Ten Tips for Selling Overseas

1. Beware of contractual sales agreements. American laws are not universal.

2. Register your trademark. If you expect to develop a customer franchise for your product, the trademark is a key element. You don't want to have to buy it from someone else overseas, because you failed to register it.

3. One country's "bargain" can be something totally different elsewhere. In some countries, promotional price discounts are equated with low quality items.

4. Try to limit agreements to stable monetary systems. Foreign exchange rates have been known to fluctuate wildly.

5. Literal translations can kill you, figuratively. When PepsiCo introduced its "Come Alive! You're in the Pepsi Generation" slogan in Thailand in the mid-1960s, it translated as "Pepsi brings your ancestors back from the dead." Don't make bonehead mistakes like this.

6. English is not always "English." Many people who speak English as a second or third language do not understand the subtle nuances of words and expressions. Don't think that they understand what you are saying just because they are nodding and can say a few words.
7. In foreign countries, you often have to haggle over media rates. Americans who are used to printed rate cards and laws that preclude preferential treatment should be prepared for a different way of conducting business.
8. When making a proposal to an overseas company, never expect an immediate response. You must be prepared to wait . . . and wait . . . and wait . . . and wait.
9. If you are invited to participate in an event, join in. The local customs are a traditional way to enjoy a relaxing environment out of the office, to talk, and to become better acquainted.
10. Always be cognizant of national pride. The quickest way to antagonize people is to tell them how to do things in their own country.

Fifteen Dos and Don'ts for Selling Abroad

1. Adapt the product to the market.
2. Pay attention to custom and tradition.
3. Exploit markets in proper sequence.
4. Remain politically tolerant.
5. Build strong local management.
6. Beware of language barriers.
7. Study differences in advertising.
8. Identify the company with the local scene.
9. Know the trade channels.
10. Understand the consumer's views of price and quality.
11. Appraise the degree of acceptance of free enterprise.
12. Explore government regulations.
13. Insulate against restrictive legislation.
14. Invest for the long term.
15. Interchange information between the home office and the foreign office.

Cross-Cultural Advertising

The basic purpose of advertising is to effectively communicate information and persuade consumers to purchase a product or service. If cross-cultural advertising is skillfully planned and implemented, it can introduce desirable new products, combat foreign competition, build goodwill, and promote sales. Skillful planning of cross-cultural advertisements requires marketeers to learn about foreign audiences, define market segments as precisely as possible, and study backgrounds and motivational influences in detail before the advertising campaign is formulated.

Cross-cultural advertising campaigns can be categorized as either multinational or global. Multinational advertisers feel that cultural differences play an important part in shaping demand for the specific types of goods and services and in determining what promotional appeals are best. Therefore they pay strict attention to cultural differences worldwide. Factors such as geography, language, religion, philosophy, tradition, and family patterns are all considered when designing the multinational advertising campaign.

Although most corporations formerly relied on multinational ad campaigns, global advertising is beginning to be taken much more seriously. For a long time, the marketing world did not have the international coordination to pursue a single idea worldwide, and local cultural differences seemed too great a chasm to try to bridge. However, in the 1980s many corporations began to make the same brand names available worldwide. Giant advertising networks arose to take the global accounts.

There are many reasons to attempt global advertising campaigns, but the most compelling are money and control. Global advertising can save money on commercial production costs and allow corporations to retain greater control over the message and content of advertisements than was previously possible.

While there are economies of scale in using the same advertising programs worldwide, there are four major problems in the global standardization of advertising: (1) translation, (2) legality, (3) credibility or image, and (4) media availability. These problems have resulted in very few global campaigns. Instead, most standardized campaigns rely upon similar types of advertisements. For example, using sports stars from every country to advertise a soft drink.

Translation may be the biggest problem for global advertisements. Obviously, if corporations are going to sell their products in countries with different languages, it will be necessary to translate their advertisements into those languages. On the surface, this seems to be easy. However, companies run into many problems. To begin with, countries with the "same" language often have different words for the same object. In Latin America, for example, the word for "automobile tire" changes from country to country.

Corporations have run into severe difficulties in choosing the correct words for advertising campaigns. Sometimes an acceptable word or direct translation in one region is obscene, misleading, or meaningless in another. General Motors thought its Nova automobile could be sold in Latin America under the same name, because Nova means "star" in Spanish. However, people started pronouncing it "no va," which is the Spanish translation for "it does not go." Obviously, people did not want to purchase cars that would not go, so car sales were very limited.

Foreign laws also provide barriers to global advertisements. What is legally allowed in one country may not be allowed elsewhere. The basic reasons for differences are national variations in views on consumer protection, competitive protection, promotion of civil rights, standards of morality, and nationalism. In terms of consumer protection, foreign laws differ with the amount of deception permitted, what can be advertised to children, whether warnings must be given of possible harmful effects, and the degree to which ingredients must be listed.

Some countries have banned advertising that is too difficult for citizens to understand. The most famous example of this involved sales of Nestle's infant formula in Africa. Nestle advertised its infant formula through mass marketing techniques. The advertisements encouraged mothers to switch from breast feeding to bottle feeding. Unfortunately, most of the mothers could not read and failed to understand product instructions for proper usage. This resulted in many cases of infant diarrhea, malnutrition, and even death. As a result, Nestle faced a 6½-year boycott of the sale of its product in less developed countries. The company's image and esprit de corps were significantly damaged.

Despite these problems, the demand for global advertising is increasing at a rapid pace. The senior vice-president and director of global marketing for Coca-Cola recently said: "The time is right for global advertising. The world has changed. There is global media now, like MTV. And there is a global teenager. The same kid you see at the Ginza in Tokyo is in Piccadilly Square in London and in Pushkin Square in Moscow." Based upon this view, Coca-Cola has designed a series of advertisements to be seen and understood everywhere. The campaign began in 1992 and was used in over 100 countries.

In developing their global ads, companies would be wise to learn from the mistakes of previous faulty campaigns. For example, Procter & Gamble made some serious errors in Japan. Japanese housewives didn't like P&G's ads. The ads stressed product benefits and user testimonials. This was very repulsive to Japanese consumers. Japanese consultants warned P&G that Japanese consumers wouldn't like the ads, but P&G wouldn't listen.

One of the worst P&G ads in Japan was for Camay soap. In the late 1970s, P&G ran an ad for Camay where a man met a woman for the first time and immediately compared her skin to that of a fine porcelain doll. Japanese consumers were insulted. For a Japanese man to say that to a Japanese woman meant that he was either unsophisticated or very rude. P&G had been warned about this, but chose to ignore the warnings of its Japanese ad-men. As a result, their ad campaign failed.

In determining whether or not a global advertisement is appropriate for a particular market, several factors should be considered:

1. The type of product: When there are certain universal selling points for some products, they are sold primarily on the basis of objective physical characteristics, for example, razor blades, automobile tires. The objective characteristics are likely to be considered by consumers to be identical, suggesting that the same appeals may work in all markets.
2. The homogeneity or heterogeneity of markets: When aggregate characteristics such as income, education, and occupation are alike, individual consumer characteristics such as needs, attitudes, and customs may also be alike, suggesting that the advertiser can use the same selling points.
3. The characteristics and availability of media: If certain media are available in some countries and not the others, certain messages and materials may not be usable.
4. The types of advertising agency service available in each market segment: If the advertising available overseas is of poor quality, the corporation may have to rely on central control of advertising.
5. Government restrictions on the nature of advertising: Certain types of messages may be prohibited by law.
6. Government tariffs on art work or printed materials: Such expenses may offset a cost advantage achieved by centralization of the art and production functions.

7. Trade codes, ethical practices, and industry agreements: In some countries, there is a gentlemen's agreement among competitors not to use a certain type of media.

8. Corporate organization of the advertiser: If a company is global, global advertising may be easier.

Human resource professionals might want to use the republics of the former Soviet Union as subject areas for their cross-cultural advertising training program. The formerly Soviet citizenry is extremely appreciative of good advertising. Foreign commercials used to receive praise as the best entertainment available on Soviet television.

In the now-defunct U.S.S.R., advertisements had consisted mostly of billboards and print ads in newspapers and magazines. Soviet television commercials were few and far between, and those on the air were amateurish. Ads were designed to tell people that a certain product was being made and might be available where they live. As a result, Soviet consumers weren't accustomed to advertising. They wanted to see the product for themselves and test whether it worked and was worth buying.

The Russia of today is evolving rapidly. Advertisements are appearing on everything from tanks to rocket ships. Companies can place their billboards at Russian launch sites, put their logos on Russian rockets, their shoes on the feet of cosmonauts in the Mir space station, and their candy bars in food kits as dessert.

Cross-Cultural Marketing Blunders

Dr. David A. Ricks has written numerous articles and books on international marketing blunders. Human resource professionals can use the books and articles as a resource for developing case examples for their cross-cultural marketing training programs. We have included several culture specific examples that can be used in training programs.

International Marketing Blunders

Blunders in Latin America

- Blunder # 1: Camellia-Scented Perfume. A famous American designer began to advertise her new women's fragrance in Latin America. The advertising campaign emphasized the perfume's fresh camellia scent. The fragrance did not sell. Why? Camellias are the flowers used for funerals in most of Latin America. Latin American women didn't want to smell like a funeral parlor.

- Blunder # 2: Airplane Lounges (Brazil). An American airline in Brazil advertised "rendezvous lounges" on its jets. The airline received the wrong kind of customers. Why? In the Brazilian brand of Portuguese, "rendezvous lounges" refer to a place to make love. Consumers expected the airline to operate as a flying bordello.

Blunders in the North American Common Market

- Blunder # 1: Bottled Ink (Mexico). An American ink manufacturer attempted to sell bottled ink in Mexico. The company used metal outdoor signs to tell customers to "avoid embarrassment" by using its brand of ink. The company used the Spanish word "embarazar" to convey the meaning of "embarrassed." Customers were astounded. Why? The Spanish word "embarazar" means "to become pregnant." Many Mexican consumers thought the company was selling a contraceptive device, and were confused when they found the bottled ink.

- Blunder # 2: Laundry Detergent (Quebec). A laundry detergent company introduced a new point-of-purchase campaign in Quebec. Advertisements stated that the detergent worked particularly well on the dirtiest parts of the wash, translated as "les parties de sale." The detergent didn't sell. Why? This phrase, "les parties de sale," was similar to another Quebecois expression for "private parts." Sales lagged, because consumers did not want to wash their private parts with laundry detergent.

Blunders in the Islamic World

- Blunder # 1: Men's Cologne (Moslem North Africa). A fragrance manufacturer tried to enter markets in North Africa that were heavily Islamic. A print advertisement for a men's cologne centered around a picture of a man and his dog in an American rural setting. The image was supposed to convey a macho feeling of a man and his "best friend," the dog. The cologne did not sell. Why? According to legend, a pack of dogs ate one of Mohammed's regiments centuries ago. They are still considered signs of bad luck or uncleanliness in parts of Moslem North Africa.

- Blunder # 2: Refrigerators (Islamic Middle East). An appliance manufacturer tried to sell refrigerators in the Islamic Middle East. Their advertisement pictured a refrigerator filled with food, including a giant ham. The advertisement was ineffective. Why? The Islamic religion forbids the eating of ham by the faithful.

Blunders in Africa

- Blunder # 1: Baby Food (Africa). A food manufacturer in Africa had pictures of a white baby on its baby food labels. The baby food didn't sell. The manufacturer reasoned that the lack of sales must be due to the use of a white baby instead of a black baby on the labels. The labels were changed to exhibit a black baby. The product still didn't sell. Why? Africans speak a multitude of languages. Therefore, it has been the custom to put a picture of the package's contents on the labels. When Africans saw a picture of a white baby on the label, they assumed that the contents were ground up white babies. They didn't want to eat any babies, white or black.

Cross-Cultural Pricing Strategy

Pricing strategy is critical to the success of an international business. It can also be boring to work on and difficult to train people in. The following presents a basic program for training managers in cross-cultural pricing strategy. Human resource professionals should feel free to modify the program to fit their particular needs. Creativity is encouraged. Otherwise, workshop participants may rapidly lose interest, and the program will be unsuccessful.

Strategically, the function of pricing is to provide an adequate return on investment (ROI). To acquire an adequate ROI, pricing strategists must set proper objectives. Pricing objectives can be either profit-oriented or volume-oriented. Trainers can use Exhibit 7-5 as a checklist for reviewing pricing objectives with workshop participants.

Exhibit 7-5
Potential Pricing Objectives

1. Maximize long-run profits
2. Maximize short-run profits
3. Growth
4. Stabilize the market
5. Desensitize customers to price
6. Maintain price-leadership
7. Discourage entrants
8. Increase the exit speed of marginal firms
9. Avoid government investigation and control
10. Maintain the loyalty of middlemen and distributors
11. Avoid increased demands by suppliers
12. Enhance the image of the firm and its products
13. Be regarded as fair by customers
14. Create interest and excitement about products
15. Be considered trustworthy and reliable by rivals
16. Help in the sale of weak products in the product-line
17. Discourage others from cutting prices
18. Make a product "visible"
19. Obtain a high price for the sale of the business
20. Build traffic

The two most important objectives to consider in a cross-cultural pricing training program are *maintaining the loyalty of middlemen and distributors* and *enhancing the image of the firm and its products*. Many international corporations have made basic mistakes in these two areas. As a result, they have severely hurt their ability to sell products in certain markets. Procter & Gamble is a good example.

Procter & Gamble performed miserably in Japan after its 1973 entry. One Japanese employee of P&G said bitterly: "They didn't listen to anybody." P&G's Cheer and Bonus laundry soaps held 15% of the market in the late 1970s. At first, Cheer and Bonus prospered through the use of a discount pricing strategy. However, this practice alienated wholesalers because it reduced their profit margins. Japanese wholesalers were much more willing to carry the laundry soaps of P&G's competitors, because they made more money on them. As a result, P&G's competitors developed excellent relationships with wholesalers and P&G was shut out of many retail outlets.

P&G's discount pricing strategy also alienated many of the local Japanese "mom & pop" stores. These small Japanese retailers have limited shelf space and turnover, so they don't like to carry discounted goods. If their profit margin is too small, they will go out of business.

Unfortunately for P&G, at least 30% of laundry detergent sold in Japan is sold at the local "mom & pop" stores. Many Japanese housewives don't have a family car to lug groceries in. They have to walk to the store and carry their groceries home. As a result, they shop in the local "mom & pop" stores, which had been disaffected by P&G's discount pricing strategy. Needless to say, by alienating Japanese wholesalers and small retailers, P&G severely reduced its ability to sell laundry detergent in Japan.

The discount strategy also devalued P&G's image in Japan, along with the image of its products. Unlike Europe and the United States, once a corporation discounts products in Japan, it's hard to raise the price later. Image is extremely important in pricing. Trainers can use Exhibit 7-6 to explore price imaging with workshop participants. For example, trainers could use the chart to explore the price imagery of Japanese, German, and American automobiles.

Exhibit 7-6
Price Imaging

The (type of product) made in (the name of the country) seem:

Inexpensive	↔	Expensive
Reasonably priced	↔	Unreasonably priced
Suits our taste	↔	Doesn't suit our taste
Luxury items	↔	Necessary items
High performance	↔	Limited performance
Reliable	↔	Unreliable
Never needs servicing	↔	Often needs servicing
Heavy duty	↔	Light duty
Underpriced	↔	Overpriced

Trainers can assist marketeers in developing overall pricing strategies by addressing certain key issues during the training program. It is important to consider the target market, costs, projected market share, brand equity, proposed discount schedules, and distribution. Trainers can use Exhibit 7-7 as a guideline for developing checklists and questionnaires.

Exhibit 7-7
Guidelines for Pricing

- The corporate pricing strategy should be tied to overall market share strategy.
- Pricing must always involve some sort of cost strategy. A corporation must hit cost targets to maintain market share.
- Pricing strategy must be derived from the price performance equation of your products versus those of your competition.
- A pricing strategy should consider the market segment your company is going after.
- The company must adequately invest in brand equity. Upward price leverage requires continuous investment in brand equity. Brand equity equals customer loyalty. A corporation must keep brand equity high, so it can keep pricing as high as possible. The corporation needs consistent positioning: "When I think of the product, I think of Brand X." A corporation must reinforce familiar associations and deliver on promises.
- Astute pricing requires that marketeers know and understand how to design a sound price discount schedule for distributors. The corporation also must reward distributors for what they do.
- Pricing plans should not be overly complex and should correspond to the most efficient shipping units identified by the company.
- The marketing department should appreciate the importance of pricing strategy. Pricing is often one of the least measured marketing activities.

A Training Program for Cross-Cultural Pricing

We have developed a generic format for a training program in cross-cultural pricing strategy. The format is an adaptation of programs that are currently being used to evaluate domestic pricing strategies. Trainers should feel free to customize it to fit their individual needs.

Prior to the training program, trainers will need to gather detailed economic data relating to the industry and the countries in question. It is particularly important to gather information on estimated demand, product costs, and average prices. Trainers will be able to get some of this information from government agencies, such as the Commerce Department or the International Trade Administration. Other good sources of industry projections include PREDICASTS and INFO-TRAC. Trainers can use Standard Industrial Classification (SIC) numbers when accessing these resources.

The training program is two days long. Enrollment is limited to thirty marketeers from a particular industry. Participants are divided into five teams. Each team represents a corporation from a different country. For example, marketeers could be placed in fictitious automobile corporations from France, Germany, Japan, South Korea, and the United States. Each corporation has three potential product lines. For example, each corporation can have a high-priced, medium-priced, and low-priced automobile.

In the two-day training period, one year in the life of the fictitious corporations will pass by. Day 1 will cover the first two quarters of the year, while Day 2 will cover the last two quarters. Participants will be given decision forms and income statements for each quarter, along with a participant's manual and a set of instructions.

On the morning of the first day, participants use the decision forms to make economic projections, keep track of decisions, and record results. In terms of economic projections, teams are required to estimate demand, average prices, and product costs for the quarter. Based upon these projections, each team will have to determine what price to charge for its products, where sales will be made, what sales support will be provided, and what sales incentives will be used.

Price must be set in dollars for each of the three product lines. Price variations are unrestricted. Price variance will depend upon economic projections, and whether or not the team decides to retain a particular product line.

Each team is allowed a total of ten salespeople. The salespeople can be divided up among the product lines as the team wishes. The team may choose not to assign any salespeople to a particular product line.

All salespersons are given a monthly salary. However, the corporation may provide incentives in an attempt to increase product sales. For example, a team may want to give salespersons a 5% commission in addition to their salary.

Sales support includes advertising, promotions, and other marketing techniques. Teams are allowed to spend as much as they wish on sales support. However, the costs must be factored into product price. If a team spends too much on sales support, sales may drop precipitously.

Teams record their products' prices, sales coverage, sales support, and sales incentives on the first decision sheet. The decision sheets are given to the trainers, who calculate corporate sales and market share. The trainer's calculations are based upon industry economic projections and cultural variables developed by the trainers prior to the workshop. Team results are then distributed, and teams fill out their income statements based upon the results, which show each team's profitability for the first quarter. All of the teams' results are posted.

After the results are posted, trainers lead discussions analyzing what occurred and why it occurred. The most relevant topics for discussion involve economic and cultural issues. Relevant economic issues include break-even analyses, foreign buyers' perception of price, preventing price objections, and how to handle price objections when they occur. Relevant cultural issues include price imagery, resistance to foreign goods, and the relative importance of distributors.

The entire process will be repeated three more times. The afternoon of Day One represents the second quarter; the morning of Day Two, the third quarter; and the afternoon of Day Two, the fourth quarter. Following each quarter, trainers lead discussions on product pricing. In particular, trainers should discuss how price affects international sales of the products.

Upon completion of the fourth and final income statement, trainers produce graphs showing the pricing decisions for each team for each quarter, as well as their market share and profitability. After reviewing the charts, teams discuss why they made the decisions they did and what changes they would make in light of their new awareness of cultural variables.

Cross-Cultural Distribution Strategy

There is little likelihood of selling products that are not made conveniently available to customers. Distribution is the path or channel that products take between production and consumption. In cross-cultural marketing, producers must choose methods of distribution to various countries, as well as the method of distribution within the country of sale.

Distribution strategies are concerned with the channels that manufacturers employ to make goods and services available to consumers. Distribution channels are made up of buyers and sellers who bridge the gap between manufacturers and consumers. Channel structure strategy involves the choice of intermediaries employed to move goods from manufacturers to customers.

The purpose of the "trade channel" or "channel of distribution" is to bridge the gap between the producer of a product and the user of it, whether the parties are located in the same community or in different countries thousands of miles apart. The components of the trade channel fall into three categories: (1) producers of products; (2) users of products; and (3) middlemen at the wholesale or retail level. Middlemen may or may not take title to the goods themselves, and may or may not handle the goods physically. However, they always perform the critical function of facilitating the transfer of title.

To transfer goods from a producer to a consumer, several functions must be performed. These include transfer of title (buying and selling), the physical movement of the goods (transportation), and any necessary storage (warehousing).

The essential qualification for a participant in the channel of distribution is that they be involved in transfer of title. Either they take title themselves, as do merchant wholesalers and retailers, or they act in a sales or buying capacity as agent for a principal. Among the latter are brokers, commission houses, manufacturer's agents, and resident buying offices. The central function of these offices is buying and selling. They may also perform additional services such as storage, financing, technical service, and risk bearing.

There are many businesses that facilitate the transfer of goods, including transportation agencies, public warehouses, advertising agencies, advertising media, market research companies, and financial institutions. However, these services are auxiliary to the distribution function. They are *not* included in the channel of distribution.

Every country's distribution system has unique aspects. European distribution systems vary dramatically from country to country, region to region, and city to city. The same is true in the Pacific Basin, South America, and the Middle East. Often, foreign distribution systems are so archaic that even established corporations find it difficult to distribute their new products.

Russia is a good example. In the early 1990s, many corporations were seeking to enter the Russian market, but there was no way to move products around. Boris Yeltsin charged that criminals were controlling Russia's supply system. Russian food distribution typified the problem. In Western countries, most food-storage facilities are located in the countryside, close to the place of production. In Russia, produce goes from the field into trucks or railway cars that haul it to city warehouses. This results in shipments of spoiled produce, along with rocks, mud and other refuse. The Russian system produces a lot of waste.

To avoid distribution problems, such as those found in Russia, global marketing managers need to ascertain the most effective channel of distribution in each of the target countries. Marketeers have two broad choices in selecting a distribution system: (1) use indigenous channels of distribution or (2) develop a global distribution system.

Marketing Realities in Developing Economies

In attempting to establish a distribution system within a less developed country, cross-cultural marketing persons must consider the following realities:

- There are vast differences between the infrastructures and mindsets of people in the First World and those in the so-called Second or Third World economies.
- Transportation and fuel may be severely strained and inadequate. Local road systems may be non-existent or in great need of repairs, and using planes or boats may be the best or only means of transportation.
- National communications are often in dire shape, especially archaic telephone systems (sometimes it is easier to place an international call rather than a domestic call). Satellite communications and facsimile machines are improving the situation.
- Maintenance of all equipment, especially high-tech, is a severe problem. The greatest need for the local distributor is training programs not only on how to use this modern equipment, but how to maintain it and obtain parts.
- Local distributors want to please and to succeed, but they operate under severe handicaps that range from obsolete banking, postal, and office systems with inadequate supplies of basic business, from lack of files, file folders to computers.

Transnational effectiveness may involve not only bringing in personnel, equipment, and supplies from the more advanced MNC, but establishing complete HRD/M systems to develop local people who are eager to learn. McDonald's did this successfully in the former U.S.S.R., developing many local entrepreneurs and suppliers in the process. For human resource leaders, it means also training expatriate personnel in cross-cultural awareness and skills, in shifting their mindset and lowering their expectations, while adapting to local realities and transforming business practice in a country that is not market-driven!

Kellogg, for example, found that its Pop Tart pastries failed in some countries not because of a cultural rejection, but because of the underdeveloped state of electric toasters and the resulting weak interest in toaster-dependent products.

Market Development Inc. in San Diego, California, proposes that a successful cross-cultural marketing system requires the marketeer to (1) evaluate consumer wants and needs on their own merits; (2) apply an objective marketing decision process to the cross-cultural situation; (3) appoint marketing managers who have the skill to keep their domestic preconceptions and cross-cultural misperceptions from intruding.

Indigenous Channels

Indigenous channels of distribution may be the most effective. Local business persons may be more aggressive in their sales approach. They also may have excellent contacts throughout the market area. Also, government regulations may favor distribution through indigenous firms. Other reasons for using indigenous distributors include:

1. Pre-existing local headquarters, branch offices, and warehouses.
2. A local sales force.
3. They are able to provide knowledge of local business practices and market demand.
4. In countries that restrict the entry of imported products, the use of local distributors sometimes provides a means of market access.
5. They may reduce political and market risk, thereby lowering borrowing costs.

To build a network of indigenous distributors, corporations need to locate candidates, narrow the choice down to a few local distributors, make a final selection, and train and work with the selection.

In evaluating potential foreign distributors, one must determine the following:

1. Does the distributor have the physical facilities, financial strength, and organizational strength to import the corporation's products? Warehouse them? Market them? Extend credit to customers? Collect payments from customers?
2. Does the distributor have a good working relationship with government agencies, including customs?
3. Is the distributor willing to consider new products and new methods of marketing?
4. Does the distributor have the financial capability to develop the market to its fullest potential?
5. Do the distributor's personnel relate well to the corporation's products and markets?
6. Is the distributor trustworthy? Does the distributor have a good reputation?
7. Is the distributor able to communicate easily both in writing and orally?

The financial resources of potential distributors are extremely important to the success of the marketing and distribution campaign. Before selecting a distributor, the corporation should obtain and analyze the candidates' most recent balance sheets and operating statements. Business and credit references should also be checked.

Marketeers must also pay close attention to legal and contractual issues involved in using foreign distributors. The distribution contract should include clauses covering geographic scope, definitions of products, terms of agreement, any necessary covenants regarding competing products, the distributor's responsibility toward maintenance of inventory, sales quotas, the responsibility of the distributor to provide local market information, credit and shipping terms, pricing, rights to modify or discontinue products, limitations regarding product warranties, and conditions of termination.

Once distributors are selected, the corporation must establish a program of regular contact and training to ensure that the distributors' sales forces have solid technical expertise in the product line. Distributors must be kept current regarding new products, new potential markets, and new sales techniques. One way to keep distributors excited about the firm's product line is to offer sales incentives. Competitive conditions must be carefully analyzed so that effective incentives are developed.

Relationships with foreign distributors are true strategic alliances. To keep the alliance on solid ground, corporations must carefully select distributors, carry out positive support and training programs for them, and continually monitor their performance. However, it is important to recognize that problems may occur no matter what the corporation does. Unless the corporation is aware of and has access to the channels used by distributors, the marketing campaign can be disrupted. Corporations should thoroughly document foreign distributors' market connections and sales techniques, so that operations can continue in the event of a breakup.

Global Distribution Channels

A global corporation may want to use its own distribution system. A company-operated distribution system is especially important if the product line is technologically sophisticated. High sales and service standards may dictate a global approach. Many corporations can win a strong competitive advantage by the quality and reliability of an effective global distribution system.

Designing a High-Performance Global Distribution System

1. Find out what customers want. The corporation must discover what end users want in the way of service. Factors to consider include delivery and convenience of shopping for the product. Do customers value around-the-corner convenience, or are they willing to deal across great distances, e.g. via a toll-free telephone number? Do customers want to buy one unit or many units? Do customers want immediate delivery, or assurance of delivery? Do customers value being able to choose between related products, or do they prefer stores to specialize? Do customers want immediate in-house repair and technical help, or do they want to use the local repair shop?

2. Find out about costs. Are the customer's wants feasible for the company? What kind of support is needed from suppliers to run a global outlet? What will each support system cost?

3. Determine the ideal. What are management's objectives? What is the ideal global distribution system for our product line?
4. Compare your options.
5. Review your assumptions. Bring in lawyers, political consultants, and distribution experts to challenge management's assumptions.
6. Confront the gap between the present system and the ideal. Develop a plan to make the ideal distribution system a reality.
7. Implement the plan.

Sometimes companies must develop their own distribution system due to an ingrained bias against and antipathy toward foreign products. For example, the Japanese distribution system is extremely difficult for foreign companies to access. Wholesalers have been a dominant part of the Japanese marketing system for several hundred years. After Japan was opened for trade with the West, the largest trading companies evolved into highly integrated organizations that included manufacturing plants, banking facilities, and wholesaling units. Wholesalers actually control the distribution of certain industrial materials and consumer goods.

Unfortunately for American manufacturers, wholesalers in Japan show extreme favoritism for local goods. Levi Strauss bypassed wholesalers in Japan and dealt directly with stores. Levi shunned the accepted Japanese practice of letting stores return unsold merchandise. Instead, they deliver to outlets weekly and offer business managers free training in running their operation more efficiently.

Another way foreign companies are entering the Japanese market is through mail-order catalogs. Land's End, Tweeds, L.L.Bean, Orvis, and other companies have joined together in making a mail-order catalog for the Japanese market. Each company has two pages in the catalog, which was sent to over 50,000 Japanese homes in late 1991. The catalog is carefully tailored to the Japanese market, emphasizing fashionable apparel, and avoiding electronics products or products labeled "Made In Korea" (Japan's arch trade rival).

Japanese consumers are not used to shopping by mail, but the market is growing. The mail-order market accounted for $11 billion, or 1.3% of Japan's retail sales in 1990. In the United States, mail-order sales in 1990 accounted for $30 billion, or 4.8% of total retail sales. If the percentage of Japanese mail-order sales can be pushed up to the American level, it will be a huge market. One way that mail-order companies are trying to increase volume is by having Japanese customers send their orders to facilities in Japan, which then fax the orders to the United States. Japanese consumers seem to be more comfortable with this approach.

While channel strategies, such as mail-order marketing, may not seem very creative to American marketeers, they can be extremely innovative and effective overseas. Global marketeers should consider using new global channel strategies to distinguish themselves from their competition. However, before changing their present distribution channel, corporations should evaluate the following factors:

1. The competition's penetration of the channel. How entrenched are other suppliers? What pricing policy is being used? Are price discounts being used?
2. The attitudes of current customers. Are customers happy with the old channel? Would old customers be willing to accept a new channel?
3. Monitor the attitudes of customers using the new channel. How close are the relationships with current suppliers? Can the corporation profit by providing superior service? What kind of reaction will customers have to a new supplier?
4. Consider distribution requirements. Can the corporation change the time frame for shipping its products? Will more outlets be needed? Is it customary to use distributors or ship directly to customers? Will the operations department be able to handle new order sizes and new requirements for meeting orders?
5. Consider packaging and merchandising. Is in-store merchandising required? Are full-time or part-time merchandisers required?
6. Test the new channel. Where should the new distribution channel be tested? Which operations personnel will be selected to test the channel?
7. Analyze the bottom line. Are there any hidden costs? How will the new distribution system affect corporate cash flow? How will it affect profits?

Partnership Marketing

"Partnership marketing" is one of the most useful concepts to evolve in recent years. Under this concept, corporations form strategic alliances to market their product lines around the world. It allows manufacturers to enter foreign markets at a cost far below that required for any singular effort, and with a marketing capability that can overwhelm competitors. By joining together, corporations are able to reduce the cost of foreign market entry and obtain economies of scale. The reduction in costs allows the alliance to use pricing strategies to gain market share.

As presently envisioned, effective marketing partnerships should not exceed four manufacturers. By keeping the number of partners down, the alliance can retain the compatibility necessary for combined global marketing. Smaller alliances are more effective at representing the corporations' worldwide interests, promoting information sharing, and developing combined research and development projects.

There are many different formats that can be used in partnership marketing. We believe that the following represents a very effective plan. Trainers should feel free to use this format, or customize it as they see fit.

1. To retain compatibility, the partnership is initially limited to no more than four members. Partners may choose to increase the number of partners in the future; however, unanimous approval is required.
2. The partnership forms a board of directors with stewardship over policy. The managing director of the partnership reports to the board, and is responsible for keeping each partner informed about ongoing business.
3. The partnership, guided by the managing director, is responsible for originating a global marketing and sales plan.
4. The partnership staff should include the managing director, two marketing executives, one highly skilled sales executive, two administrative support personnel, and a telemarketing sales support group. The sales support group uses highly qualified salespersons who contact customers directly.
5. The world is divided into manageable regions. The regions are supervised by in-field marketing professionals, who develop contacts with all major distributors and retailers. The in-field marketing professionals have negotiating authority with their customers within recognized budgetary confines.
6. The head office is linked electronically to all field locations and handles all administrative contact from customers. Toll-free telephone lines are used whenever possible. Regional managers receive reports on all problems that arise.

7. The option exists to form a field merchandising capability that will handle specific promotions, such as new product introductions, major city sales drives, product sampling, and merchandising.

The global marketplace is very fluid. The only certainty is that the world is constantly changing. To become world-class marketeers, managers must actively take steps to keep track of the pulse of their markets. Awareness of and sensitivity to the global arena and its plethora of cultural variables is a key ingredient to a successful global marketing program.

However, cross-cultural awareness by itself is not enough. To excel in global marketing, corporations must be driven as overachievers to push past the boundaries of what is presently accepted, of what sells now, and of what is safe. Global corporations must actively "grow" their marketplace. This is done by keeping a tight connection with consumers; developing a worldwide information and intelligence system; and positioning the organization to satisfy consumer demands.

Human resource leaders can make a unique contribution to global marketing, especially with reference to local consumer culture, marketing, and communications: First, in helping their own personnel to change the organization's culture to maximize transcultural opportunities to serve human needs. Second, promoting by various means a global mindset to marketing across cultures to replace the domestic focus. Third, meeting the challenges of the transcultural marketplace both at home and abroad through training in cross-cultural awareness and skills, as well as in altering domestic marketing policies and practices.

Human resource professionals should use the information in this chapter to develop cross-cultural marketing training programs. Trainers should feel free to customize our suggestions to fit their unique situations. We hope this will enable corporations to become aware of the requirements of the global marketplace and the steps that are necessary for success.

References

1. Braidwood, S., "World Products: A Threat or a Promise?" *Design,* September 1984, pp. 40–45.
2. Brown, P. B., "Over There," *Inc.,* April 1990, pp. 105+.
3. Buzzell, R. D., "Can You Standardize Multinational Marketing?" *Harvard Business Review,* November/December 1968, pp. 102–113.

4. Dentzer, S., "The Coming Global Boom," *U.S. News & World Report,* July 16, 1990, pp. 22–28.

5. Goizueta, R. C., "Globalization: A Soft Drink Perspective," *Vital Speeches of the Day,* February 9, 1989, pp. 360–362.

6. Grune, G. V., "Global Marketing: Global Opportunities," *Vital Speeches of the Day,* May 20, 1989, pp. 580–582.

7. Kupfer, A., "America's Fastest Growing Company," *Fortune,* August 13, 1990, pp. 48.

8. Machan, D., "Ici on Parle Bottom-line Responsibility," *Forbes,* February 8, 1988, pp. 138–140.

9. McCormick, J. and Stone, N., "From National Champion to Global Competitor: An Interview with Thomson's Alain Gomez," *Harvard Business Review,* May/June 1990, pp. 127–135.

10. Miller, L., "How to Keep Managers Up to Date," *Training & Development Journal,* September 1990, pp. 35–37.

11. Ricks, D. A., *Blunders in International Business,* Cambridge, MA: Blackwell Publishers, 1993.

12. Rodkin, H. H., "10 Rules to Live (and Sell) by Overseas," *Sales & Marketing Management,* April 2, 1984, pp. 63–64.

13. Slater, J. R., "The Hazards of Cross-Cultural Advertising," *Business America,* April 2, 1984, pp. 20–23.

14. Williams, M. J., "Rewriting the Export Rules," *Fortune,* April 23, 1990, pp. 89+.

CHAPTER 8

CROSS-CULTURAL NEGOTIATOR

Introduction

Human resource professionals and internal organizational trainers are often asked to recommend or conduct training programs that will assist participants to negotiate more effectively in the domestic and international arenas. Therefore, part of the HR specialist's task is to train, guide, and develop individuals to become more effective international business negotiators. This chapter discusses the basic elements and tools needed to conduct effective negotiations. Because each negotiating situation is unique, the individuals involved in the negotiating situation will have to determine which tools are most appropriate for the given situation.

The ability to appropriately prioritize the negotiating tools to suit the situation takes practice. We believe the ability of the negotiator is greatly enhanced by learning the skills. The key to effective negotiation is rehearsing negotiating situations.

The late professor Israel Unterman [15] proposed that international negotiation skills are best taught by:

1. Preparing a flexible scenario in which a student or trainee devises a set of modified, strategic plans and approaches.
2. Using negotiating teams for practice in comprehending selective barriers and gateways to effective communication, such as culturally-influenced body language or behaviors.
3. Learning exercises in use of voice, word congruence, listening skills, coping with emotional responses and stress, and closing the negotiation with some kind of agreement.

Unterman advocated the case study method for teaching negotiation skills, and his research analyzed the differences among national teams and the cultural variations that influence the process and outcome of the negotiation and decision-making.

In the last section of this chapter we include case study scenarios that will allow potential negotiators to apply the background information, the variables of the universal negotiating model, and the negotiating styles we describe in the chapter. The HR specialist or trainer can facilitate these sessions and provide feedback that will aid the negotiators in developing their negotiating skills.

One of your first tasks as the facilitator in this learning activity should be to analyze the audience to determine its needs. Once this needs assessment has been conducted, you can create a learning program that will be best suited for each audience. The last section will include exercises that will provide the flexibility to adapt to each audience.

What do all of the following situations have in common?

- During an executive meeting a manager suggests how to change a process to make production more efficient.
- A car salesman shows the new year models to a woman who is in the market for a new car.
- An American manager has been sent to the Mexico City office to "discuss" the new plans for their office.
- The management teams from Germany and Poland meet to hammer out the personnel and human resource policies of their newly created joint venture.
- American and Thai managers meet to determine labor contracts for their workers in the next year.

These are all situations that involve negotiation. The universal model for cross-cultural negotiators we describe in this chapter will help individuals in any negotiating situation be more effective negotiators.

The Why and What of Negotiating

Clearly the situations just presented identify why we need to understand the basic principles of negotiating, so that negotiating can be more skillful. When we understand the motivations of others, we can better communicate with them, which could lead to more effective negotiations. Negotiation skills are very important in today's global marketplace and they are becoming necessities for business managers and executives who deal with business transactions across national borders.

Negotiating is a difficult term to define because each author defines it a bit differently. For our purposes we will use the following definition [6]:

International Business Negotiations—negotiations that result in mutual benefit, and that are purposeful, rather than reactive, occurring between individuals with different cultural backgrounds.

Negotiation is a process in which two or more entities come together to discuss common and conflicting interests in order to reach an agreement of mutual benefit. A successful negotiation is a "win-win situation" in which both parties gain. In international business negotiations, there are cultural dimensions in every aspect of the negotiations. The surest way for a negotiator to establish good relations with foreign negotiators is to demonstrate that an agreement is of mutual advantage. According to Moran and Stripp [11], the secret of negotiation is to point out the common advantages to both parties and to link these advantages so that they appear to be equally balanced.

It is important for persons studying negotiations to understand that negotiation is a learned activity and that with practice the negotiating skills can be improved. The following information can be helpful in understanding the learned behaviors for negotiating as human resource professionals are aware of the process of learning, especially adult learning, which has different characteristics than the child learning process. HR specialists should help their audience to understand the basic principles of adult learning in order to prevent their frustration when they are learning the negotiation process.

One very important aspect of this process deals with the orientation of negotiations across cultures. The traditional American style of negotiating emphasizes the "deal." It is a single and static emphasis that stresses only the present situation. Compare this to other cultural negotiating styles and we find the "relationship" orientation. This style has multiple emphasis (what's next); focuses on the past, present, and future negotiations; and is dynamic in nature. It is important to realize that the traditional American style of deal-making must be adjusted to focus on building relationships in the international business environment.

How Does the Culture Affect Negotiations

We would identify the cultural aspect as the most important aspect when learning about negotiation. The global work force is changing and becoming more integrated culturally. For example, it would be hard to find an organization without a culturally diverse employee population. Therefore, it becomes crucial that all employees learn about the culture and how it affects negotiations because these culturally diverse employee populations often must negotiate on a daily basis.

Exhibit 8-1 [14] shows how culture affects the differing aspects of our negotiating styles.

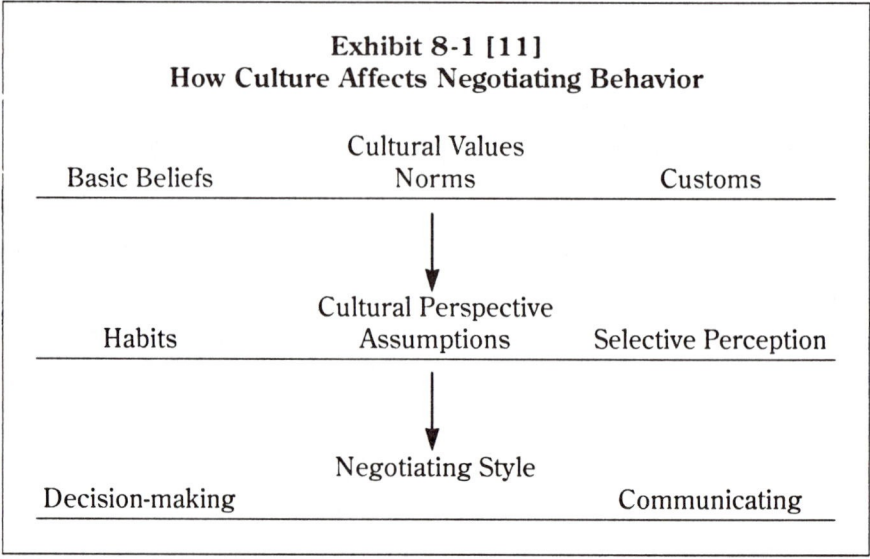

Exhibit 8-1 [11]
How Culture Affects Negotiating Behavior

Cultural Values
Basic Beliefs   Norms   Customs

Cultural Perspective
Habits   Assumptions   Selective Perception

Negotiating Style
Decision-making   Communicating

American negotiators should be aware of [2]:

1. The cultural conditioning with regard to the way negotiators view the nature of the negotiation process itself. American negotiators are often frustrated because their counterparts do not enter in the expected give-and-take, which they typically experience in domestic or labor-management negotiations in the United States. We are frustrated when we do not experience this overseas.

2. The use of a "middle man." For many cultures, such as the Japanese, to openly disagree is not a pleasant experience and whenever there is a conflict in a negotiation situation, very often a go-between or a third person is used to assist in the negotiation process.

3. Trusting the other party. American negotiators usually begin a negotiating session by trusting the persons until proven otherwise. However, the French are more inclined to mistrust until faith and trust is proven by their counterparts.

4. Viewing the process as a problem-solving exercise whereby a number of fallback positions are carefully discussed prior to a session. However, other cultures do not view it as a problem-solving exercise and their first position is the only position they have discussed and the one they wish to present and have accepted.

5. The importance of protocol. Mexican negotiators are often selected for their skill at rhetoric and making distinguished performances. Negotiation is perceived from their perspective as a time to test Mexican honor and to determine the attitude of the American negotiators towards Mexicans.

6. Selection of the negotiation team. In the United States, persons are selected primarily on the basis of technical competence. However, in other societies one may be negotiating with people who do not have a high degree of technical competence, because the members of a negotiating team are selected on the basis of personal power or authority.

7. How the negotiating team views the decision-making process. In the United States, negotiators approach the negotiation session and the decisions that result from it by essentially saying, "anything is O.K. unless it has been restricted." However, others approach the same situation with, "nothing is permitted unless it is initiated by the state."

8. Decision-making. In Mexico, decisions are typically from a top-down direction in an organization and they reflect the personalities of the individuals. And when Mexican negotiators work overseas, they prefer to work with high-level people and typically link issues with trade-offs (for example, conceding a point on narcotics control in exchange for free vegetable importation into the United States).

Selecting Effective Negotiators

Great care must be taken in choosing negotiators. Companies often send negotiators to work internationally who are not familiar with the interests, laws, customs, language, or even geography of the foreign country. HR specialists may be asked to assist in the identification of individuals most suited to international business negotiations. This determination will lead to the organizations increased effectiveness when dealing with negotiations across cultures.

Effective negotiators have many skills. The following list has been compiled from various authors and is intended to assist the HR specialist in identifying persons in the organization for training negotiations. Effective negotiators

1. Are observant
2. Have sound judgment
3. Are patient
4. Appreciate humor
5. Are not easily distracted
6. Think before speaking
7. Are open to others' ways of life
8. Present information diplomatically
9. Manage stress in ambiguous situations
10. Clearly express their ideas
11. Are sensitive to others' cultural backgrounds
12. Are forward looking/thinking
13. Are extensive planners

Skills of Effective Negotiators

To give HR specialists an analysis of the difference of behaviors between effective and non-effective negotiators the following information has been provided to clarify the importance of identifying effective negotiating skills. It includes aspects of pre-negotiation and actual face-to-face negotiation [7].

The following is a summary of a research project that analyzed *actual* negotiations. The researchers' methods allowed them to distinguish between skilled negotiators and average negotiators by using behavior analysis techniques as they observed the negotiations and recorded the discussion. They identified "successful" negotiators as those who—

1. Were rated as effective by both sides.
2. Had a "track-record" of significant success.
3. Had a low incidence of "implementation" failures.

A total of 48 negotiators were studied who met all of these three success criteria. They included union representatives (17), management representatives (12), contract negotiators (10), and others (9).

The 48 successful negotiators were studied over a total of 102 separate negotiating sessions. In the following description, the successful negotiators are called the "skilled" group. In comparison, the negotiators who either failed to meet the criteria or about whom no criteria were available, were called the "average" group.

Negotiation Planning

Negotiation training emphasizes the importance of these planning factors.

1. Planning time—No significant difference was found between the total planning time that skilled and average negotiators claimed they spent prior to actual negotiation.
2. Exploration of options—The skilled negotiator considered a wider range of outcomes or options for action than the average negotiator.
   Skilled negotiator—5.1 outcomes or options per issue
   Average negotiator—2.6 outcomes or options per issue
3. Common ground—The research showed that the skilled negotiators gave over three times as much attention to common ground areas as did average negotiators.
   Skilled negotiators—38% of comments about areas of anticipated agreement or common ground
   Average negotiators—11% of comments about areas of anticipated agreement or common ground
4. Long-term or short-term?—With the average negotiator, approximately one comment in twenty-five met the criteria of a long-term consideration, namely a comment that involved any factor extending beyond the immediate implementation of the issue under negotiation. The skilled negotiator, while showing twice as many long-term comments, still only averages 8.5% of his total recorded planning comments.
5. Setting limits—The researchers asked negotiators about their objectives and recorded whether their replies referred to single-point objectives (e.g., "We aim to settle at 83.") or to a defined range (e.g., "We hope to get 85, but we would settle for a minimum of 77."). Skilled

negotiators were significantly more likely to set upper and lower limits—to plan in terms of range. Average negotiators, in contrast, were more likely to plan their objectives around a fixed point.

6. Sequence and issue planning—The term "planning" frequently refers to a process of sequencing, putting a number of events, points, or potential occurrences into a time sequence. Critical path analysis and other forms of network planning are examples.

Typical Sequence Plan Used by Average Negotiators

A then B then C then D
Issues are linked.

Typical Issue Plan Used by Skilled Negotiators

A
B
D
C

Issues are independent and not linked by sequence.

	Number of Mentions Implying Sequence in Planning
Skilled Negotiators	2.1 per session
Average Negotiators	4.9 per session

The clear advantage of issue planning over sequence planning is flexibility.

Face-To-Face Behavior

Skilled negotiators show marked differences in their face-to-face behavior compared with average negotiators. They use certain types of behavior significantly more frequently while other types they tend to avoid.

1. Irritators—Certain words and phrases that are commonly used during negotiation have negligible value in persuading the other party, but do cause irritation. Probably the most frequent example of these is the term "generous offer" used by a negotiator to describe his own proposal.

	Use of Irritators Per Hour Face-to-Face Speaking Time
Skilled negotiators	2.3
Average negotiators	10.8

2. Counter-proposals—During negotiation, one party frequently puts forward a proposal and the other party immediately responds with a counter-proposal. Researchers found that skilled negotiators made immediate counter-proposals much less frequently than average negotiators.

	Frequency of Counter-Proposals Per Hour of Face-To-Face Speaking Time
Skilled negotiators	1.7
Average negotiators	3.1

3. Argument dilution—This way of thinking predisposes us to believe that there is some special merit in quantity. Having five reasons for doing something is considered more persuasive than having only one reason. We feel that the more we can put on our scale, the more likely we are to tip the balance of an argument in our favor.

	Average Number of Reasons Given by Negotiator to Back Each Argument/Advanced
Skilled negotiators	1.8
Average negotiators	3.0

The researchers found that the opposite was true. The skilled negotiator used less reasons to back up each of their arguments.

4. Reviewing the negotiation—The researchers asked negotiators how likely they were to spend time reviewing the negotiation afterwards. Over two-thirds of the skilled negotiators claimed that they always set aside some time after a negotiation to review it and consider what they had learned. Just under half of average negotiators, in contrast, made the same claim.

This research clearly indicates the *behavior* of skilled negotiators and which behaviors can be imitated and avoided so as to forecast success.

Knowing Oneself

Preparation is the most essential phase to any successful negotiation. Key to this preparation is knowing yourself and knowing one's counterpart.

Each culture brings to the negotiating table various aspects of their culture. Effective negotiators have done their homework and have a clear understanding of what their counterpart is bringing.

John Graham and Roy Herberger [3] suggest a combination of characteristics that American negotiators typically use. They are part of the cultural baggage such nationals bring to the negotiating table and according to Graham and Herberger, typify the "American John Wayne" style of negotiating.

1. I can go it alone. Many U.S. executives seem to believe they can handle any negotiating situation by themselves, and they are outnumbered in most negotiating situations.
2. Just call me John. Americans value informality and equality in human relations. They try to make people feel comfortable by playing down status distinctions.
3. Pardon my French. Americans aren't very talented at speaking foreign languages.
4. Check with the home office. American negotiators get upset when halfway through a negotiation the other side says, "I'll have to check with the home office." The implication is that the decision makers are not present.
5. Get to the point. Americans don't like to beat around the bush and want to get to the heart of the matter quickly.
6. Lay your cards on the table. Americans expect honest information at the bargaining table.
7. Don't just sit there, speak up. Americans don't deal well with silence during negotiations.
8. Don't take no for an answer. Persistence is highly valued by Americans and is part of the deeply ingrained competitive spirit that manifests itself in every aspect of American life.
9. One thing at a time. Americans usually attack a complex negotiation task sequentially, that is, they separate the issues and settle them one at a time.

10. A deal is a deal. When Americans make an agreement and give their word, they expect to honor the agreement no matter what the circumstance.

11. I am what I am. Few Americans take pride in changing their minds even in difficult circumstances.

Knowing the Other Culture

For a negotiator to become an effective negotiator, he or she must become adept at researching other cultures. A negotiator must know all aspects of the other culture to prevent serious negotiating blunders or cross-cultural faux pas, which could mean the end of the negotiation and the end of the business relationship.

Considerations in Cross-Cultural Negotiation

Glen Fisher presents a basic system or framework for analyzing cross-cultural negotiations [2]. He addresses five considerations: (1) the players and the situation; (2) styles of decision-making; (3) national character; (4) cross-cultural noise; and (5) interpreters and translators. Each consideration presents questions that should be answered before entering international negotiations. Fisher provides broad answers to his questions by examining international negotiations with Japanese, French, and Mexican counterparts.

The Players and the Situation

Fisher asserts that there is a cultural dimension in the way negotiators view the negotiation process. This raises several issues. Form, hospitality, and protocol may be very important to the success of international negotiations. Difficulties sometimes arise because there is a difference in what negotiators expect of a negotiation's social setting. The negotiator should discover what the foreign negotiator expects and then provide a tension-free environment that encourages cooperation and problem-solving.

There also may be a national style in choosing negotiators and in selecting negotiating teams. Negotiators can anticipate a counterpart's behavior by researching biographical data and analyzing the negotiator's organizational or institutional role. In the case of negotiating teams, it is useful to discover how corporate culture affects internal dynamics.

Styles of Decision Making

Fisher contends that there are patterns in the way officials and executives structure their negotiation communication systems and reach institutional decisions. The organizational culture of a foreign corporation may provide formal rules and regulations guiding its decision-making process. A negotiator can find ways to influence a foreign corporation's decisions by analyzing its corporate culture and structuring arguments to fit within established guidelines.

Furthermore, there are general cultural patterns by which individual negotiators develop personal styles of decision-making behavior. By discovering how foreign counterparts look at facts and analyze data, successful negotiators can provide information which will increase the probability of a successful outcome.

National Character

Studies of national character call attention both to the patterns of personality that negotiators tend to exhibit and to the collective concerns that give a nation a distinctive outlook in international relationships. Foreign negotiators concerned with international image may be preoccupied with discussions of their national heritage, identity, and language. Cultural attitudes, such as ethnocentrism or xenophilia, may influence the tone of their argument.

Fisher maintains that foreign negotiators display many different styles of logic and reasoning. International negotiators frequently find that discussions are impeded because the two sides seem to be pursuing different paths of logic. Negotiation breakdown may result from the way issues are conceptualized, the way evidence and new information are used, or the way one point seems to lead to the next.

During the discussions, the foreign counterpart may pay more attention to some arguments than to others. Greater weight may be given to legal precedence, expert opinion, technical data, amity, or reciprocal advantage. A good international negotiator will discover what is persuasive to the foreign counterpart, and use that method of persuasion.

Foreign negotiators may place different values on agreements and hold different assumptions as to the way contracts should be honored. The negotiator must find out what steps the counterpart intends to take in implementing the agreement. A signature on a piece of paper or a handshake may signify friendship rather than the closing of a contract.

Cross-Cultural Noise

Noise consists of background distractions that have nothing to do with the substance of the foreign negotiator's message. Factors such as gestures, personal proximity, and office surroundings may unintentionally interfere with communication. The danger of misinterpretation of messages necessitates analysis of various contextual factors.

Interpreters and Translators

Fisher points to limitations in translating certain ideas, concepts, meanings, and nuances. Subjective meaning may not come across through words alone. Gestures, tone of voice, cadence, and double entendres are all meant to transmit a message. Yet these are not included in a translation.

Sometimes a negotiator will try to communicate a concept or idea that does not exist in the counterpart's culture. For example, the American and English concept of "fair play" seems to have no exact equivalent in any other language. How then can an English national expect "fair play" from a foreign counterpart?

Interpreters and translators may have difficulty in transmitting the logic of key arguments. This is especially true in discussions of abstract concepts such as planning and international strategy. The parties may think that they have come to an agreement when in fact they have entirely different intentions and understandings.

Fisher's five-part framework provided scholars and consultants with a launching pad for both theory-building and practical applications.

Using Interpreters

The importance of an interpreter in business negotiations cannot be overemphasized. It is the interpreter who can assist with the accurate communication of ideas between the two teams. It is advisable to remember the following twenty tips concerning the use of interpreters.

1. Brief the interpreter in advance about the subject. (Select an interpreter knowledgeable about the product, if possible).
2. Speak clearly and slowly.
3. Avoid little-known words, such as "arcane" or "heuristic."
4. Explain the major idea two or three different ways, as the point may be lost if discussed only once.
5. Do not talk more than a minute or two without giving the interpreter a chance to speak.
6. While talking, allow the interpreter time to make notes of what is being said.
7. Do not lose confidence if the interpreter uses a dictionary.
8. Permit the interpreter to spend as much time as needed in clarifying points whose meanings are obscure.
9. Do not interrupt the interpreter as he translates, as interrupting causes many misunderstandings.
10. Avoid long sentences, double negatives, or the use of negative wordings of a sentence when a positive form could be used.
11. Avoid superfluous words. Your point may be lost if wrapped up in generalities.
12. Try to be expressive and use gestures to support your verbal messages.
13. During meetings, write out the main points discussed. In this way both parties can double check their understanding.
14. Prepare visual aids or overhead slides to facilitate the interpretation.
15. Don't expect an interpreter to work for over two hours without a rest period.
16. Consider using two interpreters if interpreting is to last a whole day or into the evening, so that when one tires the other can take over.
17. Don't be concerned if a speaker talks for five minutes and the interpreter covers it in half a minute.
18. Be understanding if it develops that the interpreter has made a mistake.
19. Ask the interpreter for advice if there are problems.
20. After meetings, confirm in writing what has been agreed.

The Process of Negotiating

Universal Model for Cross-Cultural Negotiators

As a human resource professional teaching negotiations, you must understand that negotiation is a cyclical process. Each individual in the audience must learn that within the process are four identifiable components that are key to understanding the negotiating cycle [16]:

1. Policy—the negotiating policy of each party; it defines the vital interests of a business and describes the customary course of action used to protect and promote those interests.

2. Interaction—how each party will try to persuade the other during the negotiation; it is the period of information exchange during which the negotiators propose offers and counteroffers. The process of interaction is a continual stream of acts, words, and gestures that are intended to persuade the counterpart. The flow of information permits each party to learn about the counterpart's expectations.

3. Deliberation—how each party gets the others' trust and on what will each party base their decisions; it is the process by which the negotiators evaluate the interaction, adjust their understanding of the counterpart's requirements and reformulate expectations, preferences, and proposals in an effort to resolve conflicting interests.

4. Outcome—how is agreement reached; this refers to the final understanding reached by the parties. The negotiators may come to some agreement or may conclude that agreement is impossible. Sometimes, negotiations do not have a definitive ending and either continue or are put off indefinitely. Whatever the outcome, it will cause the business to evaluate its policy.

These four components of the negotiation process establish a framework for global business negotiators to make intelligent decisions and take appropriate actions before, during, and after global negotiations by enabling them to predict and interpret the actions of their foreign counterparts.

The Framework

Again, we stress the importance of you as the facilitator in providing the necessary information to the audience participants that will allow them to become effective negotiators. The following framework describes the various parts of negotiating, and we stress the complete discussion of each of the following variables.

The components in the process of negotiation can be divided into one or more variables. These variables are intended to furnish a comprehensive and useful checklist of factors that a negotiator should consider when preparing for a negotiation session. Proper use and application of the variables can influence the success of the global negotiation.

Process Component	Component Variable(s)
Policy	1. Basic concept of negotiation
	2. Selection of negotiators
	3. Role of individual aspirations
	4. Concern with protocol
	5. Significance of type of issue
Interaction	6. Complexity of language
	7. Nature of persuasive argument
	8. Value of time
Deliberation	9. Basis of trust
	10. Risk-taking propensity
	11. Internal decision-making systems
Outcome	12. Form of satisfactory agreement

By selectively categorizing information under each of these twelve variables, negotiators can develop a profile that will show the counterpart's philosophy of negotiation; who the negotiators are and why they were selected; what the negotiators want for themselves; how they will act and how they will expect others to act; what kind of things are most important to them; how they try to persuade others verbally and nonverbally; how they use time and how long they expect negotiations to take; what makes them trust someone; how they handle risk; who makes the decisions and how the decisions are made; and what form of agreement they expect.

First, the negotiator should conduct an initial research of the relevant literature concerning the target culture and, if possible, extensively interview individuals who have negotiating experience with the target culture. The negotiator should then use the framework to organize their research findings. They should analyze the information and develop a set of provisional propositions on the target culture. These provisional propositions should be used in devising plans before the negotiation begins.

When interaction begins, the negotiator may observe deviations from the provisional propositions. The negotiator should not be disturbed by this. The initial research comes from books and other people's experiences. The past experiences of other business people are valuable, but are not always reliable. The negotiator must accept change and be prepared to face unexpected situations.

The framework is a dynamic model and, as interaction occurs, the negotiator should continually add personal observations and adjust the propositions accordingly. In this manner, the negotiator can arrive at a personal understanding of the foreign counterpart's motivations, needs, perspectives, and expectations. The framework is suited to customization by each individual negotiator who may want to add or subtract certain variables. The effective negotiators will be able to customize by adding, subtracting, and prioritizing the variables so that mutual benefit is achieved by all parties involved in the negotiation.

The framework is particularly well-suited for computer applications. The provisional propositions can be organized and stored on diskette as well as recording the negotiation. Using compact and laptop computers, the propositions can be reviewed and modified while flying overseas, in a foreign hotel room, and even throughout the actual negotiation process. In this manner, an individual or organization can build a personalized library that combines general information and personal observations on negotiating with specific cultures, organizations, and individuals. The library will then be available for future reference, providing a catalogued history of past global negotiations.

This approach is easy to understand and use. Its basic form can (and should) be adapted and changed as the situation and environment change. Also, because we continually stress the fact the each negotiation is unique, the framework must be adjusted accordingly. The skillful negotiator will learn how to make the appropriate adjustments for effective global negotiations. Exhibit 8-2 provides a better understanding of how negotiators use the framework in assessing the other party because it lists the possible ranges of negotiator profiles for each variable.

Exhibit 8-2
Framework for Global Business Negotiations

Variable	Negotiator's Profile Range	
Basic concept of negotiation	Strategic	Synergistic
Selection of negotiators	Technical ability	Social skills
Role of individual aspirations	Organization	Self
Concern with protocol	Formal	Informal
Significance of type of issue	Substantive	Relationship-based
Complexity of Language	Verbal	Nonverbal
Nature of Persuasive argument	Logic	Dogma Emotion
Value of time	Strict	Relaxed
Basis of trust	Law	Friendship
Risk-taking propensity	Cautious	Adventurous
Internal decision-making systems	Authoritative	Consensus
Form of satisfactory agreement	Explicit	Implicit

The most important aspect of this framework is that the individual negotiator should understand fully these variables and the possible ranges of negotiator behavior. Understanding the ranges will allow the negotiator to adjust accordingly to each international negotiating situation. It is much more realistic for the negotiator to be able to remember and use these twelve variables rather than to try to remember where every culture falls within the ranges. As the negotiator becomes more familiar with this framework and with various cultures he/she will become more adept in customizing the framework to fit the negotiating situation. The following discussion will provide the basic necessities for understanding the ranges of negotiator behavior for each variable in the framework.

Basic Concept of Negotiation

Although negotiation has universal aspects, negotiators are driven by a variety of different beliefs, concepts, and attitudes regarding proper approaches to the negotiation process. Depending upon custom, tradition, and/or personal preference, a negotiator will use diverse procedures, techniques, and methods of inquiry to obtain the desired ends. There are two basic opposing philosophies of negotiation: strategic and synergistic—

Strategic	**Synergistic**
Purpose	
Maximization of individual benefit.	Maximization of joint benefit.
Beliefs	
Zero sum.	Nonzero-sum.
Conflict is functional.	Conflict is dysfunctional.
Opposing interests are illegitimate.	Opposing interests are legitimate.
To solve conflict must coerce other.	To solve conflict must work together.
Attitude	
Competitive.	Cooperative.
Suspicious.	Trusting.
Hostile.	Friendly.
Ready to exploit other's needs.	Ready to respond helpfully.
Sensitive to differences.	Sensitive to common interests.
Communication	
Misleading.	Open and honest.
Confrontational.	Nonconfrontational.
Expands scope of conflict.	Limits scope of conflict.
Stimulates a sense of opposition.	Stimulates conformity and convergence of beliefs and values.

Under the *strategic negotiation* model, resources are seen to be limited, i.e., there is a fixed pie. Each side wants to get as much of the pie as it can get; however, if one party gets more, then the other party gets less. As interests are seen to be diametrically opposed, the sides are extremely competitive, often relying on trickery and coercion to obtain desired ends.

Under the *synergistic negotiation* model, resources are seen to be unlimited, i.e., there is enough for everyone; each side can "win." Each side wants to get as much pie as it can get and, by cooperating, everyone can have as much as they want. Followers of this model believe that there are several alternative ways in which the parties can obtain their desired ends without one party profiting at the expense of or interfering with the other.

Under the *strategic-synergistic* model, there are several types of resources, some are limited and others are unlimited, i.e., there are many kinds of pie, some are plentiful and some are scarce and each side has differing tastes. Depending upon the situation, followers of this model will use either a strategic or a synergistic approach.

If a negotiator has no knowledge of the counterpart's philosophy of negotiation, then many contingencies must be prepared for and planning becomes overly complex. By determining the counterpart's philosophy, the negotiator can concentrate upon developing specific plans that are appropriate to the counterpart's dispositions. Careful planning based on sound information of the counterpart will lead to an early and favorable agreement.

Selection of Negotiators

A basic fact about negotiation is that foreign negotiators are not abstract representatives of the other side. They are human beings. They have emotions, deeply held values, and different backgrounds and viewpoints. This human aspect of negotiation can be either helpful or disastrous.

Variations in prior experience, background, and outlook can affect the negotiator's manner and effectiveness. Individual differences in background (such as gender, age, political affiliation, and social class) as well as individual differences in personality (such as cooperativeness, authoritarianism, and risk-taking propensity) may shape the course of the negotiations. Therefore, it is important to know why the foreign negotiator was selected.

Foreign businesses attempt to choose negotiators who are the most capable of achieving satisfactory performance. In practice this means that most negotiator selection decisions are informal and reflect certain biases or preferences. Selection criteria can be broadly categorized under technical ability or social skills:

Technical Ability	Social Skills
Achievement	Ascription
Scientific skills	Status
Legal training	Personal attributes
General knowledge	Kinship
Language fluency	Social class

The number of negotiators considered appropriate for a negotiation appears to vary by culture. In some cases, a negotiating team will include some individuals who are socially skilled and others who are technically adept.

Technical ability is knowledge and proven ability in a particular field of expertise. Individuals who are technically skilled must have proven their ability through reputation, records of success, and demonstration of recognized skills. Negotiating skill and experience are included in this category. Also included are cross-cultural skills, such as the ability to learn new customs and procedures and the ability to improvise.

Businesses that value technical attributes attempt to make appointments and promotions "scientifically." Negotiators are chosen on the basis of measured competence. Desired characteristics include technical knowledge, scientific skills, language fluency, and legal training.

Businesses that value social skills make appointments and promotions on the basis of social criteria. Desired characteristics include personal attributes and status. Personal attributes are individual characteristics, such as affability, demonstrated loyalty, and perceived trustworthiness. Status is the candidate's relative rank in a hierarchy of prestige. This category includes seniority, political affiliation, social class, gender, age, ethnic ties, kinship, and physical characteristics.

Role of Individual Aspirations

The personal ambitions of negotiators are rarely identical with the interests of their corporations. In some cases, the position taken by a foreign negotiator may reflect personal goals to a greater degree than corporate goals. For example, an interest in personal success may lead negotiators to accept terms that are not favorable to their corporations. Negotiators have even been known to act as mediators between the two sides instead of as advocates for their corporations.

On the other hand, negotiators may want to prove that they are hard bargainers and decide to cling to a position more stubbornly than is either required by corporate instructions or warranted by any prospects that the counterpart might yield. Personal reputation may be more important than organizational reputation or success of the negotiation.

Like all human beings, negotiators have needs that they want to satisfy. Classical economic theory assumes that, as an individual, the negotiator will act in a manner that best fulfills his interests. This is deceptive in that "his" may refer to several different entities. In the extreme, "his" refers solely to the individual. Often, however, "his" may refer to the individual's family or household, and it is this entity whose interest is being maximized. In other cases, individuals act as if "his" referred to an even large entity. They appear to act in terms, not of their own interest, but of a larger collectivity or community. They might act in the interest of their profession, their nation, or even the world.

Negotiators are often put in the position of choosing between private goals and corporate goals. The negotiator may resolve this dilemma by exhibiting a "collectivity-orientations" and acting on behalf of the corporation; or the negotiator may exhibit a "self-orientation" and act for personal interests.

The dialectic between aspirations for self and aspirations for community can also be considered in terms of "relational orientation." Kluckhohn and Strodtbeck [8] discuss "individualism," "collaterality," and "lineality." When the individualistic principle is dominant, a negotiator's individual goals have primacy over the goals of the corporation. The negotiator is not allowed to ruthlessly disregard the interests of the corporation; however, it is understood that the negotiator will pursue individual interests along with corporate interests. Negotiators who exhibit a "collateral orientation" strongly identify with their corporations, but lack a strong national consciousness. Negotiators who exhibit a "lineal orientation" identify not only with their corporation, but strongly identify with their nation and history.

Concern with Protocol

Protocol lists accepted practices of diplomatic interaction in detailed codes of ceremony and procedure. Ceremony is conventional acts of politeness and etiquette. The underlying principle of ceremony is courteous consideration for the feelings of others, plus recognition of authority and vested responsibility. Procedure is the order to be pursued before, during, and after the negotiation process.

Rules of protocol may be formal or informal. Negotiators who insist on formal protocol stress adherence to strict and detailed rules that govern manners and conduct. They attach importance to explicit displays of courtesy. Parliamentary procedure may be used during the negotiations.

Negotiators who are informal attach little importance to explicit displays of courtesy and are inattentive to rules that govern manners and conduct. Procedure during negotiation does not follow any set rules. Negotiators may constantly interrupt each other.

If the counterpart's expectations of courteous behavior are not met, confusion and unnecessary conflict may result. Failure to follow protocol may be seen as a lack of respect for the counterpart's culture. Seemingly minor slights can cause confusion and conflict. In the extreme, failure to conform to protocol may cause negotiations to collapse.

Negotiators should give careful attention to the way protocol is applied. It is important to know whether or not the counterpart is using the rules of protocol to either favor or victimize the negotiator. The counterpart may be using protocol to communicate feelings ranging from a desire to see the negotiations successfully concluded to a complete lack of interest. Deliberate breaches of etiquette are often calculated manifestations of distrust.

Site selection is an important aspect of protocol because it affects psychological climate, availability and use of communications channels, and the presence of time limits. When negotiations occur in a foreign land, the host assumes responsibility for arranging the physical space. Physical arrangements, such as the size of tables and the height of chairs, have strategic implications and may become vehicles for accentuating status and power differences. An important political negotiation was held up for months while negotiators argued over the shape of the table.

The rules of protocol govern a variety of activities, including location of the negotiations, welcoming, transportation, official forms of address, presentation of credentials, business and visiting cards, dress codes, gift giving, entertainment, privileges, courtesies, ceremonies, receptions, language, use of interpreters, composition of the negotiating teams, seating arrangements, timing, documentation, departure, and precedence. These activities provide facilities and restraints, encouragements and deterrents to successful negotiations.

Significance of Type of Issue

In negotiation both parties share a common interest. They either want to share the same object or exchange different objects that they cannot gain by themselves, but can only obtain through each other. At the same time, the parties share conflicting interests in that their levels of aspiration (their highest objectives) are incongruent. The term issue, means a point arising from, or growing out of, the parties' conflicting interests.

Defining the issues is one of the most important parts of the negotiation. Before negotiations begin, each party formulates a preliminary statement of what it sees as the most important issues. The formulation of an issue may stake out the starting points and limits for concessions, fix the benchmarks for evaluating gains and losses, and circumscribe the areas in which pressures, threats, and inducements can be used.

This process continues throughout the negotiations. In fact, the negotiators may spend more time in trying to agree on what the issues are than in settling them.

An important part of issue definition is determining the counterpart's "vital interests" and "limits." Vital interests are those concerns that the counterpart views as essential to survival, security, or fundamental welfare. Limit is the counterparts' ultimate fallback position, the level of benefit beyond which they are unwilling to concede. If the parties' limits are incongruent, then it is impossible to reach an agreement.

Negotiators can gain an advantage by analyzing the issues to determine the counterpart's true preferences and priorities. If the negotiators are aware of their counterpart's limit, they can maneuver to get the best possible terms of agreement. At the same time, an understanding of the counterpart's view of the issues will enable negotiators to be more effective in disguising their own preferences and priorities.

Strategic issue analysis in negotiations should concentrate on two types of issues: substantive and relationship-based:

Substantive	Relationship-Based
Tangible	Intangible
Money	Personal, internal
Property	Values
Power	Beliefs

Substantive issues center around control and use of resources, such as space, money, power, property, prestige, and food. All business negotiators want to reach an agreement that satisfies their tangible interests because such interests are the ultimate issue.

Relationship-based issues center around the ongoing nature of mutual or reciprocal interests. Most negotiations occur in the context of an ongoing relationship. In an ongoing relationship, it is important to carry on each negotiation in a way that will help rather than hinder future relations and future negotiations. In many situations, the ongoing relationship is more important than the substantive outcome of any single negotiation.

Complexity of Language

"Context" includes the vocal and nonvocal aspects of communication that surround a word or passage and clarify its meaning. Contextual aspects of verbal communication include the rate at which one talks; the pitch or tone level of the voice; the intensity or loudness or softness of the speaker's voice; the flexibility or adaptability of the voice to the situation; the variations of rate, pitch and intensity that add effectiveness to delivery; the quality of the voice; fluency; and expressional patterns or nuances of delivery that convey meaning.

Contextual aspects of nonvocal expression include eye contact; pupil contraction and dilation; facial expression; odor; color, including changes in facial tone and match of clothing; hand gestures; body movement; personal distancing; and use of space.

Cultures can be either verbal or nonverbal. In verbal communication, information is transmitted through an elaborated code that makes meanings both explicit and specific. In nonverbal communication, the extra-verbal component of communication is the major channel for transmitting meaning.

Basil Bernstein [1] identifies two general types of code (language) for transmitting messages; restricted code and elaborated code. A restricted code arises when the social relationship is based upon closely shared identifications, upon an extensive range of shared expectations, or upon a range of common assumptions. Thus, a restricted code emerges when the culture raises the "we" above "I." Common cultural identity reduces the need to explicitly verbalize intent. The extra-verbal component of the communication becomes the major channel for transmitting messages. Meaning comes from how things are said and when they are said, rather than what is said.

The restricted code reinforces the social relationship rather than creating speech that uniquely fits the intentions of the speakers. Restricted codes do not give rise to verbally differentiated "I's." I-restricted-code meaning need not be fully explicit. A slight shift of pitch or stress, a small gesture, can carry a complete meaning. Communication is accomplished through closely shared identifications and affective empathy that removes the need to elaborate verbal meanings.

An elaborated code arises whenever the culture emphasizes the "I" over the "we," that is, whenever the intent of the other person cannot be taken for granted. Speakers are forced to elaborate their meanings by making them both explicit and specific. Meanings that are limited to the speaker's culture must be eliminated so that the speaker will be understood by the listener.

The elaborated code presupposes a sharp gap between self and others that is crossed through the creation of speech specifically fitting the differentiated "other." As the differentiated other does not share the cultural background of the speaker, the elaborated code helps the speaker make his subjective intent verbally explicit.

Edward T. Hall [4, 5] continues Bernstein's discussion of high-context and low-context cultures. High-context or low-context refers to the amount of information that is given in communication.

Similar to Bernstein's elaborated code, in a low-context communication, information is transmitted through an explicit code to make up for a lack of shared meanings. Hall sees a low-context communication as similar to interacting with a computer. If information is not explicitly stated and the program is not followed completely, then meaning is distorted.

Similar to Bernstein's restricted code, a high-context communication is one in which most of the information is either in the physical context or internalized in the person, while little is in the coded, explicit, transmitted part of the message. High-context communications feature preprogrammed information that is in the receiver and in the setting.

Hall sees high-context communication as faster, more economical, more efficient, and more satisfying than low-context communications; however, if time is not devoted to common programming, then communication is incomplete. For this reason, negotiators should be cautious of becoming involved in high-context communications.

Mushakoji [12] makes a similar distinction in his description of *erabi* culture and *awase* culture. The *erabi* culture assumes negotiations will proceed via a clear statement of position by each side; therefore, an explicit, standardized vocabulary is used to convey meaning. In contrast, the *awase* culture uses expressions with multifarious nuances that hint at reality rather than describing it precisely. Words are not taken at face value. Rather, meaning must be inferred. In negotiations, the *awase* preference is to infer the counterpart's position without clear explanation.

It is important to be aware of nonverbal cues for several reasons. First, the negotiator may unintentionally transmit false messages to the counterpart. Misrepresentation of nonverbal cues may range from feeling that an offer has been made that has not in fact been made to feeling that the negotiations have been ended when in fact they have not been ended. Second, the negotiator may not pick up on or may misinterpret nonverbal cues being transmitted by the counterpart. Third, effective communication may require the use of nonverbal messages. There may be no other acceptable way of communicating.

Nature of Persuasive Argument

Aristotle identified three means of influencing belief and action: *logos* (logical appeal); *pathos* (emotional appeal); and *ethos* (the appeal that comes from the listener's respect for the speaker as a person). In theory, pure argumentation uses only *logos,* or evidence and logical reasoning; however, this is unrealistic, because "logic" is defined subjectively.

It is better to think of argumentation in terms of its persuasive ability. Argumentation, then, is the art of persuading others to think or act in a definite way. In ideal form, argumentation unites reasoning with persuasive power. It convinces by adapting the material to the interests, prejudices, and idiosyncrasies of the audience, as well as exciting the emotions to just the extent necessary for the desired ends.

Argumentation in global negotiations involves a blend of logic, emotion, and dogma.

Negotiators who use logic try to persuade their counterparts with "substantive proof." To provide substantive proof, the negotiator must use empirical or factual evidence. Empirical evidence consists of presumably verifiable statements, including statistical reports, cost benefit analyses, and financial statements.

Negotiators who use emotional appeal try to persuade their counterparts with "motivational proofs." They provide evidence that coincides with the emotions, values, or motives of the counterpart including evidence from historical and cultural tradition.

Negotiators who use dogma try to persuade their counterparts with "authoritative proofs." They provide a statement of opinion from a person whose training and practice qualify her as an authority. This could include dogma from a religious expert, or ideology from a political expert, or even a statement of intuition from a matriarch.

Value of Time

Every culture possesses an internal clock based on rhythmic stimuli in specific environments. Cultures differ in time conception, time perspective, and time experiencing.

All individuals have a preferential orientation toward the past, the present, or the future. The preferred temporal perspective reflects cultural values.

An orientation toward the future implies an expectation of advancement or progressive development. Negotiators are able to predict, plan for, and change forthcoming events and conditions.

An orientation toward the present implies a predominance of the mental state of the moment. The negotiators' only concerns are those that are happening now.

An orientation toward the past implies a belief that everything that is or will be has already existed or occurred.

Temporal perspective influences overall strategy, especially issue formulation and important aspects of decision making. It may be impossible to enter a strict, binding agreement with cultures that have a relaxed perspective of the future.

Cultures have different ways of organizing and using time. Some cultures take a strict view of scheduling and others are more relaxed.

Edward Hall [4, 5] divides cultures into "monochronic" and "polychronic." Monochronic time emphasizes schedules, segmentation and promptness. By scheduling time, monochronic people compartmentalize events and concentrate on one thing at a time. Because scheduling by its nature selects what will be perceived and attended and permits only a limited number of events within a given period, what gets scheduled constitutes a system for setting priorities for both people and functions.

Polychronic time stresses involvement of people and completion of transactions rather than adherence to a preset schedule. The future is not solid or firm and, therefore, cannot be planned. Appointments are frequently broken and important plans may be changed right up to the minute of execution.

Bases of Trust

Negotiators face the dilemma of trust. They cannot be completely trusting, because they would be at the mercy of their counterpart's deceptions; however, to believe nothing the counterpart says eliminates the possibility of reaching an agreement.

At some point, every negotiator must face the critical problem of having to infer the counterparts' true intentions, interests, and preferences. When the negotiation is governed by mutual trust, the counterparts' behavior can be taken as a true indication of their underlying disposition. When the negotiation is governed by mutual suspicion, negotiators must develop a "translation" scheme that permits them to decipher what their counterparts really mean.

Trust has various meanings. Depending upon theoretical orientation and research interests, trust has been conceptualized as a personality construct, as a perception of equitableness and general helpfulness in interpersonal relationships, and as behavior exposing the individual to risky situations.

Trust always implies expectations of some kind, normally having to do with fiduciary obligation and responsibility. In a broad sense, trust can be viewed as expectation of the persistence of the moral social order. In negotiation, trust means reliance upon the accuracy of the counterpart's information and confidence that joint decisions will lead to the desired outcome.

In a broad sense, negotiators base trust on either law or friendship.

Risk-Taking Propensity

Decisions can be made under conditions of certainty, risk, or uncertainty. If a decision invariably leads to a specific outcome, then there is "certainty." If a decision leads to one of a set of possible specific outcomes, each occurring with a known probability, then there is "risk." If a decision leads to a set of possible specific outcomes with unknown or unmeaningful probabilities, then there is "uncertainty."

Risk implies the chance of injury, damage, or loss compared to some previous standard. Negotiators are subject to several kinds of loss including "image loss" in the eyes of other negotiators, present and future; "position loss"—the negotiator can't move back after making concessions; "information loss"—opponents can use candid information against the negotiator; and the loss of opportunity for competitive behavior [13].

Internal Decision-Making Systems

In global business negotiations, decisions are made on the basis of past company experience, existing company structure, quality of the international communications system, and personal biases.

Internal decision-making systems can be broadly dichotomized as either "authoritative" or "consensus." In authoritative decision-making systems, leaders or other powerful individuals make decisions without much concern for consensus. Decision-making power is not delegated to the entire negotiating team. The team leader may have been given the authority to make a decision without consulting with superiors; however, top management may reserve the right to overrule the team leader's decision.

In consensus decision-making systems, negotiators do not have the authority to make decisions without consulting superiors. The team leader must obtain support from team members and listen to their advice. The team may have to submit information to a committee or to a group of committees before any decision can be made.

Sometimes decision-making authority arises outside of the foreign corporation. A foreign government, unions, stockholders, or suppliers may be able to dictate the final decision.

If decision-making authority does not rest within the foreign negotiating team, negotiators must discover who does have decision-making power and formulate their argument to influence that person or persons. In such situations, it may be best to provide reports, charts, computer programs, and videotapes that can be evaluated at corporate headquarters.

If decision-making power rests solely within the foreign team-leader, the negotiator can focus persuasive appeals to fit the leader's disposition. It does little good to convince other team members if the leader won't listen to their advice.

If the decision requires unanimous team approval, the pluralistic nature of the team may prolong the decision-making process. Negotiators may have to wait a long time before they receive a final answer.

Above all else, global negotiation is a process of joint decision-making. Each party can only obtain what the other is prepared to allow. Because the parties necessarily begin the negotiations with some kind of differences between them, the process of decision-making involves a convergence. At least one party, but usually both, must move toward the other. Although there may be compromise of some sort, this is not inevitable because one party may be induced to move altogether to the counterpart's position or, alternatively, there can be a joint, integrative creation of something new that is acceptable to both parties.

Form of Satisfactory Agreement

Negotiations are entered into "ostensibly for the purpose of reaching agreement." An agreement can be defined as an exchange of conditional promises, in which each party declares that it will act in a certain way on condition that the other parties act in accordance with their promises [9].

Promises are only *manifestations of intention* to act or refrain from acting in a certain way, so a promise is less than absolute. Depending upon the individuals and cultures involved, promise breaking is tolerated, expected and, in certain cases, desired.

The fact that promises are less than absolute has severe implications for the negotiator. A promise projects exchange into the future. If the negotiator's organization takes action in anticipation of performance by the counterpart, nonperformance may cause extreme damage.

To avoid expensive complications, the negotiator must ensure that there is a means of communication understandable to the parties that will lead to a mutually acceptable agreement with an effective mechanism to enforce promises.

There are two broad forms of satisfactory agreement. One is an explicit, detailed written contract that, by covering all contingencies, requires no future cooperation and binds the parties through an outside enforcement mechanism. The other is an implicit, broad oral agreement that, in accepting unforeseen change as a normal aspect of life, leaves room for the parties to deal with the problem together and binds the parties through the quality of their personal relationship.

This chapter has attempted to synthesize some of the principal strategies and frameworks for conducting successful cross-cultural negotiations. We intend that human resource leaders would then use this information in staff meetings or training sessions to prepare cross-cultural negotiators. In essence, this is a component of a comprehensive HRD program that prepares global managers and professionals. Creative HR professionals will use this input in the form of case studies, simulations, and other group processes to promote skill in negotiating between persons of diverse cultural backgrounds.

The questionnaire in Exhibit 8-3 may be useful for the HR specialist in helping negotiators determine their individual negotiation style.

Exhibit 8-3
Negotiation Skills
A Self-Assessment Exercise

Please respond to this list of questions in terms of what you believe you do *when interacting with others.* Base your answers on your typical day-to-day activities. Be as frank as you can.

For each statement, please enter on the Score Sheet the number corresponding to your choice of the five possible responses given below:

1. If you have never (or very rarely) observed yourself doing what is described in the statement.
2. If you have observed yourself doing what is described in the statement *occasionally, but infrequently:* that is, less often than most other people who are involved in similar situations.
3. If you have observed yourself doing what is described in the statement about *an average amount:* that is, about as often as most other people who are involved in similar situations.
4. If you have observed yourself doing what is described in the statement *fairly frequently:* that is, somewhat more often than most other people who are involved in similar situations.
5. If you have observed yourself doing what is described in the statement *very frequently:* that is, considerably more than most other people who are involved in similar situations.

Please answer each question.

1. I focus on the entire situation or problem.
2. I evaluate the facts according to a set of personal values.
3. I am relatively unemotional.
4. I think that the facts speak for themselves in most situations.
5. I enjoy working on new problems.
6. I focus on what is going on between people when interacting.
7. I tend to analyze things very carefully.
8. I am neutral when arguing.
9. I work in bursts of energy with slack periods in between.
10. I am sensitive to other people's needs and feelings.
11. I hurt people's feelings without knowing it.
12. I am good at keeping track of what has been said in a discussion.
13. I put two and two together quickly.
14. I look for common ground and compromise.
15. I use logic to solve problems.
16. I know most of the details when discussing an issue.
17. I follow my inspirations of the moment.
18. I take strong stands on matters of principle.
19. I am good at using a step-by-step approach.
20. I clarify information for others.

---

*Adapted by Pierre Casse from Interactive Style Questionnaire (Situation Management Systems, Inc.) in *Training for the Cross-Cultural Mind,* SIETAR, Washington, D.C., 1979. Used with permission.

21. I get my facts a bit wrong.
22. I try to please people.
23. I am very systematic when making a point.
24. I relate facts to experience.
25. I am good at pinpointing essentials.
26. I enjoy harmony.
27. I weigh the pros and cons.
28. I am patient.
29. I project myself into the future.
30. I let my decisions be influenced by my personal likes and wishes.
31. I look for cause and effect.
32. I focus on what needs attention now.
33. When others become uncertain or discouraged, my enthusiasm carries them along.
34. I am sensitive to praise.
35. I make logical statements.
36. I rely on well tested ways to solve problems.
37. I keep switching from one idea to another.
38. I offer bargains.
39. I have my ideas very well thought out.
40. I am precise in my arguments.
41. I bring others to see the exciting possibilities in a situation.
42. I appeal to emotions and feelings to reach a "fair" deal.
43. I present well articulated arguments for the proposals I favor.
44. I do not trust inspiration.
45. I speak in a way which conveys a sense of excitement to others.
46. I communicate what I am willing to give in return for what I get.
47. I put forward proposals or suggestions which make sense even if they are unpopular.
48. I am pragmatic.
49. I am imaginative and creative in analyzing a situation.
50. I put together very well-reasoned arguments.
51. I actively solicit others' opinions and suggestions.
52. I document my statements.
53. My enthusiasm is contagious.
54. I build upon others' ideas.
55. My proposals command the attention of others.
56. I like to use the inductive method (from facts to theories).
57. I can be emotional at times.
58. I use veiled or open threats to get others to comply.
59. When I disagree with someone, I skillfully point out the flaws in the others' arguments.
60. I am low-key in my reactions.
61. In trying to persuade others. I appeal to their need for sensations and novelty.
62. I make other people feel that they have something of value to contribute.
63. I put forth ideas which are incisive.
64. I face difficulties with realism.
65. I point out the positive potential in discouraging or difficult situations.

(continued on next page)

66. I show tolerance and understanding of others' feelings.
67. I use arguments relevant to the problem at hand.
68. I am perceived as a down-to-earth person.
69. I go beyond the facts.
70. I give people credit for their ideas and contributions.
71. I like to organize and plan.
72. I am skillful at bringing up pertinent facts.
73. I have a charismatic tone.
74. When disputes arise, I search for the areas of agreement.
75. I am consistent in my reactions.
76. I quickly notice what needs attention.
77. I withdraw when the excitement is over.
78. I appeal for harmony and cooperation.
79. I am cool when negotiating.
80. I work all the way through to reach a conclusion.

Score Sheet

Enter the score you assign each question (1, 2, 3, 4, or 5) in the space provided. *Please note:* The item numbers progress across the page from left to right. When you have all your scores, add them up *vertically* to attain four totals. Insert a "3" in any number space left blank.

1. _____	2. _____	3. _____	4. _____
5. _____	6. _____	7. _____	8. _____
9. _____	10. _____	11. _____	12. _____
13. _____	14. _____	15. _____	16. _____
17. _____	18. _____	19. _____	20. _____
21. _____	22. _____	23. _____	24. _____
25. _____	26. _____	27. _____	28. _____
29. _____	30. _____	31. _____	32. _____
33. _____	34. _____	35. _____	36. _____
37. _____	38. _____	39. _____	40. _____
41. _____	42. _____	43. _____	44. _____
45. _____	46. _____	47. _____	48. _____
49. _____	50. _____	51. _____	52. _____
53. _____	54. _____	55. _____	56. _____
57. _____	58. _____	59. _____	60. _____
61. _____	62. _____	63. _____	64. _____
65. _____	66. _____	67. _____	68. _____
69. _____	70. _____	71. _____	72. _____
73. _____	74. _____	75. _____	76. _____
77. _____	78. _____	79. _____	80. _____
IN: _____	NR: _____	AN: _____	FA: _____

Negotiation Style Profile

Enter now your four scores on the bar chart below. Construct your profile by connecting the four data points.

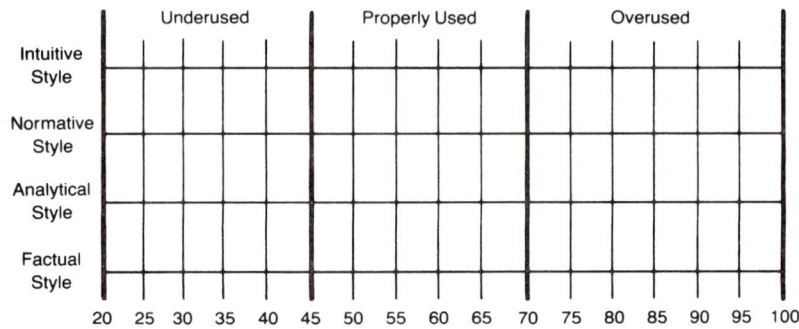

Description of Styles

Factual

Basic Assumption: "The facts speak for themselves."

Behavior: Pointing out facts in neutral way, keeping track of what has been said, reminding people of their statements, knowing most of the details of the discussed issue and sharing them with others, clarifying, relating facts to experience, being low-key in their reactions, looking for proof, documenting their statements.

Key Words: Meaning, define, explain, clarify, facts.

Intuitive

Basic Assumption: "Imagination can solve any problem."

Behavior: Making warm and enthusiastic statements, focusing on the entire situation or problem, pinpointing essentials, making projections into the future, being imaginative and creative in analyzing the situation, keeping switching from one subject to another, going beyond the facts, coming up with new ideas all the time, pushing and withdrawing from time to time, putting two and two together quickly, getting their facts a bit wrong sometimes, being deductive.

Key Words: Principles, essential, tomorrow, creative, idea.

Normative

Basic Assumption: "Negotiating is bargaining."

Behavior: Judging assessing and evaluating the facts according to a set of personal values, approving and disapproving, agreeing and disagreeing, using loaded works, offering bargains, proposing rewards, incentives, appealing to feelings and emotions to reach a "fair" deal, demanding, requiring, threatening, involving power, using status, authority, correlating, looking for compromise, making effective statements, focusing on people, their reactions, judging, attention to communication and group processes.

Key Words: Wrong, right, good, bad, like.

(continued on next page)

Analytical

Basic Assumption: "Logic leads to the right conclusions."

Behavior: Forming reasons, drawing conclusions and applying them to the case in negotiation, arguing in favor or against one's own or others' position, directing, breaking down, dividing, analyzing each situation for cause and effect, identifying relationships of the parts, putting things into logical order, organizing, weighing the pros and cons thoroughly, making identical statements, using linear reckoning.

Key Words: Because, then, consequently, therefore, in order to.

Guidelines for Negotiating with People Having Different Styles

1. Negotiating with someone having a *factual* style—
   - Be *precise* in presenting your facts.
   - Refer to the *past* (what has already been tried out, what has worked, what has been shown from past experiences . . .).
   - Be *indicative* (go from the facts to the principles.
   - Know your dossier (including the details).
   - Document what you say.
2. Negotiating with someone having an *intuitive* style—
   - Focus on the situation as a whole.
   - Project yourself into the future (look for opportunities).
   - Tap the imagination and creativity of your partner.
   - Be quick in reacting (jump from one idea to another).
   - Build upon the reaction of the other person.
3. Negotiating with someone having an *analytical* style—
   - Use logic when arguing.
   - Look for causes and effects.
   - Analyze the relationships between the various elements of the situation or problem at stake.
   - Be patient.
   - Analyze various options with their respective pros and cons.
4. Negotiating with someone having a *normative* style—
   - Establish a sound relationship right at the outset of the negotiation.
   - Show your interest in what the other person is saying.
   - Identify his or her values and adjust to them accordingly.
   - Be ready to compromise.
   - Appeal to your partner's feelings.

References

1. Bernstein, B., *Class, Codes, and Control,* New York: Schocken Books, 1975.
2. Fisher, G., *International Negotiation: A Cross-Cultural Perspective,* Yarmouth, ME: Intercultural Press, 1980.
3. Graham, J. L. and Herberger, R., "Negotiators Abroad—Don't Shoot from the Hip," *Harvard Business Review,* July/August, 1983, Vol. 61, No. 4.
4. Hall, E., *Dance of Life,* Garden City, NY: Anchor Books/Doubleday, 1984.

5. Hall E., *Beyond Culture,* Garden City, NY: Anchor Books/Doubleday, 1976.
6. Harris, P. and Moran, R. T., *Managing Cultural Differences,* 3rd Edition, Houston: Gulf Publishing Company, 1991.
7. Huthwaite Research Group Report, "Behavior of Successful Negotiators," Reston, VA: Huthwaite, Inc., 1982.
8. Kluckhohn, F. and Strodtbeck, F., *Variations in Value Orientations,* Evanston, Illinois: Row, Peterson and Company, 1961.
9. MacNeil, I., *The New Social Contract,* New Haven, CT: Yale, 1980.
10. Moran, R. T., *Getting Your Yen's Worth: How to Negotiate with Japan, Inc.,* Houston: Gulf Publishing Company, 1985.
11. Moran, R. T. and Stripp, W., *Dynamics of Successful International Business Negotiations,* Houston: Gulf Publishing Company, 1991.
12. Mushakoji, K., "The Cultural Premises of Japanese Diplomacy," in *The Silent Power: Japan's Identity and the World Role,* Tokyo: Simul Press, 1976.
13. Pruitt, D., *Negotiation Behavior,* New York: Academic Press, 1981.
14. Sunshine, R. B., *Negotiating for International Development: A Practitioner's Handbook,* Boston: Martinus Nijhoff Publishers, 1990.
15. Unterman, I., "Negotiation and Cross-Cultural Communication" in *International Negotiation* edited by D. H. Bendhmane and J. W. McDonald, Washington, D.C.: Foreign Service Institute, U.S. Department of State, 1984.
16. Weiss, S. T. and Stripp, W., *Negotiating with Foreign Businesspersons,* New York: New York University Graduate School of Business Administration monograph #89-9, 1985.

CHAPTER 9

EFFECTIVE CROSS-CULTURAL MEETINGS

Introduction

Since the beginning of human existence, people have been meeting in diads, triads, and small groups to exchange ideas, to plan, and to learn together. Our species has moved from the aboriginal village meeting house to the New England town meeting, from parliamentary convocations to United Nations assemblies. Arriving at a consensus through meetings has become the essence of the democratic process worldwide. In this Information Age, such meetings can occur face-to-face in limited numbers as in a team, or in large conventions as in an industry conference. Furthermore, the prospects have been enhanced by electronic meetings in which we move our brains instead of our bodies. Increasingly, these meetings involve cross-cultural encounters—people from different nationalities or places of origins, from different disciplines or fields of expertise, from different classes or levels of societies. Even with a common language for the meeting, such as English, participants differ in the skill and usage of that language because they speak American or British forms of English, or because English is a second language rather than their native tongue, or because they speak a dialect, such as Black English or "Spanglish."

During the last three decades, phenomenal growth has occurred in international meetings conducted by government entities and UN agencies, as well as by trade and professional associations, multinational corporations, and consulting firms. Generally, the purpose of these meetings is information exchange, especially about leading-edge technologies, new processes, and procedures. Frequently, these cross-cultural meetings are to update people in professional or human resource development. The size of such encounters may range from small, selected groups to conventions of thousands. Ultimately, meeting encounters among personnel should contribute toward improving organizational relations.

Whether these persons actually leave their home culture to convene in a host culture, or engage in a worldwide/regional video conference, careful meeting planning can ensure that cultural synergy is realized by combining human efforts through collaboration and cooperation. Advances in transportation and communication technologies have made mass travel and exchange more feasible. However, rising transportation, energy, and hotel costs, along with political and economic instability abroad, may make such travel less desirable and electronic conferencing more attractive thanks to innovations in satellites, television, and computers. From now through the 21st century, we can expect cross-cultural interchange of minds and thoughts on a scale unprecedented in human history.

Global managers developing strategies to capitalize on the challenges of the global market should carefully consider the meetings that consume so much of their people's energy and time. Specifically, potential *human resource leaders* should be concerned about the effectiveness of all meetings in the organizations, especially those devoted to education and training. A survey conducted by Burke Marketing Research in Cincinnati discovered that the average executive spends 16.5 hours per week or 21 of the 40-hour work weeks during a year in meetings [11]. The investigators concluded that if such top managers earned a yearly averagé salary of $45,000, that means that $18,559 is spent for merely sitting in meetings. Because many upper level managers actually earn more than the figure cited, the meetings may be even more costly, especially when nearly one-third of those gatherings are considered unnecessary. One waste of meeting time, talent, and money is the regularly scheduled session with no agenda. For example, a company or agency may have a tradition that certain key personnel meet every Monday or Wednesday at 8:30 a.m., and everyone involved dutifully blocks out the time on his or her schedule regardless of whether any need for the meeting actually exists or not. Corporate headhunter Robert Half, who commissioned the cited study, lamented that America does not lead the world in productivity but in number of meetings!

The concern of this book is exercising leadership in cross-cultural management and high performance. One way to achieve that is by finding innovative substitutes for the classical face-to-face meeting, whether video phones or electronic mail are used. Another way is to make better use of people's energies and talents when they gather for meetings, which may in part involve removing cultural and language barriers to interaction. Those in attendance may then participate and contribute more fully.

In the subsequent sections the input on cross-cultural meetings focuses on (1) critical issues, (2) increasing cross-cultural meeting effectiveness, (3) using new meeting technologies, (4) providing examples of organizational successes in that regard, and (5) suggesting human resource development (HRD) strategies for consideration. The chapter concludes with an instrument for improving cross-cultural meeting planning and management.

If we view our organizations as energy exchange systems, then HR leaders must be concerned that the energy flows properly, to channel human activities and achieve optimal organizational goals. When assessing institutional energy, management also must evaluate meetings that consume personnel effort in preparing, conducting, and following-up on these events. For example, is the human and financial capital invested in meetings being well spent? From an energy conservation perspective, the next question becomes: Does a better way exist to confer and communicate than in the person-to-person format? If personal presence is required in a group encounter, then how do you facilitate better participation by culturally diverse personnel?

Cross-Cultural Meeting Issues

Why Do We Need to Meet?

Meetings for meetings' sake should be discouraged. Taking personnel from their regular work is costly; the underlying rationale for the meeting should be to help employees better accomplish their work, or to live better in the case of a community meeting. When a company or association justifies a meeting, perhaps the impetus for gathering employees or members together is to exchange information and insight, to promote on-the-job learning, to solve or prevent a problem, to raise morale, or to reward high performance.

Do We Use an Electronic or Personal Medium?

Megatrend author John Naisbit observed: "The more technology in this society, the more people want to get together. Meetings will be one of the great growth industries in this country because of technology; people want to aggregate more, in a compensatory way." Convenience and cost considerations may dictate that initial exchanges be by telephone or video phone, or other forms of telecommunications and networking. For in-depth encounters and the development of relationships that promote trust however, personal meetings may prove to be preferable. Some training may be accomplished through programmed learning or interactive video, but there are occasions when bringing trainees together in a group enhances the preliminary self-instruction.

What Is an International Meeting?

There was a time, according to Virginia Lofft, associate publisher of *Successful Meetings,* when the term "international meeting" meant a conference of U.S. participants at a non-domestic location, or going beyond one's national borders to a foreign site. Another interpretation was a meeting of internationals, people from different countries, gathering for reasons of trade, profession, economics, politics, or global concern, such as an ecological issue. Today, we prefer the term *cross-cultural* to describe meetings at home or abroad that involve people from varying cultural backgrounds and languages.

How to Plan and Manage Meetings?

In the past, such arrangements were often delegated to a secretary or staff person. In the new work culture, managers are involved directly in such matters because of the costs and complexity of subject matter, participants, and other factors that ensure meeting success. Just as marketing and sales executives have always been actively engaged in group meetings with sales personnel and customers, other managers now use meetings to help subordinates and clients use information, products, and services to achieve timely and better results. In large systems like a transnational corporation, meeting planning and management may be complex enough to require assistance from human resource development specialists or professional meeting consultants.

A true professional in meeting planning and management develops a computerized knowledge bank about resource personnel, presenters, meeting sites and facilities, technology and equipment, meeting methods, and group dynamics. Such a database may contain diverse information about site services and weather, travel and transportation variables, translators and suppliers, participant demographics and needs, and/or other special requirements for a successful meeting. Emerging emphasis on professionalism now prompts practitioners to join Meeting Planners International and become Certified Meeting Professionals (Convention Liaison Council, 1575 I St., Suite 1200, Washington, D.C. 20005, USA).

What Are the Cultural Influences on Meeting Dynamics?

Cultural background impacts the meeting planner, operator, presenter, and audience. When outside one's own borders, and sometimes even within one's own country, semantic differences may imply that signs, symbols, and gestures that are perfectly acceptable at home could have a different meaning or be unacceptable in another country. Even when meeting on home territory the make-up of an audience from foreign cultures may preclude the use of certain procedures and practices.

In Europe, there is a definite protocol about meetings, especially those involving people of many different nationalities. Large conferences tend to open with a social reception involving local dignitaries. The regular sessions are more formal and automatically involve simultaneous language translations or similar equipment. There is a tendency for more speeches and fewer group encounters, and often banquets or formal social events are considered the highlight. Because Europeans have been meeting together for thousands of years, there is often a sophistication among them not found among their former colonials, including such practices as printed invitations and published proceedings in several languages.

North American meeting planners have a tendency to be highly organized and very concerned about details, timing, and procedures. When abroad, they find locals who are anxious to please visitors and create a favorable impression of their country and its people. For the sake of national "face," they sometimes say things they think the "Yankee" wants to hear and even make promises they cannot possibly keep. The native supplier or conference coordinator may not be as concerned about details and may have a different "time" consciousness. It is not uncommon to experience the "mañana" syndrome in which other things are more essential now, so put off this one until tomorrow. Sometimes those from more developed nations go into a developing economy and overwhelm local colleagues, contractors, or providers with too much information and too many demands, often not allowing sufficient time for such requests to be fulfilled given the local constraints and the ability of the indigenous person to deliver. Though there may be many telephone, fax, or mail communications from the "on-site" meeting arranger assuring the planner of no problems, that "all is well and on schedule," be prepared with alternative plans in the event that expectations cannot be met. Whether in Latin America, the Middle or Far East or anywhere else, be prepared for the unanticipated; be flexible in responding to the meeting challenges. Upon arrival, planners frequently discover that an insufficient number of handouts have been translated into the foreign languages, that the menus have been changed by food shortages, or that audio or video equipment is not available as ordered or is not electronically compatible. The local arranger may then be very apologetic, try hard to please, and mean well. Fortunately, the chances for successful meetings are improving in the great international hotel chains that attempt to maintain global standards and services that satisfy customer meeting needs.

It is important to realize that a meeting or conference may not only reflect the macroculture of a country, but also the microculture of the organizational sponsor. If the latter's work environment is very formal, status-conscious, and businesslike, one can usually expect the meetings to be conservative and dignified with emphasis on people's roles or ranks. On the other hand, the global high-tech firm is generally more informal and spontaneous, operating with a team management mode of equality and a norm of competence. Thus, such a U.S. corporation is likely to use informality and group process to promote interaction, reporting, and action. Foreigners familiar with hierarchy and lectures with little meeting discussion may be unfamiliar with the former approaches. Although the Japanese are group-oriented, their managers in the United States are not accustomed to American candidness and sharing. Transnational enterprises must "educate" personnel throughout the world to their particular corporate meeting culture and preferences.

Asians become disturbed at meetings when Occidentals are direct in feedback or express heated emotions. As a consultant abroad, author Harris observed during training sessions in the Philippines that locals became upset when French Canadian community development workers gave angry or highly emotional responses to one another. Filipinos are not culturally disposed to frank exchanges and prefer to create harmony at meetings. Yet, such internationals can be oriented to new meeting techniques ranging from simulations and brainstorming sessions to interactive videos. Likewise, although Americans tend to be open, friendly, and even gregarious upon first meeting, sometimes talking freely about their families or even their personal lives, non-Westerners frequently are reluctant to reveal such information until real friendship is established; the latter would usually never inquire about the wife of a business acquaintance. For instance, German or Dutch participants at an international meeting tend to be more formal and reserved, especially in initial exchanges. With people from diverse backgrounds, the usual, accepted way of meeting in one's own country may not be known or understood by others from outside that culture.

Furthermore, a corporation can be defined through its meeting procedures. Meetings provide a showcase for reinforcement or delineation of organizational culture, such as in the prescribed roles of management and other participants, or in the manner of listening and problem solving. NASA has set procedures for its meetings that include extensive use of carefully constructed overhead slides and rehearsed sessions, particularly if the press or public are involved.

When an agency like NASA is forced to seek international partners, meetings may be strained and unproductive if the institutional culture is not altered. Exhibit 9-1 [10] points up the problem, and may explain why the appointment of a new agency director came from outside industry, rather than from within the bureaucracy.

In meetings of both the public and private sectors rituals are observed, such as displaying the organization's heros, repeating its myths and victories, and articulating its goals and aspirations for the future. Organizational meetings serve as opportunities to transmit and reaffirm values, customs, and beliefs, while building morale and team spirit. Anyone who has attended meetings of the U.S. Navy or Amway Corporation understand this spirit. Strong corporate cultures use meetings to gain commitment and involvement, to motivate and increase productivity, and/or to give recognition and reward. A company with a reputation for a "touch of class" employs these strategies in its conferences and social events, especially in the treatment of guest speakers or employee spouses. Cheap outfits on the other hand

---

Exhibit 9-1 [10]
Lower the Drawbridge

The specter of a united European-Russian space effort should give pause to Americans who still cling to the notion that the United States cannot be surpassed in space. In the United States, meanwhile the space community is marking time, and risks being left out of this new international partnership. NASA's isolationist culture is not attuned to international space ventures. International affairs officers in government agencies should be multilingual strategic thinkers who can clearly see the plus and minuses of tying NASA efforts to those of other nations. NASA officials who travel abroad should be carefully selected and well prepared to represent the agency. The Office of International Affairs within NASA needs to be elevated, so that international relations receive the administrator's attention and to prevent the State Department from further steamrolling of NASA cooperation. . . . A U.S. executive recently described the current situation as a drawbridge mentality, in which NASA has decided if it just disregards unsettling changes overseas, perhaps they will go away. It is time to lower the drawbridge!

---

run seedy, sloppy, and sometimes chaotic meetings with an emphasis on making money and little regard for people or long-term outcomes.

Organizational culture is communicated in the:

- Selection of meeting site (e.g., a university conference center or posh resort, domestic or international location).
- Arrangement of schedule (e.g., balance in structured and unstructured sessions, provisions for recreation and entertainment).
- Provisions for formality and informality (e.g., in meeting tone and procedures, in business and/or causal dress, in accompanying sightseeing or field trips).

Meetings are ideal when there are major changes in organizational structure and environment; a merger/acquisition occurs, or a new owner wants to meet key personnel to share a different vision. Meetings are dynamic mechanisms for keeping a work force or members informed, for achieving organizational goals and profitability, and for creating synergy among various entities in the system. Excellence in organizational culture measures meeting results, establishes accountability for post-meeting activities, ensures wide dissemination of findings, and reinforces the principal meeting messages.

Because most meetings today are cross-cultural in nature, HR leaders ensure that meeting planning and management are culturally astute. At the very least, such meetings should contribute to increasing cultural awareness among participants.

Increasing Cross-Cultural Meeting Effectiveness

Ineffective meetings can undermine and even divide organizations. One of the authors (Harris) was once vice-president in a corporation that held weekly executive meetings at which the same pattern always prevailed: the president presided, made small talk and jokes, and then dominated the proceedings. Rarely did the other executives present contribute to deliberations, and no real decisions were ever made in these meetings. No agenda was ever set, no meaningful business was ever transacted, and everyone left frustrated, except the CEO's cronies who flattered his ego. After having resigned from the firm, the writer discovered a few years later that not only had the company gone bankrupt, but at the time of the meetings in question, the former president was going deaf, refused to admit that he was unable to hear the contributions of others, and would not wear a hearing aid. Thus, the strange meeting behavior contributed to the business failure. If that organization had welcomed and acted upon feedback from personnel, it might be alive and well today.

To discover how meetings in an enterprise can be improved, ask the people who work there. This topic is perfect for action research by HR leaders, as long as replies are anonymous and respondents are free to "tell it like it is." A properly conducted survey can be done by questionnaires or interviews to ascertain:

- What meetings are considered boring and/or unnecessary?

- What disturbs employees most about existing meetings, such as obstacles to authentic communications and involvement?

- What suggestions do participants have for making group encounters more productive as well as culturally sensitive?

When the survey results have been assembled and analyzed, top management should assemble to make decisions regarding meeting improvement based upon the findings.

Bradford D. Smart, president of Smart and Associates in Chicago, conducted a similar study to determine what meeting characteristics particularly bothered executives, especially in team sessions. The respondents (14 board chairpersons, 358 presidents, 142 vice-presidents, and 121 general managers) complained about:

- Poor and/or inadequate preparation for the sessions by meeting planners or participants.
- People straying from the subject under discussion.
- Members not listening properly during the presentations and analysis.
- Participant verbosity during questioning or discussions.
- Lack of active participation by some attendees.
- Emotional outbursts and conflicts.
- Questionable effectiveness of methods or discussions.
- Length of meetings.

The same executives surveyed reached some consensus as to the ground rules they preferred during business meetings, including training sessions or team building:

- Each member must feel totally responsible for group effectiveness and team solutions, ensuring the maximum use of time and human resources available (e.g., inviting quiet ones to speak up and requesting those who usually dominate to listen more).
- Telephone call interruptions should be banned except for urgent issues of "life and death importance."
- Circular seating arrangements are opted for, even without tables.
- Participants should contribute to structuring the agenda and establishing priorities, usually at the beginning of the meeting and always in team meetings.
- Participatory decision-making achieved through group consensus is the desirable form of group action.
- Conflicts should be confronted and resolved, lest they hamper group effectiveness.

- Teams should learn how to diagnose and deal with problems of group process, including the appropriate use of instruments for this purpose.

Here are sixteen *cross-cultural meeting guidelines* to enhance effectiveness:

1. *Recognize that meetings have different purposes,* requiring both participants and methods appropriate for the type of meeting proposed (e.g., meetings for regular staff business, for work programming, for unit feedback on progress, for problem-solving, for information sharing or training); therefore, plan accordingly.

2. *Realize there are meeting skills to be acquired* relative to planning, chairing, controlling, facilitating, and coping with problems or obtaining solutions; acquire these competencies.

3. *Consult resources that can assist in improving the technical presentation during meetings* (e.g., seek training in multimedia methods, production of slides or videotapes, group dynamics).

4. *Use meetings as coordinating tools* to provide interaction opportunities for managers or supervisors of complex, interdependent operations.

5. *Control the meeting location and services.* Hold meetings, if possible, on one's own "territory," but ensure that facilities are adequate for optimal performance, including all necessary supplies and equipment. If the meeting is held off-site, carefully control the selection and monitor the services provided.

6. *Seat participants for minimal conflict or collusion* (e.g., divide antagonists and comrades) and maximum exchange (e.g., round tables, U-shaped table arrangement, or other set-ups to promote eye contact and interaction).

7. *Formal agendas are normally helpful* to focus efforts and save time, while avoiding undesirable and irrelevant subjects (except in unstructured meetings when the group itself develops the agenda); issues are who sets the agendas, how to get items on the docket, and when the agenda is distributed (e.g., Does the leader establish the agenda or delegate that task? Is there a procedure for members to contribute items for discussion? Is the agenda set in advance to allow for preparation or held until the actual meeting?).

8. *Control time in business meetings* so that it is used productively (e.g., provide necessary materials in advance, set a time limit, use a timing device, limit individual input, establish meeting procedures).

9. *Facilitate the meeting process.* When a diverse group gathers for the first time, it might be wise to go around to each member and ask them to briefly state what they see as the purpose of the meeting and what they hope the outcome will be. The facilitator may at that point note the level of language or communication proficiency that each possesses, clear up misunderstandings, and engage in various helpful activities (e.g., provide for note taking and recording when desirable, invite and foster participation, encourage compromise and conflict management, replay people's ideas and synthesize input, use audio-visual aids, articulate clearly and non-defensively, divide the group into sub-groups or task forces to study critical issues, obtain support beforehand on critical decisions, offer positive reinforcement of sound strategies and positions, seek and obtain consensus, and if necessary at times call for a vote).

10. *Conclude the meeting by clarifying action steps,* establishing accountability, setting deadlines if necessary, confirming noteworthy contributions, encouraging feelings of accomplishment, and ending punctually.

When an international meeting is held outside the borders of one's homeland, these "tips" for meeting planners may help ensure an effective conference abroad:

11. *Personally inspect the overseas meeting facility and negotiate directly with suppliers and other contractors.* Use this pre-meeting visit to not only assess the situation, but develop relations and rapport with hotel or conference center staff and other locals providing support services. It is important to ascertain equipment compatibility relative to electrical systems (i.e., voltage). When such a visit is not feasible, you may wish to use the telephone and fax to accomplish some advance planning or obtain a local representative to take care of it for you. In any case, discuss your needs and concerns quietly and avoid being demanding or overly businesslike. Examine meeting and guest rooms, as well as kitchen facilities. Do request bids in writing for all services to be rendered by external contractors. If you do not speak the local language, speak more slowly than normal

when conversing in English with representatives for whom English is a second or third language. Having business cards printed in both their language and yours is useful. If a large facility is required, remember to make reservations well in advance of the event (e.g., a year to two years prior in places where desirable space is at a premium, or when a special request is being made for an estate chateau or manor house converted into a conference center).

12. *Food service negotiations and planning are critical* before arrival. Some considerations are:

    a) Determine if continental breakfast is included or if the European plan is required, then inform your members in advance.

    b) If possible sample meals selected with the catering manager and discuss the accepted prices (avoid selections that may lead to intestinal or preference problems for visitors).

    c) Order bottled water and ascertain brands/prices of all wines and other beverages to be served.

    d) Obtain information about the reputations of local restaurants, finding out if a special meal or banquet arrangement might be available at a nearby castle or royal estate, with transportation provided for your members.

13. *Contract for translation services.* Interpreters are sometimes supplied through hotels or local commercial outlets. It is not unusual in Europe for instance to have translations, visual aids, and handouts in three different languages (English, French, and German). The use of portable headphones permits simultaneous translation in several languages. If English is the only meeting language, translations of the agenda and supplementary materials are recommended.

14. *Conference materials and equipment* may be shipped or obtained overseas depending on reliability and cost of local suppliers. Prior to departure for the event the following should be considered:

    a) Travel cards or memorandum with information on group travel arrangements and expected expenses (including tipping practices), the foreign climate and suitable clothing, crime and safety, meals and special event provisions, programs for spouses, recommendations on transportation abroad and other pertinent local lore, as well as organizational expectations of members within the foreign culture.

b) Brightly colored, group-identifiable luggage tags, as well as personal conference badges and nameplates for tables.

c) Information desk onsite with details about hospitality arrangements, local tours, local customs (e.g., in regards to smoking, etc.), and special services (e.g., babysitting).

d) Audio and/or video recordings of the sessions to be available to participants at a later date or for purchase (note language options).

15. *Fully use international resources.* Planners may obtain assistance to improve their meeting or conference from:

a) Travel and transport agencies which provide booklets on local customs regulations, money exchange, sightseeing opportunities, cultural events, etc., and may advise on local vendors.

b) Hotel and conference center operators, who can often provide additional services beyond the use of their facility or can at least recommend reliable suppliers; sometimes a hotel does not have meeting facilities but can arrange for the use of a nearby government convention facility.

c) Government tourist and convention bureaus both at home and abroad, which can supply a variety of helpful information and services.

d) Overseas colleagues, partners, or subsidiaries, who may provide an employee or department to help with meetings in their country.

e) Security precautions cannot be ignored in international meetings due to political unrest and changes that some countries are undergoing; these could potentially result in varying degrees of terrorism, revolution, or even civil war.

Such security arrangements may be made with local police or private services, or be provided by the hotel itself to protect both participants and equipment. Meeting planners must be informed about the safety factors involved in a local situation and weigh all risks before selecting an exotic Third World locale that may provide luxurious services at relatively low cost but be surrounded by a sea of poverty and strife. International meeting planners have an obligation to keep participants out of "harm's way," such as when the locals suffer from extreme xenophobia and are hostile toward visitors.

16. *Allow for the local differences* in people, facilities, equipment, and laws. The more informed and prepared a professional planner becomes about local traditions and peculiarities the less likely the chance that one will be embarrassed or inconvenienced by differences in customs, currency, and voltages (AC versus DC power). In a country where people are unfamiliar with group dynamic techniques, such things should either be avoided in programming, or else participants should be carefully instructed in the process. One must also be informed on current customs regulations and charges for bringing equipment into a specific country or taking things out of it. U.S. Customs has practical booklets on foreign travel and goods exchange. The "carnet system" facilitates the transfer of equipment and materials into many nations if the items are used for a meeting and then removed; one must file a customs document beforehand declaring what will be temporarily taken in and then out, promising not to sell onsite. The U.S. Council of the International Chambers of Commerce is an official agent for the forms for this system. Local World Trade Associations can also provide helpful data in this regard. When it comes to currency and liability differences, an organization's banker and insurance agent can be a mine of useful information. Money conversion charts are also available from Universal Currency Converter (1 News Plaza, Peoria IL 61601, USA).

Sometimes international meetings are offered as incentive awards to employees who have performed exceptionally well. To heighten member interest and increase attendance, the meeting may be held aboard an ocean liner, at a historic site, or in a resort. It is important to maintain a balance between the real business of the meeting and the opportunities for personal and professional growth offered by the foreign location. The American compulsion for work and "getting your money's worth" from employees is not stressed in many civilized societies, so include some social events in the program that highlight the local culture.

To further international goodwill and cooperation, HR people should provide meeting leaders and participants with guidelines for appropriate behavior in the host culture in advance. Here is a summary of pertinent insights from the famous motivation psychologist, Dr. Ernest Dichter:

- Avoid national stereotypes and generalizations, ascertaining beforehand the accuracy of your assumptions about the "natives," especially when they are part of the audience.
- Practice sensitive intercultural behavior and communication that avoids brashness and seeks to do what is appropriate in the local situation (e.g., showing deference to some participants, such as managing directors, because of their positions; avoid "back-slapping" and political or off-color jokes; use preferred titles like "Herr Doktor Engineer" or local forms of greeting such as a bow).
- Advise invited dignitaries in advance, in writing, of expectations regarding their part in the proceedings (e.g., time frame, whether merely official greetings or a speech is sought); make proper arrangements for welcoming and facilitating such honored persons.

B. Y. Auger, vice-president for program development at the 3M Company, has the following suggestions for a speaker's preparation and presentation at a cross-cultural meeting:

- Speaking English through an interpreter requires that the presenter articulate clearly and slowly, avoiding colloquialisms and shouting, while concentrating on conveying one thought at a time.
- Visuals help with multicultural audiences, but ensure that what is displayed corresponds to the translation of text; outlining major points with overhead slides for instance organizes thoughts in a logical way for the receiver; limit the number of points per slide to six categories or less; learn to speak in your own language while the illustration displayed may relate the message in a foreign language.

International meetings can be effective when well-organized, well-executed, and culturally sensitive. Whether personal or through electronic means, they are a powerful tool in the global marketplace for promoting free enterprise as well as intercultural collaboration.

New Meeting Technology

Meeting performance can be enhanced by appropriate use of the many new electronic devices available to promote human interaction. "Children of the television age" expect nothing less when they attend meetings, conferences, and conventions. They have not only high expectations regarding the use of multimedia in presenting knowledge and information, they want it done professionally in terms of content, format, and technical expertise. Soundtracks must therefore be clear and understandable, live commentary has to be dynamic, pertinent and stimulating, and visuals must be crisp and the pace fast. Whether dealing with a serious subject or a sales pitch, today's products of mass media—the "now" generation—demand that both medium and message be informative, sophisticated, and entertaining. This applies equally to live meetings, teleconferencing, or combinations of the two.

Because of these expectations, an added burden is placed on meeting planners to ensure that the use of films, video, slides, audio, computers, synthesizers and/or other such AV technology is carefully selected and combined for maximum impact. Therefore, planners must consider whether

- The proper hardware and/or software has been identified and chosen.
- The pre-meeting testing of the above proves satisfactory, especially in terms of sequence and integration of equipment and presentations.
- The provision of alternative programming has been made in case of technical breakdowns, power failures, and other emergencies.
- The plan makes for optimal use of the audience's senses—the more senses called upon, the better the chance that the message will be retained through the use of multimedia technology.

People enjoy variety at meetings, a change of pace, and opportunities to directly participate in what is happening. The new communication technologies make all of this possible in dazzling ways. Live input can be alternated with mass media, group process, and even electronic interactive involvement. Multiple projectors can be synchronized for maximum impact. The planner might begin with a training film, supplement it by offering new dimensions of the same subject with two slide projectors, and conclude the demonstration with active participation by actors or the audience. Such methods can be used sequentially or simultaneously with multiple screens. Because annual corporate conferences may represent a considerable financial investment, multidimensional transmission of a message may establish the right mood and learning environment. In addition to professional conference consultants, most professional conference facilities have personnel to assist planners with meeting rooms, including appropriate colors, lighting, ventilation, seating, sound and/or musical background. It then becomes possible to immerse a group in a kaleidoscope of sight, sound and feelings, providing a stimulating and at times almost psychedelic learning environment.

In this era of mass communication, imaginative meeting facilitators have numerous mechanical and technical aids, as well as traditional means, with which to stimulate the senses and transmit the message more effectively. Indeed, there can be a message in the media chosen, as rock concert promoters have demonstrated with their use of laser lights and satellite dishes.

Educational media now offer a variety of instructional kits, learning packages, and other seminar aids to assist the manager or trainer conducting the meeting. For example, CRM Films (2215 Faraday Ave., Carlsbad, CA 92008, USA) support their management development films not only with instructor's guides, but also with supplementary materials ranging from videocassettes and computer discs to case studies and diagnostic instruments. A film or video on "Meeting the Meeting Challenge" for example has both a Leader's Guide and an optional workbook for the trainees. Going International (302 23rd Ave., San Francisco, CA 94121) has several films and videos that are useful in cross-cultural training. Longman Crown of Reston, Virginia offers computer-based, user-friendly, interactive systems that can be used on personal computers and include learning strategies for drill and practice, tutorials and inquiries, simulations, and computer-managed instructional methods. The subjects range from time and project management to decision-making and management performance.

When these capabilities are combined with television receivers and videocassettes, a learning system is created for individual or group training. Interactive video is the marriage of computer to videotape or videodisc and represents a powerful new meeting and training tool. TV Answer, also of Reston, Virginia, has developed a technology using a satellite link that allows consumers to use computer program cards, a joy stick, and a black box attached to a TV receiver not only to provide answers, but also participate in television productions, as well as access their bank accounts and place orders for products and services.

The prospects for improving meetings through technology are staggering—satellite communications, word processing systems, fiber optics, paging devices, new uses of long lines, and even the newly emerging technology of virtual reality. High technology offers exciting opportunities to present graphics and simulations at meetings or conferences, to survey an audience for rapid response or texting purposes, to promote interactive, self or group learning, and to encourage networking.

Cases in Point

One high technology firm in Silicon Valley discovered that its meetings were ineffective because so many of its engineers were of foreign origin and spoke English as a second language. Although technically competent, they were unfamiliar with American business meeting purposes and methods. The Northern California company hired an EASL consultant to design and conduct a training program for all personnel on "How to Benefit From Staff Meetings." It was treated as an organizational problem rather than singling out the foreign-born employees. The end result was increased meeting productivity for all those involved.

Consider the following mini-cases and their implications for improving your own cross-cultural meetings:

Intel Corporation. Andrew S. Grove, founder and president of the computer company said that in the course of a workday he normally engages in 25 separate activities, but that ⅔ of his time is spent in meetings. Obviously then, this time must be used productively. Meetings provide the medium for most managerial activity and when conducted effectively provide managerial leverage. Grove [2] describes two basic types of business meetings:

1. *Process-Oriented meetings* in which knowledge is shared and information exchanged. They should take place on a regularly scheduled basis and be recorded on people's calendars for minimal interruption of productivity. They are generally of three kinds:

a) One-on-one—such as supervisor-subordinate, for mutual information exchange, learning, coaching, and problem-solving; number and length may vary but agenda is normally set by subordinate in outline form for note taking; usually is performance-oriented; participants may "batch" together key issues for discussion or establish a "hold" file for those things that are less urgent and can be put off until another encounter; supervisors welcome authentic communication and see these meetings as an opportunity to build organizational relationships; the face-to-face encounter may be supplemented by telephone and note exchanges.

b) Staff meeting—supervisor and subordinates confer; opportunity for peer interaction and decision-making; leader plays multiple roles of observer, expediter, questioner, and decision-maker, and may share authority with the group in this context.

c) Operation reviews—bring together managers and peers from various parts of the organization to motivate, share progress and problems, and generally report on the larger operational activities; usually formal presentations, well-organized format; an opportunity for senior management to provide behavior models and share the "big picture."

2. *Mission-oriented meetings* for ad-hoc affairs aimed at producing a specific output, such as a decision in short time-frame. The key chairperson, who must understand why the meeting is necessary, what specific accomplishments are required, who should attend, and what logistic arrangements are critical. That person is also responsible for follow-up action—minutes of the meeting, commitments pursued, etc. No more than 25% of time devoted to meetings should be of this infrequent "emergency" type.

When one estimates a manager's time on an hourly basis and multiplies it by the number of managers attending a meeting, a large amount of corporate money is being invested. Therefore, meetings must be justified and expedited if the participants and the company are to be seriously committed to them.

Entrepreneurial Companies. Meeting planners or facilitators need to use their imaginations and be innovative about the manner in which people are brought together. Dr. Martin Apple, president of San

Francisco's Adytum Inc., used a unique meeting formula in one of his previous start-up companies. As chief executive, Apple held a daily stand-up meeting for all key researchers at 8:30 a.m.; the normal workday for this bio-tech plant began at 9 a.m. During the opening half-hour the group would brainstorm ideas for possible patents while the session was tape recorded. During the course of the day, the CEO would play back the ideas kicked around by the group. Before leaving work that day, each member received a brief typed memorandum to the group from the president regarding which of the concepts seemed feasible for patent filing. In this way, the knowledge workers were energized and enthused, knowing that each day they had an opportunity to meet with top management and actively contribute creatively, with the potential for future reward. The entrepreneurial activity of the company prospered as a result of these unusual meetings and a record number of patents were actually filed and recognitions given.

American Society of Association Management (1101 16th St., NW, Washington, DC 20036, USA). This organization of association executives reported that more than half of its 4,000 association members hold meetings, conventions, and trade missions outside the continental United States. Foreign locales are sometimes chosen as travel incentives to reward employees or members, or to bring together personnel from a transnational organization that operates in various parts of the world. Reasonable group transportation rates, promotability, and the ability to schedule field trips to foreign operations are often cited as the rationale behind such decisions, as well as opportunities for professional growth.

Electronic Cross-Cultural Meetings. The emerging teleconferencing services industry in the U.S. is expected to produce revenue of $3.4 billion in 1992 alone. Ford Motor Company used this technology, flying 400 journalists from around the world to a Los Angeles conference at which Ford introduced two new cars, while they simultaneously beamed the event via private satellite network to Ford locations around the globe. New York advertising agencies are using Inter-Continental and Hilton Hotel video conferencing facilities to make presentations to potential clients in Europe; during the sessions, they develop storyboards and pass hard copy back and forth across continents by electronic transmission. Merrill Lynch uses "SAT conferences" for seminars ranging from investments to instructing CEO's on how to capitalize on video opportunities. General Motors has linked up via satellite to 31 GM training centers and 24 plants to discuss a new labor agreement under negotiation with 3,500 senior managers.

Residential Cross-Cultural Training. The Shell Corporation has 5,000 expatriates worldwide, 35% of whom undergo a week's residential pre-departure training course at either The Centre for International Briefing in the U.K.'s Farnham Castle or in the Netherlands. In the future, Shell expects to provide all its graduate entrants with cross-cultural training regardless of whether they are earmarked for foreign assignment or not; the company is aware that new employees need such indoctrination early in their careers.

Unilever, BP, and Phillips also regularly schedule personnel meetings at England's Farnham Castle. Other worldwide corporations have established their own cross-cultural training facilities: Scandinavian Airlines System has its Inter-cultural Communication Department and Center (ICC) in Sweden, which also offers its services to external clients such as SKF, Pharmacia, Scandia International, DuPont, Ford, Intel, Kodak, and Procter & Gamble. Similarly, NEC in Tokyo has its own Institute of International Studies, which offers the Japanese a grueling six-day course on how to do business in the West. Other organizations prefer to send their management for telescoped cross-cultural training at universities and educational institutions such as the American Graduate School of International Management (Thunderbird) in Phoenix, Arizona, or INSEAD in Fontainbleau, France.

In this post-industrial age, information and learning are the means to establish the authority of competence and to further career development, as well as being the solution to problems and challenges. Global leaders who are sensitive to their human resource development responsibilities realize this and make effective use of meetings to accomplish such purposes. Whether the situation requires a live or electronic meeting, innovators master the professional methods or know where to obtain support services to achieve high performance through meetings, especially with cross-cultural trainees or audiences.

Action Learning and Research

Today's information society values knowledge that is power. Both students and the work force are increasingly engaged in acquiring, analyzing, processing, distributing and/or servicing this precious resource. Just as data are pieced together to formulate information, information is shaped and paired to create knowledge. When knowledge contributes to enlightenment, it can then be profitably applied to improve human performance and productivity. This occurs through the study, analysis, and sharing of knowledge; lifetime learning is thus a central characteristic of the new work culture [3-5].

Managing Cultural Differences [6,7] and other books in this series contain a body of information and insights that can lead to knowledge for students or trainees. It is, however, the instructor or trainer who facilities the process of learning, the systematic acquisition of this knowledge and the mastery of skills. More often than not this process happens through a meeting, whether in a university classroom or in corporate training centers. One way to conduct such programs is through *action learning,* an instructional strategy that promotes learning by doing, a means through which to facilitate "andragogy," the art and science of helping mature people to learn. The action by the learners occurs both during and after the formalized class or training session. The action *during* the instructional period occurs through variety and participation. Action learning as a methodology achieves this during the group meeting through:

- Input—from the instructor and guest speakers, or from the class or training group; from audio-visual aids, handouts, or a textbook.
- Interaction—informal discussion of the content, or planned group process (such as a case study, brainstorm, simulation, or some other exercise in group dynamics).
- Instrumentation—inventories, check-lists, questionnaires or other data-gathering instruments that collect information or opinions for analysis and reporting, as well as sensitizing learners to the subject matter or serving as a basis of formal group discussion.

The above I/I/I method is placed within the context of a "learning module," a 2–4 hour instructional period. If the HR leader is planning a one-day seminar or workshop, then this may involve two to three learning modules (morning and afternoon or possibly an evening session). The material in our previous chapters, for instance, can be covered—depending on the time available for instruction—in one or two learning modules per chapter. A training or university course can be organized around the table of contents from any book in the MCD series by framing the contents in terms of modules. If working under schedule constraints, the instructor must decide how many learning modules to use to cover a chapter's content, i.e., whether the material is to be condensed or expanded upon. To achieve action during the learning module, the authors propose this approach of *input, interaction,* and *instrumentation.*

The action *after* the group learning experience occurs in two ways. First, the learner develops specific action plans at the end of each session. That may mean writing down individual activities one plans to engage in or try out as a result of the learning gained, and can be done at the end of a learning module or the end of a day of training. In industry and government this is sometimes done in duplicate by using carbon paper—one copy of the *action plan* goes to the instructor or the trainee's supervisor. Traditionally, teachers and trainers have given assignments to be performed after the instructional period and reported upon in the next meeting. Whatever the strategy adopted, the rationale is that learning is not only to be informative and entertaining if possible, but also lead to personal and professional development. By sharing the action plans with a supervisor, the action plans can be incorporated into performance evaluation.

When employing action learning strategies for cross-cultural learning, the instructor is primarily a facilitator rather than an information-distributor. The rationale behind this is:

- Situational—it depends upon the learning group and circumstances (whether in a university class, on-the-job training, or a group preparing to go overseas), but always aims to promote the internalization of knowledge through practice and application.
- Personalized—it individualizes learning so as to make allowances for the student/trainee's unique needs, perceptions, and expectations while setting performance standards that are realistic and appropriate to that particular person (e.g., a foreign student in comparison to a native American).
- Experiential—it builds upon the members' experiences, provides a learning experience through participation, and balances "learning by doing" with cognitive input ("I feel" + "I think").
- Problem-oriented—it deals with issues for problem-solving and decision-making which can result in personal or organizational change (e.g., confronting ethnocentrism and prejudices rather than merely memorizing definitions of culture.

- Systematic—it takes not only a learning systems approach but views this course of instruction as a sub-system in a larger human resource development effort or educational system.

Action learning is based on the assumptions so well articulated by the guru of adult education, Dr. Malcolm Knowles:

- Adults enter a learning activity with an image of themselves as self-directing, responsible grown-ups, not immature, dependent learners; they learn better in a threat-free learning climate that fosters acceptance, freedom, and participation.
- Adults enter a learning activity with more and different quality of experience than youth, and therefore have a broader basis for new learning and contribution.
- Adults enter a learning activity with more immediate intentions to apply the learning to work or life problems. Instructors engaged in cultural awareness education therefore build action learning sessions upon such basic assumptions.

The instructor using action learning is seeking attitudinal and behavioral change in the learner as a result of the knowledge, understanding, and skills acquired. If the learner represents an organization (e.g., on a sponsored scholarship or as an employee) then the needs of the corporation, association, or agency must also be considered during the educational planning and implementation; the organization should be changed or improved as a result of the learner's better performance. Thus, each learning module should have clearly stated objectives and measurable criteria or means for achieving learning goals. The instructor in turn should demonstrate competence not only in the subject matter but as a learning facilitator. Action can also result from this learning methodology through *action research,* engaged in by either the learner or the instructor. This is a systematic study undertaken as a result of some problem or challenge discovered in the course of the training session. Suppose a class were intrigued by the information gained from some questionnaire or other instrument. A group project could be undertaken to compare trainees' own results on that inquiry form with those of another group such as foreign managers or international students. Extra credit or higher grades might be given to participants in this action research project if it is completed in a creditable manner.

Another example is a trainer in a government agency who might wish to use a management development course as a means for organization development research. (This is called the MD/OD strategy—management development sessions used for organization development purposes). Data can be collected through pre/post instruments created by the instructor, or during the interaction sessions (collecting the newsprint paper or flip chart reports of small groups who report on their discussions or findings). In any event, the data obtained in or through the learning encounter is analyzed and reported upon, perhaps by the instructor feedback to the learners or through a briefing to administrators or executives. The information and knowledge obtained can become the basis for promoting personal or organizational development.

Values of Action Learning and Research

Action learning is a dynamic process appropriate for mature trainees because it involves adults in a variety of intensive, educational experiences. Its advantages for use during meetings or training programs are:

- It stimulates learning at both the cognitive and affective levels—that is, by rational thinking and through the emotions or feelings.
- It is carefully prepared, timed, and paced to make optimal use of the training period.
- It promotes individual and group learning through variety of input, interaction, and instrumentation.
- It focuses upon results and requires planning for action that occurs because of the training or meeting.

The principal value of action learning is that the intention is to promote positive and constructive change in people and their systems through increased awareness, knowledge, and skills.

Action research complements this approach because it seeks to further an organization's effectiveness by gathering information from its membership on individual and institutional performance. Meetings and training sessions are viewed as opportunities to further this data collection. With a systematic analysis of findings, the merits are:

- It aids organizational diagnosis and development, helping to validate the need and the means for planned change.

- It evaluates the effectiveness of human resource development efforts.
- It provides measures of performance, productivity, and profitability.
- It improves the basis for decision-making, planning, accountability, and career development.

When synergy exists, action learning becomes a means for action research. Combined, both strategies are powerful for maintaining both personal and organizational health. These are managerial tools suitable for an Information Age with knowledge and service workers who seek more participation and input. Many corporations have realized the value of marketing research and include such specialists on their staffs. The new work culture requires expansion of such inquiry to go beyond surveys of public preferences and customer concerns, to broaden the human factor research and include all employees or members.

Since every manager has a responsibility to develop his or her people, as well as oneself, action learning and research enable HR leaders to fulfill that role. When technicians and other specialists are assigned a training task, these HRD strategies permit them to be more professional in their approach. Action learning and research are means for capitalizing upon human assets and having significant implications for improving cross-cultural meetings!

Preferred Meeting Methods

In a survey of its membership, the American Society for Training & Development found that its professional trainers and HRD specialists preferred these meeting and training techniques for the following six categories of learning:

- Knowledge acquisition—programmed instruction, lecture, conference method, and case study.
- Changing attitudes—role playing, sensitivity training, conference, and case study methods.
- Problem-solving—case study, business games, conference method, and role playing.
- Interpersonal skills—role playing and sensitivity training.
- Participant acceptance—conference and case study methods.

- Knowledge retention—role playing, programmed instruction, conference, and case study methods.

Ninety-three percent of these respondents ranked leadership training skills as the most important learning subject, while giving priority also to problem-solving skills, decision-making skills, performance appraisal, and time management. Note that the use of electronic technology, such as when the computer is used for programmed instruction or business games, can enhance some of these preferred training methods. The disappointment in this survey is that none of these so-called HR leaders identified cross-cultural skills as an area for meeting and training, unless the subject is assumed under knowledge acquisition and retention.

Meetings Can Be Fun and Productive

The key to high performance is energized people who are interested and involved. One of the best ways to energize people at meetings is through play, games, and simulations. As first mentioned in chapter 3, further possibilities are described here. When people enjoy themselves at work, they tend to be more productive. The meeting, especially for training purposes, can be a useful mechanism for unleashing hidden creativity through play. Play permits employees to reveal a joyful, spontaneous, and even silly side of themselves that is often restrained on the job. Enlightened management takes advantage of this approach for creative problem solving and education, as well as the mental health and recreational factors involved.

Over many years in leadership development, we have found that management games are very worthwhile because they:

- Provide a change of pace in the training or meeting schedule
- Foster experiential or affective learning·
- Reveal behavior in a simulation that often occurs on the job.
- Entertain while teaching important lessons of teamwork.
- Build upon the competitive spirit while teaching the disadvantages of unrestrained competition and the synergistic value of cooperation and collaboration.
- Offer the opportunity for meaningful analysis and discussion after play as to what happened and why.

- Give an incentive to extra team effort that can be rewarded, literally or figuratively.

In a meeting simulation, a real-life experience is simulated or replayed through a "game-like" experience in a condensed time span. As previously indicated, a manager or trainer may purchase, borrow, or create a simulation game to meet a specific need. Three examples of helpful commercial games for management development are distributed by Simulation Training Systems, (218 Twelfth St., Del Mar, CA 92014, USA): "Bafa, Bafa" provides a learning experience in cross-cultural relations; "Starpower" teaches a group about the realities of power and its influence on behavior; "Relocation" examines the issues involved in moving a corporate headquarters, from the viewpoints of both the community and the employees.

On the other hand, innovative trainers may use cardboard, sticks, glue, tinker toys, or other household items to create a structured learning experience that teaches managers the importance of cooperation or win-win situations. Dr. Allen Zoll produces *Dynamic Management Education,* which describes a variety of adult education techniques from cases and in-basket exercises to action mazes and business games (Management Education Associates, 2003 33rd South, Seattle, WA 98144, USA). Other major creators and distributors of management simulations include:

- Didactic Systems, Inc., PO Box 457, Cranford, NJ 07016, USA
- Education Research, PO Box 4205, Warren, NJ 07060, USA

Local stores that sell computer software can also advise on what is available on the market in terms of computer simulations.

Dr. Matt Weinstein has developed a company that teaches adults how to play: Playfair, Inc., based in Berkeley, CA, with offices in Dallas and New York City. His corporate clients use these services at meetings and conferences to help their employees decrease stress, increase productivity, and improve morale or camaraderie. As a replacement for the cocktail hour, he can take hundreds or thousands of meeting attendees gathered in a ballroom and engage them in free form play. There are no winners or losers, only celebration, bonding, and community results.

When the meeting sessions are spread over several days or weeks, building opportunities for physical and emotional release into the conference design is essential for participants to recharge themselves for further intellectual effort. This "re-creation" can serve as a learning experience when planned intentionally. Team golf is an example of a game that uses the rules of "Scramble" in which a group tally replaces individual scores (combining the best performance of each member for each shot on every hole). Many resorts that cater to conference groups have a variety of silly games to relax tired registrants: water-balloon tosses, egg-carrying relays, sand castle building contests, or creative party themes. The resulting laughter is good for morale, encourages conviviality and comradeship, and puts attendees on an equal footing. Meetings, a part of the work environment, can be made enjoyable in a variety of ways.

The principal conclusions to be drawn are simply that HR leaders should invest more care and professionalism into meeting arrangements and implementation. Whether the meeting is a weekly staff meeting, an annual stockholders' gathering, a regional sales conference, an employee retreat, an appraisal interview, or a regular meeting between supervisor and subordinate, performance can be enhanced through well-orchestrated meetings. The first way is by using established guidelines and group dynamics in the planning, conducting, and evaluating of such events. Secondly, the employment of multimedia technology to interest and the involvement of participants are effective. Thirdly, by remembering the human element, one makes provision for people's comfort and relaxation. The manager or trainer has many resources upon which to call for assistance to improve meetings: the organization's HRD specialists, the staff at the meeting site, the external speakers or consultants employed as presenters, and the suppliers of meeting or game materials and services.

Instrumentation

As indicated throughout this text, meetings can be used for data gathering, especially by means of instruments. This same device can provide information during a meeting for group discussion and analysis of the findings. Apart from their feedback and other values, questionnaires, inventories, and checklists can be devised to improve the performance of the manager or trainer.

Although the purchase of instruments produced by commercial publishers is possible, managers and trainers should not hesitate to construct their own data-gathering forms to suit their specific purposes. Regardless of the format chosen, the HR leader wants to select a survey approach with these features:

- Ease of administration and collection of data.

- Appropriate and understandable wording or questioning.

- Convenience for scoring and interpreting the results.

- Viability for validity and comparative studies.

Today the computer can be used to score responses, as well as undertake statistical analysis of the results. Such data-gathering has several values:

- It creates awareness and sensitivity in the respondents relative to some of the key learning issues.

- It provides information on the trainees that can be used in program design and preparation or in post-project reporting for purposes of organizational development and HRD planning for future programs.

- It helps in evaluating the program's effectiveness, particularly regarding change in the learning group as a result of the training.

In whatever form, pencil-paper instruments are diagnostic tools that facilitate the identification of people and program needs. Obviously, they also serve as a means for assessing performance, such as during meetings, and contribute to both the actualization of human potential and organizational effectiveness. For example, an evaluation form may be designed for administration at the end of a major meeting, conference, or training session to ascertain participant reaction to the learning experience.

Exhibit 9-2 will help leaders to assure that cross-cultural meetings are planned and conducted effectively, as well as provide a means for further performance evaluation in the workplace.

Exhibit 9-2
Cross-Cultural Meeting Planner*

Name of the organizational sponsor: _____

Date of the meeting: _____

Site of the meeting: _____

Purposes of the meeting: _____

Number and type of attendants expected for the meeting:

Audience: Multicultural/international ( )   Home culture ( )

Language needs of the participants: _____

Type of Meeting being planned: Conference ( )   Seminar ( )

Operational review ( )   Regular staff meeting ( )

One-on-one encounter ( )   Large audience ( )   Small audience ( )

Other: _____

Organizational sponsor (review history/mission/needs): _____

Site Selection (who makes decision/criteria/flexibility): _____

Instructions:

   In planning this meeting, please rate yourself on a scale of 1 to 10 as to how you have carried out the following functions. Use the box on the right for your score: 1 is lowest, 5 is average, and 10 is the highest rating for excellence. If the item is not applicable, skip the item and continue to the next number.

Assessment Issue   Rating

1. Input came from both management and potential participants on the purposes and agenda for this meeting.   [ ]
2. Sufficient research is conducted on the attendees and their backgrounds and special needs, especially when the audience is multicultural.   [ ]

---

* This *Meeting Management Planning Inventory* by Philip R. Harris and other instruments are available in quantity orders from Harris International (2702 Costebelle Drive, La Jolla, CA 92037, USA, Tel: 619-453-2271). Catalogs available upon request.

3. The objectives were stated clearly and circulated with an agenda to the intended audience or attendees. [ ]

4. Adequate and comfortable site/facilities selected and successful negotiations conducted with operators. [ ]

5. Proper budgeting or provisions were made for the meeting expenses (and income, if any). [ ]

6. Adequate arrangements were made for the selection and/or pre-registration of attendees, as well as on-site registration and/or welcome of meeting participants. [ ]

7. Adequate negotiations and arrangements were completed for all guests, presenters, exhibitors, and other human resources required for this meeting. [ ]

8. If meeting off-site, adequate provisions were made for transportation, and registrants were informed of such transportation. [ ]

9. If a residential meeting, adequate arrangements were made for housing and alternatives; registrants, guests, exhibitors, and staff were informed. [ ]

10. Adequate design planning as to program activities, variety, sequence, time, and pacing. [ ]

11. If appropriate, adequate provision included time for relaxation and play. [ ]

12. Satisfactory arrangements ensured for ordering all program equipment, learning materials, and exhibits. [ ]

13. Adequate provisions ensured for on-site monitoring and management of external support service, meeting staff, and procedures (e.g., registration and hospitality desk, refreshment and food services, exhibits, distribution of handout materials, security, etc.). [ ]

14. Adequate pre-meeting briefing of registrants and resource staff, plus coordination with on-site management. [ ]

15. Arrangements made for special needs of participants (e.g., handicapped, non-smokers, spouse program, etc.) [ ]

16. If off-site, necessary shipping or mailing arrangements completed for all materials and equipment at site (or for their purchase/lease/rental on-site). [ ]

17. Final checking executed satisfactorily on functional logistics (e.g., the details and set-up of meeting rooms, media equipment, exhibits, food and beverage services, etc.). [ ]

18. Final confirmation of arrangements and site opportunities to all concerned (e.g., mailing of schedule or agenda with travel directions

to participants, staff, presenters, and possibly entertainers, exhibitors, suppliers, and site managers). [ ]

19. Provisions made for staff person or contractor to select, communicate, and coordinate with resource persons (e.g., speakers, facilitators, panelists, entertainers, exhibitors, travel guides). [ ]

20. Provisions completed for entertaining and informative program alternatives if spouse or family accompany attendee. [ ]

21. If appropriate, arrangement completed for public relations program in conjunction with meeting (e.g., press release, media coverage, follow-up stories). [ ]

22. Arrangement completed for recording the meeting or conference (in writing, stenotype, or audio/video); if appropriate, for editing and publishing the proceedings, and distribution and/or sale of recordings/proceedings. [ ]

23. Arrangements completed for evaluating the meeting as to its effectiveness and implementation of action plans set at the meeting. [ ]

24. Provision for payment of all gratuities and invoices for services contracted, including any reimbursements owed to participants. [ ]

25. Provision for letters of appreciation or commendation to be sent to appropriate persons connected with meeting's success (e.g., participants, presenters, suppliers, etc.). [ ]

(*NOTE:* If this meeting is international, especially if held outside one's homeland, then one should continue with the inventory).

26. Prior to the meeting, personal visitation ensured that:

- The overseas facility and services were adequate. [ ]
- Equipment and power incompatibilities were resolved. [ ]
- Negotiations with contractors had achieved mutual cultural understanding and agreement as to what is being provided. [ ]
- Problems of overseas shipping and entry of materials, equipment had been resolved with customs in home/host countries (whenever possible, equipment should be leased or rented abroad, while contracting for local supplies). [ ]

27. Observance of all the foreign formalities regarding international meeting amenities, such as:

- Invitations and confirmations to government or corporate officials invited to receptions, luncheons, and banquets. [ ]

- Selection of local representatives to welcome participants, give addresses or lectures, and bestow honors/rewards. [ ]

28. Preparations made to facilitate intercultural communication with the locals or among participants from other countries (e.g., business cards in both languages, proper use of titles and seating arrangements, multilingual presentation of learning materials and slides, interpreters, and simultaneous translation equipment, etc.). [ ]
29. Communication with contractor for translations clearly established purpose and general goals of meeting, type of audience, and scope of special interpretation requirements. [ ]
30. Arrangements made for participants to enjoy the international resources, such as:

- Extra group services and discounts of airlines and travel agencies. [ ]
- Use of local stately mansions, grand estates, or convention centers. [ ]
- Optional offerings for local or supplemental sightseeing tours and appropriate field trips. [ ]
- Incorporation into schedule of host culture's food/dress, as well as music/festivals. [ ]
- Cultural briefings on the foreign customs, protocol, opportunities, and dangers. [ ]

31. Pre-departure briefings provided to all participants by mail or in person on customs regulations, currency issues, tipping, security issues, and other relevant matters (e.g., host country cuisine "pros & cons," public safety, and terrorism, cultural differences regarding meeting activities and participation, role of women in country). [ ]
32. Arrangements made for translations of meeting/conference proceedings in the major participant languages, as well as editing, printing or recordings' reproduction, and distribution of volumes or cassettes. [ ]
33. If minutes or proceedings are required following the sessions, arrangements adequately made for production and distribution (possibly in several languages). [ ]

(*NOTE:* To obtain a total score among the 41 possible selections, add up the number of items to which it was appropriate for you to respond; then tally up the number of rating scores. To attain an evaluation average, divide the total number of items into the total number of ratings.)

HRD Strategies

Cross-Cultural Meeting Resources

Sources of Periodicals/Annual Directories of Suppliers and Sites

- *Successful Meetings* and its *Annual Meeting Planners Guide* (633 Third Avenue, NY, NY 10017, USA)
- *Meeting News* (1515 Broadway, N.Y., NY 10036, USA)
- *Corporate Meetings and Incentives* (P.O. Box 6238, Duluth, MN 55606, USA)
- *Meetings & Conventions* (Reed Travel Group, 44 Cook St., Denver, CO 80206) free monthly magazine
- *Marketing Meetings* (The Marketing Federation, Inc., 7141 Gulf Blvd., St. Petersburg, FL 33706, USA)
- *Training, The HRD Magazine* and *Creative Training Techniques,* a newsletter (Lakeside Publications, 50 So. Ninth St., Minneapolis, MN 55402, USA)

Sources of Books, Manuals, and Computer Software

- *The Annual Meeting Handbook* (The Corporate Shareholders Press, 271 Madison Ave., New York, NY 10016, USA)
- *The Successful Meeting Master Guide for Business and Professions* by B. and K. Palmer, 1983 (American Management Associations Book Club, 135 West 50th Street, NY, NY 10020)
- *The Teleconferencing Handbook: A Guide to Cost-Effective Communication),* annual edited by E. Lazer (Knowledge Industry Publications, 701 Westchester Ave., White Plains, NY 10604)
- *Conducting Successful Meetings,* a computer software program by DSI Micro, Inc. (770 Broadway, New York, NY 10013)
- *We've Got to Start Meeting Like This!—A Guide to Successful Business Meeting Management* by R. K. Mosvick and R. B. Nelson (Scott, Foresman/Harper Collins, 1900 E. Lake Ave., Glenview, IL 60026, USA; 1987)
- *Intercultural Communication: Preparing to Function Successfully in the International Environment* by Janice C. Hepworth (University Centers, Inc., 1190 S. Colorado Blvd., Ste. 201, Denver, CO 80222, USA; 1990)

■ *Intercultural Press, Inc.* (P.O. Box 768, Yarmouth, ME 04096, USA). A central source of cross-cultural learning materials.

Sources for Professional Development of HR Leaders

■ *American Society for Training & Development* (630 Duke St., Alexandria, VA 22313, USA)
■ *Center for Creative Leadership* (5000 Laurinda Dr., Greensboro, NC 27438, USA)
■ *East-West Center* (1777 East-West Center Road, Honolulu, HI 92848, USA)
■ *SIETAR International* (Society for Intercultural, Education, Training and Research—1414 Twenty-Second St., NW, Washington, DC 20037, USA)
■ *University Associates* (8717 Production Ave., San Diego, CA 92121, USA)

References

1. Dichter, E., *Motivating Human Behavior,* New York: McGraw-Hill, 1971.
2. Grove, A., *High Output Management,* New York: Random House, 1983.
3. Harris, P. R., *New Worlds, New Ways, New Managements,* Ann Arbor, MI: Masterco Press/AMACOM, 1983.
4. Harris, P. R., *Management in Transition—Transforming Managerial Practices and Organizational Strategies for a New Work Culture,* San Francisco: Jossey-Bass, 1985.
5. Harris, P. R., *High Performance Leadership—Strategies for Maximum Productivity,* Glenview, IL: Scott, Foresman/Harper/Collins, 1989.
6. Harris, P. and Moran, R. T., *Managing Cultural Differences,* 4th Edition, Houston: Gulf Publishing Company, 1991.
7. Moran, R. T. and Harris, P. R., *Managing Cultural Synergy,* Houston, TX: Gulf Publishing, 1982.
8. Naisbit, J., *Megatrends,* New York: Warner Communications, 1982.
9. Rheingold, H., *Virtual Reality,* New York: Summit Books, 1991.
10. *Space News,* April 13–16, 1992.
11. *Time,* December 16, 1985, p.50.

CHAPTER 10

DEVELOPING HR LEADERSHIP IN GLOBAL ORGANIZATIONS

Introduction

Organizations, like people, must constantly adapt to changing realities. Ideally, key management should lead the process, but too often many executives are dragged kicking and screaming into the 21st century. It is for precisely that reason that prestigious groups such as The Conference Board (845 Third Ave., N.Y., NY 10022, USA) strive to provide their membership organizations with reports and programs that will alter policies and practices in global business. In 1991, the Board conducted a conference on "Frontiers for Management Development," which focused on the need to break paradigms in order to reshape human resource development (HRD) systems. At these sessions *Fortune 500* corporate executives were reminded that "paradigm" came from the Greek word "pattern," and that the aim was to foster new patterns of thinking, especially about HRD functions such as identifying, selecting, training, and developing personnel, in particular management. The conference topics highlighted some of the very same themes discussed in this book: managing across boundaries by leveraging the power of teams; helping managers to become architects of their own learning; transforming managerial perspectives; meeting the challenges of the diverse work force.

The admirable exchange overlooked one critical subject, however, one in which another training company has developed an entire seminar entitled "Globalization: A Strategic Perspective." This HRD program is designed around *globalization* as the art of positioning an organization beyond national boundaries, adapting to changing local environments wherever markets and resources may exist. The presentations are based on the new realities of rapid technological advances, worldwide socio-economic and political changes, increasing environmental awareness, and other such forces impacting the global business environment.

To gain a competitive edge, global operators are taught skills in environmental scanning, acculturation, global area networking, and even chaos theory.

A sampling of their forecasts underscores the importance of our discussions here. Among growing trends cited by Coates, Jarratt, and Mahaffie [5] are:

- Increasing diversity in the work force within the U.S.A.—more, older workers, more Hispanics and high-achieving Asians, more educational and professional advancement for both blacks and women.
- New focus on workers as an asset and greater investment in the training and education of personnel.
- Requirements of the emerging global society are diverging from the knowledge base of the U.S. population—more knowledge and education are required than are currently being provided in this country.

Supplementing these predictions, Cetron, and Davies [4] add:

- The world economy will become increasingly integrated—it will be increasingly difficult to label a product by national origin, but within new economic blocs multinational corporations will grow and become far more powerful and socially responsible; companies will be increasingly judged on how they treat the environment and be forced to clean up any damage resulting from their activities.
- Major corporations are collaborating in greater numbers with universities to establish degree-granting corporate schools and programs for their employees.
- Companies will continue to expand operations beyond their national borders and eventually even into space.

The implications of these observations are that HR leaders must not only retrain personnel to cope with such emerging realities, but also lead in the transformation of organizational culture, an issue we have analyzed previously [7, Ch. 6]. In Chapter 1 we discussed training leaders for a work culture entirely different from that with which we were raised and are familiar. We indicated that transformational leadership requires the *creating of a new vision* as framed by the following observations: The rationale for that has been offered throughout this book, but to reinforce the message we turn to selections from other astute authors:

- From Robert B. Reich [12]—"Today's corporations are part of a 'global web.' Goods are designed in one country, produced in a second at facilities financed in a third, and sold in a fourth ... About 20% of the work force have good jobs that pay well in a global economy. These are the symbolic analysts who define problems and design solutions for them. They have unconventional career paths; they perceive themselves as part of a network, rather than climbing a hierarchical ladder. ...

  "The best form of national industrial policy is investment in people, concentrating on producing educated citizens who can participate effectively in a world economy as do symbolic analysts."

- From Hon. Elliot L. Richardson [9]—"The very concept of national sovereignty is being submerged by the flow of financial transactions and information exchanges which diminish the relevance of national boundaries ... The vastly expanded marketplace for innovative technologies and products will carry cultural identities across many borders ... Cultural sensitivity, which is reflected in respect for national differences may appear at first too intangible and unmeasurable to figure in the equation. But if one tries to identify all the various qualities distinguishing a corporation that has won respect and admiration in its quest for worldwide economic success, one finds that such sensitivity is invariably one of them ... As global involvement increases, business leadership takes on new dimensions. The corporation that asks who it is, what it shall become, and how it shall be perceived in foreign settings, is asking statesmanlike questions."

- From Robert J. Radway [9]—"In the new global marketplace, technological, financial, and other competitive challenges are helping to seal different kinds of strategic alliances that would not have been possible less than a decade ago ... The rules of the game are not yet well understood, and cultural differences are preventing the successful integration of management strategies and teams in these new alliances ... U.S. companies in particular are learning that key factors for success in these, be they joint ventures for manufacturing, research, and development, financial consortia, or technology transfer, demand much more careful planning and training than has been required in the past."

- From Professors Nancy J. Adler and Fariborz Ghadar [9]—"The central issues for multinational enterprises is . . . to find the fit between the firm's external environment and overall strategy, and its human resource management policy . . . Cross-cultural interaction takes place both within the firm and between the firm and its external environment. Consequently, understanding and managing cultural differences has become essential both internally and externally . . . Trans-global managers today use cultural diversity to balance three organizational tensions. First, they minimize the impact of cultural diversity when integration is needed. Second, they use cultural diversity to differentiate products and services when culturally distinct markets or work forces must be addressed. Third, they use cultural diversity as a primary source of new ideas when innovation is needed. Balancing cultural integration and differentiation affects all aspects of the human resource management system."

Such insights confirm why would-be HR leaders must innovate in transforming themselves and their organization's culture and people.

Globalization

This is a way of thinking and acting that moves us away from parochialism towards transnationalism, a state of mind that enables us to use our personal and organizational resources more effectively. Globalization is creating a world without walls, made possible by advances in communication and transportation technologies. This new perspective is seen in the rapid movement of ideas, capital, technology, and people across national borders. For those who would become HR leaders adopting this global viewpoint implies moving beyond both mental and geographical boundaries.

To accomplish this, Russell [13] advocates acting upon three principles of the paradigm:

1. *Envision the "big picture"* so that one may better understand macroeconomics, social and demographic developments, and respond by adapting your personal and business strategies. Do this by abandoning outdated paradigms or conceptual models, by anticipating and adapting to change, by monitoring different information sources and seeking underlying patterns, by developing systems thinking that pro-

vides a framework for seeing interrelationships rather than isolated events.

2. *Bridge cultural gaps* so that one may communicate more effectively with people who are different, thereby increasing the capacity for success at home and abroad. Think of culture as socially transmitted behavior patterns that are becoming increasingly diverse within North America; diversity should be perceived as a source of strength for an organization, providing everyone equal opportunity to contribute and advance.

3. *Adopt a global spirit* so that one has a mind-set for operating effectively in the new global economic landscape. Remember that the old rules do not apply and "reciprocity" is becoming the integrating principle of the world economy; transnational enterprises crisscross national economies, market segmentation by cultural niches is increasing and transnational consumers are becoming the norm; international trade relationships are having greater influence than are political ones.

Russell's vision for the year 2000 is that it will be natural to think globally because (a) organizations will be almost indistinguishable in terms of national character—they will be owned and staffed by people from all over the world; and (b) strategic alliances, as well as global locating, marketing, and distribution systems, will cause an intricate integration and synergism among economies; globalization will be the norm.

Any scanning of current business literature such as the following will confirm these observations.

Obviously, the "mind shift" we are proposing in globalization and the other forces of change may lead to culture shock for both individuals and institutions. The new global realities cause the restructuring of economic systems, reorganization of roles and procedures, reorientation of industries and organizations, and formation of alliances with those formerly viewed as competitors or even as enemies. For example, such cultural trauma is being experienced not only by leaders in the Eastern bloc but also by many of their Western counterparts now being asked to form joint ventures with partners from Soviet republics and Warsaw Pact members who have up to now been conditioned to doing business under forty years of totalitarian bureaucracy. Diverse cultures around the world are presently going through a profound questioning of their present way of life, assumptions, etc. The movement toward free market economies and enterprises is but one global indicator of this.

Empowerment

This second major change force is occurring globally, but is manifested locally at different paces and levels because of cultural conditions. Empowerment as a concept originates in North America and refers mainly to the work force; that is, altering management style and transforming organizational set-ups from hierarchial to more participatory, sharing authority and responsibility with workers in a variety of ways. This form of more open, team management is spreading rapidly in Western Europe but only selectively in Japan. The Japanese are group oriented, but have yet to empower women and other minorities within their organizations. In Eastern Europe and Asia empowerment is revealing itself in political restructuring from authoritarianism to democracy and free enterprise, in which managers are freed from government or party controls and begin to involve their co-workers in the process of reshaping factories, cooperatives, and businesses.

Block [3] maintains that organizational politics work against people taking responsibility; personnel should be empowered, helping them to acquire positive political skills. He believes that middle managers in particular should be the focus of such efforts.

While globalization "tears down walls" between national economies and peoples, empowerment does the same between management and labor. The high-speed, global marketplace suffers from top-down, slow, unresponsive, bureaucratic management. Empowerment requires another mind shift in the way we think about the world of work and its human resources. The latter are now perceived as organizational assets to be enhanced and supported. HR leaders, then, search for opportunities to assist workers, remove blocks to their productivity, and facilitate their career development for the good of the enterprise. Practice the 3 Es with co-workers: Educate, Enable, and Equip them. Because the average employee is better-educated and informed, empowerment is an idea whose time has come. As Richard King of the Los Angeles King International Group said:

"Empowerment is being able to participate in the creation of substances around you, rather than having to cope with what is given to you."

For a mind shift in this direction to occur, organizations must:

1. *Update Continuously.* Self-renewing individuals are able to keep pace with rapid work place changes. Knowledge workers routinely seek to develop new and higher skills. Learning managers read the latest in management and technical books, attend seminars, and join information networks, then share these insights with their co-workers. Realizing the rapid obsolescence of past skills, systems, and procedures amid increasing complexity, HR leaders create conditions so that the organization becomes a learning environment that encourages mind expansion. The outcome of this HRD thrust should be increased competency and improved quality of thinking, products, and services.

2. *Collaborate with Others.* Organizations must share information, power, and decision-making, as well as improve organizational relationships. The cooperation extends from individuals to groups to organizations to regions and even nations, resulting in improved international relations. Collaboration demands practicing more effective communication and team skills while creating synergy among people differences and resolving conflict. Enlightened management seeks to understand personnel needs in an effort to motivate workers, encourages workers to take responsibility and solve problems on the spot, and promotes work groups and teams as well as project management. To foster high performance, the cooperation extends outward to suppliers, customers, joint venture partners, and even competitors.

3. *Seek Creativity and Quality.* This ensures that information, service, and/or products are constantly being improved, so that the organization is better tomorrow than it is today. As a norm creativity means that organizational renewal is ongoing, with quality embedded in the organization's "genetic code" enabling members to meet increased competition and heightened customer expectations. The concepts are interdependent; quality or mastering fundamentals are prerequisites to creativity. The HR leader helps all personnel make a commitment to creativity in all aspects of work, and encourages a systematic approach to quality. Leading edge, world-class organi-

zations facilitate the creative process at every level and work unit, thus contributing to the quest for quality.

How the above may be accomplished will become more evident in the section on HRD Strategies. Some corporations have worked toward this by adopting quality circles based on W. Edward Deming's Fourteen Points [6], which contributed to the Japanese quality revolution. Tatsuono [14] explores how the cultural traditions of Japan enabled their scientists, engineers, and workers to eventually become world-class innovators. The principal path to empowerment seems to be team management, which was discussed in detail in Chapter 3.

Women can contribute much to the improvement of organizational vitality. Astin and Leland [1] completed a cross-generational study about women leaders and their contribution to social change despite sex discrimination and harassment in both society and the work place.

Landmark research on this subject is being done by Ann Morrison and her colleagues at the New Leaders Institute (P.O. Box 1110, Del Mar, CA 92014). Their studies [10] examined the transparent gender barriers to top management—"the glass ceiling"—for women seeking executive positions in America's largest manufacturing and service companies. It analyzed the factors that determine success or derailment in the corporate environment and the ways in which women can overcome the obstacles to career development.

In 1991, the U.S. Department of Labor belatedly adopted the "glass ceiling" terminology and provided statistics to underscore this problem in the work place.

Morrison then spearheaded another research project [11] on "Organizational Policies and Practices that Aid Advancement of Women and People of Color in Management," and interviewed 200 managers from 16 model organizations to address the following questions:

- How can corporations and other institutions better integrate women and people of color in middle and upper management ranks?
- Which policies and practices being used in organizations are most effective for this purpose, and what are the characteristics and/or circumstances responsible for their effectiveness?
- What can organizations incorporate into existing practices and how can they otherwise improve current practices to facilitate advancement prospects for women and people of color in management?

Such HRD research is vital because the nation can no longer condone the under-utilization of females and minorities in management at a time when the new work culture norm favors competence as the only norm for performance and promotion. This issue goes beyond the matter of empowerment and confronts an emerging reality: the Hudson Institute [8] forecasts that by the year 2000, 80% of the net additions to the labor force in the U.S. will be women, minorities, and immigrants. By the end of this decade, such persons will be rising not only into general management, but also into the executive suite. The culture of American corporations will then change, for it will become less dominated by white, Anglo-Saxon males.

A recent study conducted by the Cranfield School of Management in England also confirmed that women managers are an under-utilized international resource. The researchers found that few European companies anticipated the growth in number of female expatriates. It has been suggested that women are especially adept at cross-cultural management skills because they use behavior patterns emphasizing sensitivity, communication skills, community, and relationships. This personal orientation is valuable in globalization, which requires the formation of alliances, collaborative efforts, and joint ventures. Europe's Kleinwort Benson was cited as an organization with a large number of women expatriate managers or professionals abroad.

HRD Strategies

Preparation for globalization and the other changes highlighted in this book should begin in the home and be developed at every level of formal education. The former governor of Virginia, Gerald L. Baliles, reminded us that "the future is not a gift; it is an achievement." While chairman of the Advisory Council for International Education for Southern Governors Association, he lead in the publication of a remarkable report in 1986, "Cornerstone of Competition." Although directed to the southern region of the USA, the book was an example of thinking and acting both globally and locally. The monograph called for a revolution in international education with support from public sector policies and programs, as well as private sector projects underwritten by business and education. Its significance for human resource development may be judged by these excerpts:

- The Council found that as a country we are doing an inadequate job in teaching geography, culture, and foreign languages; that we do not adequately prepare teachers to deal with international issues; that both the federal and state governments have failed to address the problem in our school systems.

- Only recently has business realized that we operate in a global economy; that we must compete and to do that, we must be able to communicate; that we consistently fail to take advantage of the work produced by the brightest minds in other countries because we are language illiterates.

- The Council examined the state of international awareness among business, governmental, and educational leaders and made specific recommendations for education of school children, their teachers, and other professionals in foreign languages and cultures, as well as geography, as integral to a state's economic development program for an informed citizenry and investment arena to attract foreign capital and partners.

- To better use information to understand people elsewhere and world events, the Council proposed that business people with international experience work with local teachers; that state funds be used to promote exchanges of local teachers with their foreign counterparts; that "sister cities" programs abroad be expanded to include "sister schools" from overseas; that State Education Departments become more involved in promoting international education programs within their systems.

- Because a state's economic health and the well-being of its citizens is somewhat dependent upon world trade, business school curriculum should have required courses in this subject matter; schools and universities should make better use of satellite television and distance education technologies to link students with international resources; regional forums on international business should be sponsored for the local business, labor, government, and educational communities; small business operators need more training programs on how to export, particularly with reference to customs and tariff regulations.

- Because international ignorance affects national security, the U.S. Departments of Defense, Education, and Commerce should be actively engaged in promoting citizen area and language studies, as well as expanded educational exchanges; federal funding and scholarships for this purpose should be coordinated with regional government and corporate efforts.

Here is an international HRD agenda to which global managers should respond on their own state and local areas! The governors challenge us to take individual and organizational responsibility for a fundamental change in attitude toward international education at all levels, with all segments of society.

With increased internationalism in economic, political, and social arenas, Black and Mendenhall [2] reviewed the literature and determined that cross-cultural training is effective in facilitating international interactions. Their extensive analysis of existing studies and programs found a significant relationship between intercultural training and improved performance. They made recommendations for a theoretical framework for future cross-cultural research that would examine the training in terms of dependent variables such as cross-cultural skill development, adjustment, and performance in a foreign setting. Using social learning theory and adjustment as a context, these researchers urged more use of similar behavior modeling in which cognitive and behavioral rehearsals facilitate retention of the models of novel behavior.

The New Work Culture of Wellness

As a more affluent society shifts to a different work culture centered around information processing and new technologies, many people are exhibiting the symptoms of "future shock"—increased substance abuse, personal and systems breakdowns, burnout and techno-stress, self-abuse, and suicide. Such destructive trends point out the need for corporate strategies to counter these negative adjustments and improve employee coping skills during the profound social transition underway. Management efforts in this regard go beyond traditional medical benefits and safety training, advocating instead *wellness in life and the workplace*. Such strategies begin first with improvements in the physical and psychological quality of the work environment itself. Next, pragmatic policies to contain rising health care costs for business as well as individuals are needed. Following that is the addition of innovative benefits and services that ultimately contribute directly to enhancing performance and productivity on the job. As an example, to reduce stress among single parents or dual career couples with young children, the HR leader may promote a preschool facility within the organization or provide a directory of such resources for employees, or offer an employee benefit to subsidize such child care. Another illustration would be developing and implementing a flextime work schedule, work-at-home programs, or a compassionate pregnancy-leave policy for both male and female workers.

To create a truly "healthy" organizations thinking managers lead in developing healthier lifestyles for themselves and their corporate colleagues. They foster preventive health efforts to avoid illness, as well as to limit medical and hospital expenses (such as by company campaigns encouraging employees to wear seat belts or give up smoking). Real HR leaders promote a *behavioral health* approach—personnel take responsibility themselves for their own *wellness and quality of life.* In this context, management encourages "turning on naturally" to life rather than a dependence on artificial substances such as alcohol or drugs. Metaindustrial managers are actively involved in stress management programs for themselves and their subordinates. They inform their colleagues about wellness resources while creating personnel support systems. Smart managers realize that corporate health—literally and financially—requires their active involvement in programs to protect and enhance the health and well-being of personnel, as well as the public affected by corporate activity.

There are three major categories for healthiness that deserve management's support:

- *Preventive health services*—high blood pressure control, family planning, pregnancy and infant health, immunization, and curbing sexually transmitted diseases.
- *Health protection*—through toxic agent control, occupational safety and health, accident prevention and injury control, fluoridation and dental hygiene, surveillance and control of infectious diseases.
- *Health promotion or wellness*—through reduction or elimination of tobacco smoking, curtailment in misuse of alcohol and drugs, control of undue stress and violent behavior, promotion of balanced nutrition, physical fitness and exercise, use of seat belts, child day care provisions, other such practices contributing to a healthier lifestyle.

References

1. Astin, H. S. and Leland, C. *Women of Influence, Women of Leadership—A Cross-generational Study of Leaders and Social Change.* San Francisco, CA: Jossey-Bass, 1991.

2. Black, J. S. and Mendenhall, J. "Cross-cultural Training Effectiveness: A Review and a Theoretical Framework," *The Academy of Management REVIEW,* Vol. 15:1, Jan. 1990, pp. 113–135.

3. Block, P. *The Empowered Manager—Positive Political Skills at Work.* San Francisco: Jossey-Bass, 1991.

4. Cetron, M. and Davies, O., *Crystal Globe: The Haves and Have Nots of the New World Order,* New York: St. Martin's Press, 1991.

5. Coates, J. F., Jarratt, J., and Mahaffie, J.B. *Seven Critical Forces Reshaping the World.* Bethesda, MD: World Future Society Bookstore, 1991.

6. Deming, W. E., *Out of the Crisis,* Cambridge, MA: Massachusetts Institute of Technology (Dept. 93/Rm.9–234).

7. Harris, Philip and Moran, Robert T. *Managing Cultural Differences,* 3rd Ed., Houston: Gulf Publishing Company, 1991.

8. Johnston, W. B. and Packer, A. E., "Work Forc 2000; Work and Workers for the 21st Century" (Executive Summary), Indianapolis, IN: Hudson Institute, 1987.

9. Moran, R. T., ed. *Global Business Management in the 1990s* Washington, DC: Beachman Publishing, 1990.

10. Morrison, A. M. et al *Leadership Diversity: Women and People of Color in Management.* San Francisco, CA: Jossey-Bass, 1992.

11. Morrison, A. M., White, R. P., and Van Velsor, E. *Breaking the Glass Ceiling—Can Women Reach the Top of America's Largest Corporations?.* Reading, MA: Addison-Wesley, 1987.

12. Reich, R. B. *The Work of Nations—Preparing Ourselves for 21st Century Capitalism.* New York: Vintage Books, 1992.

13. Russell, L. and Williamson, B. H. *Tearing Down the Walls: The GEO Change Forces* (1991); *Handbook for the Future* (1990). Irvine, CA: The GEO Group (5405 Alton Parkway, 92714).

14. Tatsuono, S. M. *Created in Japan: From Imitators to World-Class Innovators.* New York: Harper & Row, 1990.

INDEX

Form of satisfactory agreement, 251–252
Framework for negotiation, 236–250
  concept of process, 239
  decision making, 150–151
  individual aspirations, 241–242
  language complexity, 245–246
  negotiator selection, 240–241
  persuasive argument, 247–248
  protocol, 243–244
  risk taking, 250
  satisfactory agreement, 251–252
  trust, 249–250
  value of time, 248–249

G

Geocentric corporations, 128
  training programs, 140
General Electric, 30
General Electric Medical Systems (GEMS), 17
General Motors, 182, 201, 279
Glass ceiling, 303
Global advertising, 202–203
Global business analysis, 42–43
Global competition, 30
Global corporation, 140
  strategy implementation, 140–141
Global distribution channels, 215–217
Global managers, 8, 53–54
Global marketing, 183, 185–186
  multinational vs., 186
  Pepsi vs. Coke, 184
  strategy, 186
Global mindset, 54–55, 75
Global objectives, 10, 46
Global opportunities, 39–42

  internal analysis of, 43–44
Global philosophy, 38–39
Global products, 191–192
  design, 190–192
Global strategy, 50
  framework for developing, 35
Global trends, 297–298, 304
Globalization, 4, 127, 139–140, 184, 187, 296–297
  CEO and, 142
  Coca Cola and, 185
  effective, 2
  mission statement for, 47
  multinationalization and, 188, 191
  paradigm shifts, 299–300
  product design, 190
  problems, 59
Gomez, Alain, 43
Groupthink, 66

H

Hagakure, 32
Hamel, Gary, 44
Health, 306–307
Hierarchial organizations, 60
High Performance Workshop (HPW), 22–23
Homogeneity, 28–29
Human resource(s)
  challenges, 64
  function, 7
  management, 7
  strategies, 21–24
  strategist, 55
  transforming of, 17–21
Human resource professional(s)
  concern for meetings, 260, 267
  conflict resolution options, 95
  as corporate strategist, 55